Words of Praise for Iyanla Vanzant

"Iyanla Vanzant taps the universality of spiritual yearning."
— **USA Today**

*"The message of Iyanla Vanzant comes right
from the heart and goes straight to the soul."*
— **Julia A. Boyd,** author of *The Company of My Sisters*

"Vanzant's spirituality is powerful and motivating."
— **Publishers Weekly**

*"Iyanla Vanzant has been down and
now her books are pulling others up."*
— **Linton Weeks, *The Washington Post***

Tapping
the Power
Within

Also by Iyanla Vanzant

Acts of Faith

Faith in the Valley: Lessons for Women on the Journey to Peace

Every Day I Pray: Prayers for Awakening to the Grace of Inner Communion

In the Meantime

One Day My Soul Just Opened Up: 40 Days and 40 Nights Toward Spiritual Strength and Personal Growth

Until Today Cards: A 50-Card Deck

Tips for Daily Living Cards: A 50-Card Deck

The Value in the Valley: A Black Women's Guide Through Life's Dilemmas

Please visit Hay House USA: **www.hayhouse.com**®
Hay House Australia: **www.hayhouse.com.au**
Hay House UK: **www.hayhouse.co.uk**
Hay House South Africa: **www.hayhouse.co.za**
Hay House India: **www.hayhouse.co.in**

Tapping
the Power
Within

A PATH TO SELF-EMPOWERMENT
FOR WOMEN

Iyanla Vanzant

SMILEYBOOKS
an imprint of Hay House, Inc.

Carlsbad, California • New York City
Sydney • London • Johannesburg
Vancouver • Hong Kong • New Delhi

Copyright © 2008 by Iyanla Vanzant

Published in the United States by: SmileyBooks, an imprint of Hay House, Inc.

Distributed in the United States by: Hay House, Inc.: www.hayhouse.com • *Published and distributed in Australia by:* Hay House Australia Pty. Ltd.: www.hayhouse.com. au • *Published and distributed in the United Kingdom by:* Hay House UK, Ltd.: www. hayhouse.co.uk • *Published and distributed in the Republic of South Africa by:* Hay House SA (Pty), Ltd.: www.hayhouse.co.za • *Distributed in Canada by:* Raincoast: www. raincoast.com • *Published and Distributed in India by:* Hay House Publishers India: www.hayhouse.com

Send inquiries to: SmileyBooks, 33 West 19th Street, 4th Floor, New York, NY 10011.

Design: Tricia Breidenthal   *Interior photos:* © Iyanla Vanzant 2008

Grateful acknowledgement is made to Lucinda Drayton of Blissful Music for permission to reprint the excerpt from "A Hundred Thousand Angels" © Blissful Music 2004

Library of Congress Cataloging-in-Publication Data

Vanzant, Iyanla.
Tapping the power within: a path to self-empowerment for women / Iyanla Vanzant.
-- 20th anniversary ed. p. cm.
ISBN 978-1-4019-2188-0 (hardcover)
1. African American women--Psychology. 2. African American women--Life skills guides. 3. Self-actualization (Psychology) 4. Vanzant, Iyanla. I. Title.
E185.86.V365 2008
305.48'896073--dc22
                                  2008011302

ISBN: 978-1-4019-2188-0

11 10 09 08   4 3 2 1
1st edition, August 2008

Printed in the United States of America

This book is dedicated to

OrisaSami
Gemmia Lynnette Vanzant

My Life, My Love, My Heart
Nisa Camille Vanzant

My Baby, My Buddy
Niamoja Adilah Afi

The best part of all that I am
Kimani Vanzant and Ashole Vanzant

Contents

Acknowledgments   xi
Introduction   xiii

Chapter 1:   Spirit   1

Chapter 2:   Spirituality   29

Chapter 3:   Blessing Your Head   57

Chapter 4:   Breathing   77

Chapter 5:   Meditation   95

Chapter 6:   Looking in the Mirror of Self   111

Chapter 7:   Prayer   133

Chapter 8:   Affirmation   153

Chapter 9:   Forgiving and Releasing   169

Chapter 10:   Ritual   187

Chapter 11:   Altars   199

Chapter 12:   Spiritual Bathing and Purification   213

Chapter 13:   Help from Planet Earth   225

Chapter 14:   Spiritual Code of Conduct   243

Chapter 15:   Precautions for Your Journey   267

Suggested Reading   279
About the Author   283
Inner Visions Institute for Spiritual Development   284

Acknowledgments

With humble gratitude and love I must acknowledge the following people for the re-birth of this work and the transformation I have experienced in my life.

Tavis Smiley, my brother who has, always, in all ways, been there for me.

Kenneth Browning, my Maestro who has stood with me and for me when I could not stand for myself.

Reid Tracy, for taking a chance and bringing me into the fold.

Cheryl Woodruff, whose quiet, gentle, patient spirit made the re-birthing of this work way more pleasant than I could have ever imagined.

Blanche Richardson, for being my birthing coach and breathing me through my writing process.

Suze Orman, for being brave enough to tell me what I needed to hear exactly when I needed to hear it.

Tom Joyner, for trusting my voice and giving me a place to share it.

Michael Baisden, for your unconditional support of who I am and what I do.

Bliss, for the incredible music that has taken my spirit to new heights.

Susan L. Taylor, for always being the example that reminds me of who I am and teaching me how to appreciate myself as a black woman.

Oprah Winfrey, for generously inviting me to teach in America's living rooms.

Almasi Wilcots, Andriette *"Asabi"* Earl, Anna Marie Troutman, Adara Walton, Beverly Biddle, Barbara Perkins, Carmen Gonzalez, Carol "Seshmi" Small, Candas "Ifama" Barnes, Charlotte Wilson, Claudia Thorne, Danni Stillwell, Deborah Lee, Deanna Mathias, Ebun "Laughing Crow" Adelona, Dr. Edna Olive, Elvia Myrie, Janice Rush, Janet Barber, Judith Hokmah, Helen Jones, Irene Robinson, Laura Rawlings, Linda *"Sharheerah"* Stephens, Lois Paris-White, Lydia Ruiz, Marge Battle, Marcia L. Dyson, Marcie Francis, Marie Brown, Maxine LeGall, Muhsinah Berry-Dawan, Nancy Yeates, Pamela Bryant, Susan L. Taylor, Tania Wallace-Bey, Terrie Bowling, Tehree "Adisa" White, Rainy Bundy, Renee Kizer, Rickie Byars-Beckwith, Viviana Hentley-Brown, Vivian Berryhill, Yahfaw Shakor, and the student body of The Inner Visions Institute for Spiritual Development. I never would have made it this far without each of you!

Introduction

It is hard to believe that 20 years have passed since I presented the first copy of the first edition of *Tapping the Power Within* to the world. I produced it on an electric typewriter and made copies at Kinko's. At that time, I was a single mom just finishing law school, ending a long-term relationship, and I had no clue about what to do next with my life. My dream at that time was: "Lord, let me have enough money on my credit card to make 20 copies of this book." Since that time, I have discovered that what we dream about is usually only a minuscule fragment of what is actually possible. That first edition of my first book was my initiation into a world and a life that I had never imagined to be possible.

When I wrote the first edition of *Tapping*, I was a recently initiated Yoruba priestess. When people asked me what that meant, I said simply: "I am a minister in an ancient African tradition." I was both excited about and eager to share what I had come to know about the ancient customs and traditions of my matriarchal lineage. Most of what I knew and shared was grounded in a linear and limited interpretation of my experiences and what I had been taught by my elders about the indigenous religion of the Yoruba culture.

Twenty years ago, I wore predominantly African garb. My hair, rich brown and finely braided, was usually draped over elaborate head wraps. Whenever I spoke, I began with a traditional Yoruba prayer, calling upon Olodumare, God, my ancestors and elders for guidance and support. I was, in essence, a neophyte: someone "new" to what I knew. It was from that place of newness, excitement, and inexperience that I first wrote this book. I knew then, as I still believe today, that the spiritual philosophies and traditions of African culture must be at the table of knowledge and teaching if the world is to heal emotionally and evolve spiritually.

I am now a 25-year initiate of the Yoruba tradition, and I recognize myself as a cultural custodian. In my mind and heart, this means it is my personal life assignment to promote and maintain the cultural and spiritual tenets of the Yoruba culture, which include the spiritual beliefs of the indigenous people. The difference between my neophyte stage and today is that I now recognize that those tenets are not confined to the Yoruba tradition; they are universal principles viewed from a particular cultural perspective. Faith, trust, compassion, forgiveness, love, kindness, joy, and devotion to God are the same tenets of psycho-spiritual development and evolution that underpin the world's major spiritual philosophies and most of the world's religions. Today I realize that Yoruba is not what I wear or what I do to my hair. Yoruba is who I am. It is what I bring into the room; it is what I say when I open my mouth to speak; it is how I bless my children and grandchildren. It is the cultural foundation that manifests in particular spiritual beliefs and practices that, when practiced in faith, will facilitate and support the evolution of my individual consciousness and my purposeful functioning in the world.

Yoruba culture provides me with a framework for how I honor the Creator in all that I do; how I view myself in the world; how I view and treat other people; and even how I handle my financial matters. Today, I understand that Yoruba is not only a religion. It is a cultural framework that embraces a specific and particular spiritual and religious philosophy. By religion, I mean the sacred beliefs that create uniformity in practice and harmony among a community of people in their approach to God as the Supreme Being of life. And, along with that philosophy come certain practices that honor the cultural traditions through which the philosophy was born. Today, I am not wed to the practices as a demonstration of my faith; I am committed to living the tenets of the philosophy.

Over the years, I have taken a lot of heat for my ability to bridge the philosophies of the modern and ancient worlds. The Yoruba community felt that I wasn't a strong enough advocate for the spiritual philosophy and practice of African culture, while the Christian community felt that I was inappropriately mixing two religions in a way that denigrated what they believe about Jesus being the only way. The Yorubas wanted to know if I had become a Christian. The Christians wanted to know if I practiced Voodoo. Some folks even believe me to be the anti-Christ, out to dupe others into moving away from Judeo-Christian beliefs and into some form of paganism.

Twenty years ago, other people's response to who I am and what I believe was a major concern for me. Now, not so much. Twenty years of experience has taught me that every living soul has a right to honor the validity of their experiences with God, and that there is considerable value in bringing the ancient traditions to the table of modern beliefs. What I know now is that you cannot separate the culture of a people from the spirit of a people. To do so is to dilute the power and presence of the Spirit of God that exists as a unique expression in every person, of every culture.

Rekindling the Flame

I grew up without my mother. There were many women in my life—strong, proud, beautiful women who did their best to usher me into womanhood. But they were not my mother. My mother's absence left a void in my identity that I was unable to name or speak in the face of the sincere, earnest efforts of the relatives who were doing their best to provide me with a home. My father's part-time presence and emotional unavailability only deepened the pain of being motherless. What I did have was a cousin, who was raised with me as my sister.

It was my sister's profound love and understanding of African culture that ultimately became my saving grace. It was through her that I discovered the richness of Yoruba culture and its spiritual traditions. Yoruba not only gave meaning to my broad nose and round hips, it made the color of my skin beautiful. In the pantheon of the Yoruba spiritual beliefs and practices, I found an image of the Creator that looked like me—dark-hued and feminine. I was also introduced to the concept of "ancestors," which reinforced my new understanding that my mother was not simply dead. Instead, she had been transformed. She was Spirit, eternal and ever present with me, as me, and around me. The cultural and spiritual philosophy of Yoruba opened my heart and mind to the meaning and presence of the spirit of God in all of Its forms and manifestations. It gave me an identity and filled the void in my soul in a way that human efforts and Sunday school had failed to do.

Yoruba, like other African and Native American spiritual traditions are technically defined as pagan religions because these traditions are not Christian, Jewish, or Islamic. What I know now is that language is a major challenge when attempting to explain the beliefs and practices of indigenous traditions. Quite often, there are no words in Western languages that can accurately translate the vastness and depth of indigenous cultures. Simultaneously, there is the challenge of interpreting spiritual phenomena from an intellectual perspective. Language can be limiting, and the intellect is programmed to discard or discount what is does not recognize and cannot rationally understand or explain.

How, then, are we to bridge the gap that exists between what the modern world defines as religion and spirituality, and what indigenous traditions offer? I believe that we must affirm the legitimacy of these ancient traditions by virtue of how we live. I have learned to do just that with much more grace, conviction, and elegance in the past 20 years. I have learned to be the demonstration of what I know and believe, without defense. I have learned to lean on and look to the place of commonality and oneness that touches all people and all beliefs. For me, that place is principle; the living, breathing tenets that are familiar to all leave little room for debate.

"There Is Only One Woman"

In presenting this revised edition to the world, I had to make some decisions. One of the decisions dealt with the subtitle: *A Path to Self-Empowerment for Black Women.* When my editor asked if I would consider changing the subtitle to *A Path of Self-Empowerment for Women,* I cringed. Over the years, this book has become a primer for many women of African descent seeking elementary knowledge about their cultural and spiritual identity. The information and the practices I originally offered—as I have been told many times—saved minds, hearts, and lives. Just like me, many black women embarked upon their spiritual journey feeling unworthy, unloved, and unfit to pray or practice spiritual rites.

Though times have changed, the experiences of many women of color remain the same. Many of us were raised in religious and spiritual communities that did not honor the contributions or the presence of women. Many of us have had emotional and spiritual experiences with religious leaders that were in total contradiction to what was being preached from the pulpit. Though many of us felt the call, the pull of our African-ness, we had no idea how to incorporate that into a spiritual philosophy or practice. We had, in fact, been taught it was wrong to do so.

Today, it is still common for women to feel unwelcome, invalidated, and inept when it comes to sharing our voice and addressing our needs in spiritual communities. It was this unique experience of women of color that I addressed in the first edition of *Tapping the Power Within.* So, "what to do?" was the issue I faced. How, 20 years later, shall I present what has been deepened and refined in my own consciousness? How do I honor all that I am within, and honor my sisters—all women—at the same time?

I have been blessed! Just as I always knew that my mother's lineage was African, I learned that my father's lineage was Native American. In the same way I was called to embrace my African heritage, I learned to embrace my Native side. My African, Native —and some Latin—heritage has afforded me the opportunity to grow in cultural sensitivity, diversity, respect, and knowledge. One of my dearest teachers, Wallace Black Elk always said:

"There is only one man and his name is All men.
There is only one woman and her name is All women.
There is only one child and its name is All children."

I, therefore, am not my sister's keeper. I *am* my sister. So I have changed the title of this book to: *Tapping the Power Within: A Path to Self-Empowerment for Women,* with the prayer that all women will find within these pages some one thing that supports her in a commitment to live a life guided by the Creator of life.

It is my vision that through the principles, practices, ceremonies, and rituals of their private spiritual practice, women will find both their internal and external balance; that they will find their own voice, song, and dance; that they will find value and worth. It matters not to me what a woman's spiritual or religious affiliation may be. What matters to me is that each woman, all women, find that place of God within themselves and live from and through that place, whether that place is called Obàtálá, Buddha, Jesus, Krishna, or the Great Spirit.

In today's world of haste, waste, anger, and violence, my mission is for women to know the love of God; live the love of God; and share the love of God in their homes and communities. I am wise enough to know, after 20 years of experience in dealing with the public, that not everyone is going to believe what I believe, nor embrace what I choose to embrace. I also know that no matter how much we fight and argue about it, we may never see eye to eye on the "right" way to approach our spirituality. My concern and purpose in presenting this work and living my life is to ensure that the traditional African and Native ways have a place at the universal table of spiritual knowledge. While each of us is free to utilize what is helpful and discard the rest, at the very least, we have a right to know these traditional ways exist.

Spiritual Evolution

The final challenge in re-presenting this work was how to integrate my learning, knowledge, and experience of the past 20 years since *Tapping* was first published. You will find that the basic information contained in the original edition is in tact. The chapters— 15 in all—including "Spirit," "Breathing," "Meditation," "Prayer," "Forgiving and Releasing," and "Spiritual Code of Conduct," appear just as they were in the first edition with relevant revisions and amplifications. At the end of each chapter, I have written a new section called, *What I Know Now*, which shares new information gleaned from my most recent years of experience and learning. It is designed to enhance and enrich the original text. These additions explain how my original 30,000 word first edition grew into this 90,000 word anniversary edition.

When this work was first presented 20 years ago, the concept of spirituality was not as commonplace as it is today. In fact, many people were afraid to speak the word aloud, much less explore the concept or its practices. Today, spirituality is almost a fad. *"Ceremony," "ritual," "affirmation,"* and *"spirituality"* are now terms commonly used in newsrooms as well as sports arenas. People proudly boast, "I am spiritual, not religious." At the same time, our children are ending up on death row or dead, our relationships are a mess, HIV/AIDS has reached epidemic proportions, and our schools are failing miserably. Yet, the mega-churches are building overflow sections. How do such contradictions exist? Take heart! We are all walking contradictions. We all have those things we talk about and present publicly, and those things we deem private or secret about which we remain silent. With the growing popularity of spirituality come increased misconceptions about what it actually means to be spiritual.

What I know now is that the concepts and principles of living a Spirit-directed, Spirit-filled life have not changed since the beginning of time. The methods and practices have evolved, deepened, and been transformed. However the underlying principles that allow us to function from a spiritual perspective are still the same. We must discover and share the true meaning of love; we must learn to forgive all things and all people, including ourselves; we must find the source of our joy and share it with all people; we must walk harmlessly, peacefully on the earth; and, we must faithfully acknowledge, embrace, and honor God, the Creator of all life.

The original text of this book, as well as the additional text added to this revised edition, is offered to assist you on your journey toward peace, love, success, and the freedom to be who you are—even with your personal contradictions. It is the first step in your journey back to the beginning—your journey in "spirit." Written from the perspective of ancient Yoruba culture and universal knowledge, the information presented is based upon the premise that you are a divine expression of the Creator (Olodumare in the Yoruba language). As you pass from the world of spirit (the womb) into the physical world, God gave you the gift of life. That gift is *breath*.

You are, in essence, spirit, housed in a physical envelope, brought to life by the breath of God to fulfill a divine mission. Your mission, while different from that of all other living beings, is directed toward a common goal—harmonious interaction among all living creatures and service for the good of the universe. As spirit, you know your destiny. You were informed prior to your birth. You choose, as spirit, the time, place, location, and circumstances of your physical life. As spirit, you are fully aware of what you must do, learn, and overcome in order to fulfill your mission.

In the physical form, you were given hands, feet, intelligence, and the discretion to fend for yourself. To be able to clearly understand and accomplish your mission, it is necessary to align and integrate your spiritual essence and nature with your physical essence and nature. How do you achieve this spiritual/physical integration? How do you determine your spiritual mission? How do you find the correct path for your spiritual mission? How do you fulfill your divine destiny? You do this with your breath and with the quality of your thoughts. It is by breath and with breath that you can direct the course of your life.

Sounds simple, right? Well, believe it or not, life is simple! Life is the simple in-and-out flow of events, circumstances, and people. We make it difficult by cutting off, holding on, and otherwise trying to control the flow of our breathing and our loving. All we ever need to do is be conscious of the presence of God in all people and situations. We must breathe consciously and live consciously and love consciously. We must learn to let things flow just like breath, and life will do the rest.

Your spirit will guide you through the ebb and flow of events in life. As your link to the Creator, your spirit is all-knowing, all-powerful, and ever-present. Spirit is divine, and so are you! It is sometimes difficult to accept that people are so divine. It is particularly difficult for African Americans who have been oppressed, disenfranchised, mis-educated, culturally and spiritually raped. The key is to "believe" you are divine; to "accept" that you have spiritual rights and to "know" that your ancestors, the universe and the Creator are supporting you spiritually.

You should understand, whether or not you are of African descent, that spirit and spirituality are an essential and necessary aspect of your basic nature. You are not replacing or undermining God by developing your spirit—you are trying to make contact with the powerful force that is God within you. What you are seeking and searching for has always been with you. Spiritual growth, development, and empowerment is a conscious choice. Now is the time to explore, accept, and understand how to make the divinity within you work with you and for you.

The Principles of Understanding

The principle element of your spiritual growth and physical evolution is the understanding of your self and your experiences. Nothing in this world is new. It has all been done and said before. Africans, as the parent race, have established the principles of understanding and confronting life issues. The principles are what we call tradition and culture. It is through these mediums that our ancestors developed a standard of behavior, and a code of morality, ethics, and values, which should govern thoughts and actions for the fullest expression of life. Our ancestors determined five principles that, if applied to daily activities, will reap positive spiritual and physical results. They are: (1) Truth, (2) Order, (3) Love,

(4) Faith, and (5) Patience. These principles, when followed and utilized as the foundations of our actions, decisions, and interactions will put us in touch with the highest universal forces. When we act in contradiction to these principles, our lives become chaotic, disorderly, and stagnant. In our pain, misery, and confusion, we lay blame and seek solutions outside of ourselves. The key is to "begin within;" to survey, explore, and become intimately familiar with your internal landscape.

Anything and everything you have experienced has been purposeful; it has brought you to where you are now. If you are fat and happy, thin and sad, wealthy and miserable, poor and sick, you have a collection of experiences to use as steppingstones to take you where you want to go. Like cotton which grows as an ugly, thorny pod and is transformed into beautiful, colorful cloth, you can transform your experiences into beautiful lessons. How? By changing the way you think about them.

As you embark upon this journey, be gentle with yourself. Do not think this is a "quick fix" to the challenges you face, and do not set unrealistic goals for obtaining spiritual insights. You must eat the mountain one bite at a time! You must be willing to release worn-out thoughts, habits, and situations in order to receive and put to use the information Spirit will bring you. Be patient. Be open to know the truth about yourself. Above all, be open to receiving the guidance that will support your spiritual growth. Do not be afraid to look at your faults, for when you recognize them, you have the power to change them.

When you begin your quest for spiritual growth, keep your own counsel. Do not try to convince others that what you are doing is right for you or for them. Everyone will get what s/he needs, when s/he needs it. As you grow and develop, everything and everyone in your environment will respond accordingly. Very often, things and people will fall away from you. Do not hold on. Know that you cannot lose anything or anyone within the "divine" order of your life. You can pray for your beloved ones and others without seeking their approval of your spiritual growth. Remember, *you cannot want more for others than they want for themselves.* Your first responsibility is to yourself! Be good to yourself; be honest with yourself and others, understanding that we all, in our own way, are perfect expressions of the Creator's life force!

The energy of Olodumare is with you through spirit. Your mission is to tap into it! The time is now!

Toward Enlightenment,

Iyanla

Chapter 1

SPIRIT

Growing up as a dark-skinned child with short hair, a broad nose, and thin legs, it was difficult for me to find anything beautiful about myself. Being black was not fashionable back in the 1950s. In fact, the prevailing standard of beauty in my family and in the world was the polar opposite of what was reflected in my mirror. My brother didn't help matters any. He told me that I had graduated from ugly to *oogly;* a cross between a mistake and a disaster. It became a family joke. He told me, "When God said beauty, you thought he said doodie, and ran off to the bathroom." That's how he explained his perception of my lack of good looks. I was convinced I was ugly and I "knew" everyone else thought I was ugly, too.

As a young girl, I spent many hours peering in the mirror, praying for beauty. My mother's lipstick, barrettes, and hair bows from Woolworth's and her Lady Ester's cold cream offered little help. If I was going to find beauty, I would have to look someplace other than my reflection in the mirror. One day, a strange thing happened. I was about 12 at the time. I was sitting at my normal spot on the bathroom sink with one foot propped on the toilet for balance. I was staring at myself in the mirror when I saw a burst of colors behind me. I froze. My heart was racing. I was looking at a reflection of myself I had never seen before! I was tall, dressed in a long, flowing white robe. My hair, eyes, and mouth were the same, yet there was a glow around my face! I was beautiful!

1

The reflection in the mirror reached out to me. I panicked, and my foot slipped into the toilet. The reflection smiled. I heard someone say, *Take my hand. Come closer.* My mind was a blur, but I remember repositioning myself and peering deeper into the mirror. My reflection now had a bright blue glow. I heard the voice again: *All your beauty is within. It is your power. All you need do is look within.* The reflection faded. As I was jolted back to the present moment, I fell off the sink. On the way down, I hit my head on the tub and my mouth on the tile floor. Somebody knocked.

"You okay in there?"

"Yeah, I must have fallen asleep," I said, scrambling to my feet and glaring at myself in the mirror. I had a huge bump on my head. My bottom lip was swollen and bleeding. I looked an awful mess! Tears welled up in my eyes. I wanted that beautiful reflection of me to reappear, but it didn't. So now, not only was I oogly, I was bruised. What was a girl to do?

In Search of Spirit

The beauty I was looking for in the mirror as a young girl was my Spirit; the divine spark that exists in every expression of life. In essence, *Tapping the Power Within* means connecting to the beauty, power, wisdom, love, and divine intelligence that exists at the core of our being. This spark of divinity is what beckons each of us to a higher, fuller experience and expression of life. The unfolding and conscious awareness of this divine presence within is the ultimate, common goal of all religious beliefs and spiritual traditions. Our awareness of and conscious connection to this divine essence is the intention that belies our religious affiliations and spiritual practices.

Each one of us is an eternal, physical manifestation of the Creator. For this reason "Spirit" is capitalized when it is being ascribed to or associated with God. As human beings, we are covered by a physical body, a specific form, for a specific purpose. As Spirit in human form, we each have a soul. Our soul is the invisible, intangible expression of all that we have been taught, as well as what we have come to believe, to think, and to experience emotionally about how life functions and how we are to function in life. While it is common to use the words "spirit" and "soul" interchangeably, this usage can lead to a misunderstanding and misrepresentation of who we are and how we are connected to God. Spirit is universal, while the soul is unique and specific to each human being.

God is Spirit. Spirit is the eternal, omnipresent (ever-present), omnipotent, (all-powerful), omniscient (all-knowing) presence of God, the Creator of all life. Spirit is the authentic identity of every living thing. As used here, "authentic" means the intangible, invisible essence of what can be known or seen. Every animal, plant form, and body of water that supports the reproduction and evolution of life is a manifestation of the Creator's omnipresent Spirit. Human beings, made in the "image and likeness" of God, are a specific physical manifestation of the eternal Spirit of life. In the same way that electrical currents move through a wire into a lamp, television, or toaster to make it function, Spirit is the source of current that runs through and gives all life-forms the power to function in a precise way. Spirit has no specific race, color, or gender.

The Spirit of the human being is the eternal essence, true identity, and the presence of God. By contrast, the soul represents how the presence of God is manifesting in a unique way, in a particular form, for a specific purpose. Spirit is the power. The soul is what makes up the personality, or the unique expression of Spirit. In human beings, the soul may express as a specific race, or gender, with unique physical attributes (such as weight, height, eye color), or the propensity to be or do a particular thing. The soul is the intermediary, that links the presence of Spirit to the physical mind, emotions, and body.

Everything that has life can create life, can nurture life, or serves a purpose in life is Spirit. The Creator's goal is for all spirits to learn to serve one another and to live in peace-filled harmony. Spirit, therefore, exists and expresses on many levels, as many expressions of life; those we can see and those we cannot see. A living being is a form of Spirit we can see. One who has lived and no longer breathes is a form of Spirit we can no longer see.

Most indigenous cultures teach that Spirit also exists in many forms, some of which we do not recognize. This concept helps us to understand why and how minerals, plants, and animals are also considered Spirit. Water, for example, is an expression of Spirit. It is a form of life that sustains and supports the reproduction and evolution of other life-forms. Whether in the womb of a human being or the depth of a river in which human and other life-forms can find food, water is an expression of Spirit that nurtures life.

Fire is another example of a living form we may not recognize as an expression of Spirit. The energy of fire can be constructive, as in a cooking flame, or destructive, as in the burning of a forest or home. Like all other life-forms, fire is an expression of Spirit that can support life. When, however, the essence of fire is misused or misdirected, it destroys life.

Likewise, when the soul is not properly educated about or connected to the presence and purpose of Spirit, it can become the source through which misuse of Spirit manifests. The most common result of this abuse is the destruction of the physical form.

As human beings, our primary purpose in life is to express the presence of Spirit in a manner that is constructive and supportive of all other life-forms. This constitutes what Native American and Buddhist traditions refer to as "learning to live harmlessly." When the soul expression does not live harmlessly, it can become the source through which misuse of Spirit manifests.

In Yoruba spiritual tradition, the essence of the human being—the Spirit—is called "Emi." Emi is the link between man and God that is sustained by breath. Emi is that part of man which returns to God at the end of the physical existence. Emi is the pure, impersonal, divine energy that exists in everyone.

What governs and guides Emi is the sacred energy called "Ori," the spiritual knowledge that is housed in the physical head. Ori is the soul that controls the individual mind. It represents a unity between the spiritual identity and physical being. Ori is the inherent knowledge of the individual's physical life purpose: what an individual is to do in life, what her spiritual mission is, how her unique purpose will be fulfilled. The Emi knows what we must learn and accomplish during a lifetime. Ori determines and directs how we will go about our learning process in order to fulfill the purpose. It is the Ori that takes on and expresses the characteristics of a specific race and gender that will ultimately govern the abilities and motivations by which we make choices and decisions throughout our life.

From the perspective of a rational mind, there are many parallels between the foundational beliefs of Judeo-Christian religions and the Yoruba or other indigenous spiritual traditions. Every individual is a Spirit with a soul. As practiced, however, both language and cultural expression become barriers and points of demarcation between Judeo-Christian belief systems and those of most indigenous faith systems, including those of the Yoruba.

For the Yoruba, our primary purpose in life is to keep the Emi and Ori in alignment so that our life is a demonstration of the power and presence of Spirit at the core of our being. Our unique expression of alignment is also considered a source of evolution and pride for our clan; those people living now and those who lived before us, with whom we share a bloodline or community connection, i.e., our tribe. Among the Yoruba, the alignment of Emi and Ori is called "A'se" (pronounced *a-shay*), meaning power or truth. It is only by purifying our Ori, the expression of our own soul, and following the promptings and guidance it receives from the Emi, the power and truth of the presence of God within, that we can successfully fulfill our spiritual and physical life mission.

While each indigenous spiritual tradition may have a different name and theory about how this purification process must unfold, there is one common thread that links many spiritual traditions of most indigenous cultures. It is that you *do not* need an intermediary to govern or guide your individual spiritual purification or evolutionary process. Unlike Christianity, which recognizes Christ as the specific and necessary intermediary, Yoruba and many other indigenous faiths hold that the quality of the individual's thoughts and the condition of the individual's heart either demonstrate or deny the individual's awareness of, connection to, and ability to live life as purposed by God.

In my early years, I was introduced to a religious belief system that considered God to be an external, vengeful, and powerful force. From my earliest memories, I was not considered to be a unique expression of God. Instead, I was taught that I was wretched, sinful, and born to suffer, until and unless I verbally and consciously embraced a specific intermediary for my salvation. Salvation was dependent on my willingness and ability to be aligned with, and connected to, one legitimate intermediary. I lived under an edict, a specific set of rules, that I was mandated to follow in order to prove myself "worthy" of God's blessings.

As I was taught, any deviation from the rules would result in even greater suffering while I was alive and eternal damnation at the occurrence of my death. The way I was introduced to God and taught to please God was not only quite difficult, it was frightening. I never seemed able to do enough, in the right way, to earn earthly rewards or heavenly acceptance. In my mind, it seemed that all the fun stuff in life—listening to music, wearing nail polish, getting a first kiss without the benefit of marriage—went against the rules and would ultimately result in my soul being banished to a fiery and uncomfortable place. As a result, as soon as it was humanly possible, I moved as far away as I possibly could from the rules I had been taught about religion and God. I convinced myself that they didn't really matter, as evidenced by the number of people who fearlessly enjoyed secular music, slow dancing, swearing, and kissing. What I did not realize at the time was that my experiences and interpretations of the rules affected my willingness and ability to accept, acknowledge, or become aware of the presence of Spirit within me.

Culture also provides us with rules to live by. The distinction between rules of culture and rules of religion is that cultural rules are created to meet and advance the needs of the people as determined by the leaders of the culture. These rules become traditions or practices that direct, evolve, or, in some cases, hinder the quality of life experienced within the culture. Religious rules are born within the culture to assure uniformity and conformity of religious and spiritual practices. Culture determines how religion is practiced and how religious leaders are identified or chosen. Depending on the intention of the culture leaders at the time, there is room and great opportunity for culture and religion to be held as separate entities. This, I believe, is the case with many modern religious practices of the Western world today.

While many indigenous cultures hold fast to the beliefs and traditions that unify and advance the culture of the people through spiritual practices, the Western world separates the business of Spirit and the business of humans into church and state. While most indigenous cultures still consider God to be the Spirit in all, expressing as all things, Western culture advances the concepts of *sacred* and *secular,* limiting God to distinct parts of life. For the most part, indigenous cultures consider the sacred purpose of Spirit in all life-forms and experiences. The unfolding of all experiences is considered to be an indication of how individual souls are evolving and expressing recognition and honor of God. Western culture has created many divisions within culture that do not honor or recognize the spiritual implications of certain practices and experiences on the souls of its people.

When I was introduced to the spiritual traditions of Yoruba culture, I found four essential ingredients that were missing from my early religious indoctrination. I found a belief system that acknowledged and honored Spirit in many forms, both tangible and intangible, visible and invisible. I discovered a system of beliefs and practices that offered me a way to be both responsible and accountable for developing and sustaining an intimate, personal relationship with Spirit, without an intermediary. I learned how to recognize and honor the various forms and expressions of Spirit in the world around me. Finally, I came to understand my own divinity. I learned that Spirit accepted me just as I was; a feminine being, of African decent, born to serve a purpose.

I was taught that "Orisa" is the name given to identify the various forms and ways Spirit is expressed in the world. The ocean, for example, is recognized in the Yoruba spiritual tradition as "Yemonja" (often pronounced *Yemaya* in the Western world). This name is a shortened version of the Yoruba concept "Yey Omo Eja," meaning: "The mother whose children are like the fish; they are to numerous to count." The ancient indigenous cultures have always seemed to know and teach what modern cultures study to determine, which is that life begins in water. Whether the seminal fluid that brings forth a sperm to meet the egg or the amniotic fluid that facilitates the unfolding life of an embryo, life begins in salty waters. Yemonja, representing the salt water that covers 96 percent of the earth's surface, is not considered a god, per se. Instead, it is the name given to the presence of Spirit manifesting as the salt waters where all life begins. As such, ocean waters are considered sacred.

In the Native American Lakota tradition, "Ina Maka" is the name of Mother Earth, the essence of feminine energy, the source and substance of all life. Unlike the Yoruba, the Lakota culture holds that all life begins in the darkness of the earth. Women in Lakota spiritual tradition represent Mother Earth because they bring forth life from the darkness of the womb. Earth is to the Lakota what water is to the Yoruba. Different cultures, different understandings—each with a different name for the manifestation of the Creator within its midst as a natural element.

In the Western world, the ocean is considered a place to play, relax, and sunbathe; while the earth is dirt—good or bad depending on whether or not is can be farmed to produce food. While most people willingly acknowledge that a day at the ocean calms the nerves and relaxes the mind, there is little if any sacredness ascribed to the ocean as the presence of Spirit. Children are warned to stay out of the dirt so that they won't mess up their clothes. Different culture, different understanding, different experience, and recognition of Spirit.

Life Never Dies

"LIFE" is the acronym for a phrase I often use to define and describe our process here on earth: "*Learning Inspired For Evolution*." The evolution of life is the process of preparation, refinement, and improvement for a greater purpose. Our physical life is the learning process through which we are spiritually purified. The purification takes place when we learn as a result of our experiences in life. Learning is a spiritual process by which we are refined and prepared to be of greater service to other living beings. However, in order to be physically and spiritually purified, we must bring our Ori and physical mind into alignment with the laws of nature. The Creator has established these natural laws to facilitate the purification and learning process we call life. These laws are what we call seasons, causes, effects, righteousness, and order.

Our Ori knows, in intricate detail, which of the laws we must learn and align with during our lifetime. Ori guides us to the experiences we will need in order to learn. Ori also serves as the recorder of the choices and decisions we make, those that are and those that are not in alignment with the natural laws. When we are in contact with our Ori and follow its guidance (what we know as our "first thought"), we are continuously provided with opportunities to bring ourselves into alignment with natural law. When we are in alignment, we can recognize and accept the lessons that will lead us to a fuller, more peace-filled, and more purposeful sense of living.

Think Less! Live More!

Our greatest challenge in the learning, purification, and alignment process of life is our mind. The mind, expressing our will and ego, is developed as a result of our experiences, emotions, and intelligence. However, mind, ego, and will are not in alignment with natural or spiritual laws. They are concerned with the way things "appear" to be, not what our experiences teach us on the spiritual level. It is only with a conscious effort that we can infuse the will and ego with the energy and power of the spirit. When the will and ego are not in alignment with our spiritual mind, we have what the Yorubas call "a bad head!" A bad head is one that functions on its own without the guidance of Spirit or more experienced elders. It is what grandmothers in this country call being "hardheaded" or "stubborn;" insisting that things are the way you want them to be when there is evidence to the contrary. Having a bad or hard head means that we are not listening internally to the voice of Spirit, or externally, to voices of wisdom, which means we are not in alignment with Spirit or the laws of nature. In most cases misalignment also indicates that we live for physical pleasures and pursuits without concern for conscious contact with the true essence of our being. When we have a bad head, we rely on the distortions of the ego to determine what we need and how we are to go about meeting those needs.

When we lack conscious contact with the true essence of our being, our perceived needs lead us to actions that create what we call negative experiences. These needs are also created by emotions that result from our negative experiences. Our mind will mesh together what we experience and desire in order to form a thought. Although thoughts govern how we respond throughout life, they may not be in alignment with the spiritual purpose or meaning of the experience. When we respond to physical thought alone, we are distracted by opinions, fears, the limitations of our experiences, and the influences of others. It is on this level of thinking that we encounter the challenges and obstacles we often refer to as the problems of life, or "issues." As individuals, we are responsible for integrating our experiences and the spiritual interpretation of those experiences into our lives. In doing so, we must be mindful that our experiences will, in all ways, align with our belief system. In order to determine if your individual development process is working, you will need to ask yourself: (1) How do I feel about what I am doing? and (2) What do I believe is possible for me and my life? Remember: What you believe determines what you see!

Aligning with Spirit's Energies

African Americans, torn away from our ancestral cultures, have lost touch with the process of connecting with our Spirit-self. We are no longer socialized or encouraged to pursue a spiritual life-style. We have been taught/told who we are, what we need, why we need it, and how to go about getting what we have been told we need. Our perceptions have been molded in a hostile environment. Our egos have been attuned to the physical world in pursuit of social and material gain. We rarely trust or follow our natural instincts. We seek validation from external forces and other people. We pursue credentials with hope that we will be accepted by others who are also out of alignment.

In this process, our Ori, which is endowed with the knowledge of our true spiritual mission and our unique life lessons, lies dormant. Spirit will never push or ask to come forward. It will wait to be invited. If we are to realize the true essence of our being and meaning in life, we must turn within to find the guidance of Spirit and bring ourselves, individually and collectively, into alignment with Spirit. What I saw in the mirror when I was 12 was my Spirit. My true identity. The intensity of my thought, fused with the emotional desire to be beautiful, drew the essence of my being to the physical level. Spirit was clothed in a form I could recognize. It spoke in a manner I could comprehend. My Spirit let me know on that day many years ago that what we seek without, we must first find within. I wanted physical beauty. What I failed to realize is the physical body has no power or meaning of its own. The body exists only as an extension of Spirit.

What we think and feel will create our reality, because Spirit creates from the inside to the outside. We must, therefore, see it within first. "Tapping the power within" is a process of recognition and reliance on the Spirit that exists within us all. Spirit is the presence and the power of the Creator, which is sustained by breath. It is that Spirit within that will provide us with the power to control our lives. Control from a spiritual perspective means "knowing." When you know what to do, how to do it, and why you are doing it, you are in control. Knowing brings you into alignment with the law. You are learning lessons. You are creating divine order in your life. You are fulfilling your unique mission. You are experiencing the purification that will prepare your spirit for its path of evolution.

Beyond the spirit of self are various levels of energy that can be instrumental in spiritual growth. African culture teaches that we must recognize Spirit on all levels. Spirits of air, water, fire, and earth are called "nature spirits." They provide us with the essential elements that support our physical life. Animal spirits represent the basic instinct of all living creatures to survive and thrive on the earth's provisions. Ancestral spirits represent the energy of those who have departed the physical plane and now exist on another level of energy. They represent the energy of life purifying itself. Ancestral spirits are represented by the standards, structures, values, and institutions that are an integral part of life as we know it. Ancestors may be of the family, community, race, or nation. According to Yoruba culture, ancestral spirits are called "Egungun."

Ancestral Spirits: Honoring Those Who Paved Our Way

When Spirit leaves the body in the experience we call death, the soul ceases to exist except in the memory of those who encountered it, but the Spirit remains connected to God. Spirit, as the eternal presence of God, never dies. It can and does, however, change form. What was once tangible and visible transforms into an intangible, invisible presence. It is this concept that supports a principle foundation of African spiritual philosophy and culture: the practice of ancestral worship. Spirits, as an expression of life eternally connected to the Creator, take on various forms, at various times, in order to fulfill a mission. Spirit may move from the visible to the invisible level as part of the evolutionary process. In its visible physical form, Spirit is the person. In its invisible form, Spirit is energy expressing as a unique form. Ancestral spirits are those persons in the family, community, race, or nation who no longer house a physical form, yet whose energy is still among us as a result of their having lived.

Ancestral worship is an integral element of the Yoruba spiritual culture. It is the method of staying connected to those who have laid the foundation for our lives. It is important that women have a clear understanding of this principle before they accept or reject the practice. In calling the name of, giving praise to, or honoring an ancestor, you are not worshipping the person—you are connecting with that person's spirit.

Remember: Spirit is energy! It is not a personality! When Spirit leaves the physical body, it is no longer hindered by the physical nature, character flaws, personality disorders, or emotional imbalances that may have been present during the individual's lifetime. The individual spirit moves into a new experience, a new level of enlightenment, as a result of life experiences. The prayers and mental energy offered to the spirit of an ancestor serve to lift the energy of the spirit in a process of evolution.

It is perfectly acceptable to call upon an ancestor you did not know or one you did not have favorable relations with in your life. Your lesson in life is to practice forgiveness and acceptance. The mission of all spiritual energy is to become aligned with universal law and achieve purification of its essence through love. Just as people in your life have helped you to heal, grow, learn, and evolve during your physical life, your prayers will do the same for the spirits of those who have passed over from physical life to spiritual life. When one calls upon—prays to—an ancestor, it helps that spirit achieve alignment and purification. You win by opening your heart through love and forgiveness. The spirit of the ancestors is freed from the debts created during the physical incarnation. It is a win-win situation.

Family ancestors are sustained by virtue of your life. Their blood runs through your veins. They are a vital link in your chain of existence, since without them, you would not be who you are. By virtue of your living, family ancestors have contact with the physical *and* spiritual planes. Community, racial, and national ancestors are those who, through their work and contributions while on the physical plane, benefited the community, race, or nation. In the African American community, Harriet Tubman, W. E. B. Du Bois, Frederick Douglass, El-Hajj Malik El-Shabazz, and Sojourner Truth (to name a few), are racial and national ancestors. We pay homage to them through the furtherance of their work and the maintenance of the institutions they built. The maintenance of a property or land that had significance to an ancestor is one of the highest forms of honor or worship.

According to African spiritual philosophy, recognition of ancestral spirits is vital to spiritual growth and evolution. The spirits of our ancestors exist as energy in our environment and influence how we approach our day-to-day life experiences. Think back to what your grandmother, aunt, mother, father, or any one of your family ancestors did for you during their life. Even if the relations between you were strained, seek to recognize the energy contribution they made to your life. In the spiritual form, the energy of these ancestors has changed. The spirit, freed from the physical body, has a duty to assist you. This assistance may come in the form of a dream, an inspiration, or an opportunity. It is spirit helping Spirit to fulfill the Creator's work. Your job, on the physical level, is to keep that energy alive through recognition, honor, and veneration.

The simplest form of honoring ancestral spirits is by calling their names. You can do this formally through prayer, or informally. Formally, you may want to set up an ancestral altar or shrine. You may offer prayers or affirmations to thank them for protection and guidance. Remember, you are not dealing with a person, you are incorporating energy. Informally, you may keep pictures or other possessions of the departed person in a special place or in a sacred way. Worship as it relates to your ancestors is not an attempt to replace God or dishonor God. It is in remembrance and honor of the essence and energy of those individuals who contributed to your life.

When we praise and uplift the energy (spirit) of our ancestors, we are simply saying, "Thank you for paving the way." It is not primitive, irreverent, nor is it anti-Christian. In fact, many indigenous traditions consider Christ to be a powerful ancestor! We should, and do, praise his energy. We do remember the importance of his life and the influence it has on our lives today. It does not matter what your religious affiliation may be; everyone and anyone can pay homage to their ancestors. Ancestral altars and shrines provide a place for symbolic offerings, or you can praise the ancestors daily in your heart and mind.

Prayer for Ancestral Spirits

I give praise and thanksgiving to the omnipotent Creator.
I give praise to the light and energy of the four directions.
I give praise for the light of my life
and the energy of the air I breathe.
I offer you food as a sign of gratitude for all that I have.
I give you praise so that your spirit
may grow stronger and more powerful.
I offer you a flower, a gift of the earth, so that you will know
there are descendants who remember and respect your presence.
I ask you, spirit Mothers, Fathers, Brothers,
Sisters and friends, to remember me in your travels.
Protect me. Guide me. Assist me and
all members of our family, living and dead.
I am in need of your assistance at all times to
overcome challenges and obstacles with money,
health, employment, and my own mortal progress.
I thank you for your guidance. I thank you for your
intercession in the matter of _____.
[State the area in which you need assistance].

Good spirits carry my prayers with you to the feet of the Creator.
Still my heart and mind with perfect peace and resolve.
I thank you for bringing the perfect solution,
in the perfect way, at the perfect time, for the best of all involved.
So be it.

Guardian Spirits

Every living being has a God-appointed guardian spirit that walks through life with her or him. This good spirit unites with you at the moment you are born. Some refer to it as "guardian angel" or "protector spirit." In African culture, guardian spirits are called "Egun." It is the duty of your Egun to assist you on your life path. Like the Ori, the Egun waits for acknowledgment and recognition. It will not interfere with the choices or decisions of your conscious mind. However, in times of need or danger, this spirit will give guidance and insight in the form of thoughts or presentiments. When you follow the direction given by your Egun, also called your "first thought," you can overcome many challenges and obstacles.

A guardian spirit may be an ancestral spirit or some other benevolent force whose spiritual evolution is dedicated to assisting living beings. While ancestral spirits have a vested interest in the survival of their descendants, they are not always guardians for their living family line. A guardian spirit may be an acquaintance from a previous life existence or a highly evolved soul who is appointed to assist in your care. Unlike your Ori, the guardian exists outside of your physical body. However, it is within your spiritual reach at all times.

Guardian spirits may or may not have names. You may call it "my guardian," "Egun," "my protector," or any common name you choose. In a state of relaxation and meditation, you can ask the spirit for its name. The response will be in the form of a thought. You may have a dream in which you see a person who is familiar, but whose name you cannot remember. Chances are it was your guardian spirit. Males may have female guardians; females may have male guardians. They are appointed based upon their past life experiences and your present life mission. Consequently, your Egun is most probably of the same race or ethnic background as you are.

In addition to your principal guardian spirit, there are other benevolent spirits who assist you in life. Those of the Catholic faith refer to them as "saints." Others may acknowledge universal spirits or earth spirits. These highly evolved, sympathetic forces unite with your guardian at various times to assist you in confronting your challenges. You may experience this uniting as a burst of energy or as an onslaught of information or opportunities. The key is to become focused and centered, and to ask your Egun for clarity and guidance.

To contact or communicate with your guardian spirit, you must simply be open and willing to do so. Your guardian spirit remains with you whether or not you recognize its presence. However, recognition, praise, and thanksgiving of your guardian spirit will strengthen its presence and influence in your life. Guardian spirits are ministers and messengers of the Creator. They provide another valuable link to universal intelligence and divine power. They walk with you, stand beside you, and care for you throughout life.

Prayer is the best method of communication with your Egun. You may want to erect an altar for your guardian spirit to assist you in maintaining constant contact and recognition. To set up an altar, you will need the following:

- A small table covered with white cloth (which indicates that the area is a sacred space, consecrated to receive divine light and energy)

- A large vessel of water (which purifies the channels of spiritual communication)

- White flowers (nature's gift of beauty, birth, and love)

- A white candle (to foster energy and communication)

The guardian spirit/angel altar is established with water, candle, crystal, and symbols of divinity—the Holy Bible and the Tao stone representing peace.

This guardian spirit altar features water, flowers, candle, money offering and a doll representing the essence or energy of a specific spirit.

This basic setup brings the four power elements of the universe together—air, water, fire, and earth—and provides a source of concentrated energy. (For more details on creating an altar, see Chapter 11.)

The key to any spiritual process is your mind. You must be willing to surrender your ego to a higher spiritual force. As a living being, you are linked to the power of all spirits. Through your Ori, you have the keys and secrets to your unique mission. Your challenge is to surrender what you think to what you are intuitively told to do. This is not an easy task. You must overcome years of conditioning, the influences of your environment, and the desire to be in control. You cannot receive spiritual consciousness with reasoning or intelligence. You must focus. Trust. Have an unquestioning faith—recognizing ancestral spirits, guardian spirits, and the spirit of your head—is the foundation of spiritual evolution according to African culture.

For women, it is a process by which we can overcome all physical limitations and live a life of service and healing. It does not matter what religious path a woman chooses. What will determine destiny is the degree to which we strive to bring forth the essence of spirit. At the spiritual level, a woman is the divine expression of love. She is co-creator with God, capable of bringing forth new life. A spiritual woman is a healer, teacher, and nurturer of life, because it is her ability to love that will soothe all who come into contact with her. The following is an ageless prayer dedicated to universal guardian spirits. Daily repetitions of this prayer will provide spiritual strength and guidance.

Prayer for Guardian Spirits

Prudent and benevolent spirits,
Messenger of God [the Creator, Divine Spirit].
Your mission is to assist me and guide me
by the good path. I thank you for your support.
Help me to endure the tests of this life
and accept them without complaint.
Deviate from me all negative thoughts.
Please do not let me give access to dark spirits
who intend to make me fail in the progress
of love for myself and all fellow beings.
Take from my eyes the veil of pride which prevents
me from seeing my own defects and
from confessing them to myself.
Above all my guardian spirit, I know you are
the one who protects me and takes an interest in me.

You know my necessities. Please guide me and assist me
in accordance to the will and in the Grace of the Creator.
I welcome your presence, your guidance, and your assistance.
Thank you Pure Spirit!*

What I Know Now

*Spirit is the omniscient (all knowing), omnipotent (all powerful),
omnipresent (ever present, everywhere present) essence of God.
Each of us possesses the same quantity, quality,
and essence of God at the core of our being.
Spirit, as created by God, and as it
exists in God, is eternal. It never dies.
Race, gender, personality, and ego do not exist in Spirit.
Spirit is the essence of love,
where all things begin and beings are equal.*

My Sister's Keeper

When I stopped, everyone in the room stopped. I am sure they
felt the surge of energy as it moved through my body. I am sure
they noticed that my eyes were fixed on the walker sitting in the
corner of the room. I am not sure they heard the sound of my
heart as it broke into pieces. That is probably when I gasped.

"She didn't want anyone to know," her childhood friend half
whispered to me.

If I heard that one more time, I was going to grab something
and rip it apart with my teeth.

"I cannot believe that no one had the decency to call me and
tell me that my sister was sick enough to be on a walker." I was
both outraged and amazed.

"I know how you feel, but she didn't want anyone to know."

---

*Adapted from *Collection of Selected Prayers* by Allan Kardec. For additional reading,
see the other prayers in this title, as well as *Spirit's Book*, also by Kardec.

"So what did you think? Did you think once she died you would put her over in the corner of the room and act like she wasn't there? Did you think that I would never find out she was dead? Are you crazy, or what?" I was done with the foolishness!

"No. I mean she didn't want anyone to know that she was sick."

"But you knew! You knew she was sick! Aren't you somebody? What you *really* mean is that she didn't want *me* to know."

I believe this is what made everyone so nervous, and now that I did know, no one knew how to explain her part in my *not* knowing.

It was earlier that morning when I got the news from my long-time friend, who took a long breath between "Hey, there" and her next statement, "I'm sorry, but your sister is dead."

My knees didn't buckle, but my mouth went dry. My stomach didn't flip, but my head was swimming.

"What do you mean *dead?*"

"She died this morning . . . in the hospital. When they called me, they told me not to tell you. I told them that they were crazy! That she was your sister and I was not going to be involved in something that crazy."

"Who told you not to tell me? What are you talking about?"

"Well, the person who called me told me that she didn't want you to know."

"To know what? That she was dead? When did my sister tell them not to tell me, before or after she died? Please don't tell me in the midst of dying she raised her head and said, 'Don't tell my sister.'"

"Calm down, sweetie. Just calm down. Apparently she had been sick for a while. I'm not sure about the details, but you need to call the house. Maybe you'll get one of the kids."

I'm not even sure if I said good-bye, but I did hang up and call my sister's house. My niece answered.

"Hi, sweetie. What is going on over there?"

"Well, Mommy passed this morning."

"I know that, baby, and I'm so sorry. What happened to her?"

"Well, she was in the hospital 'cause she'd been sick for awhile. I guess it got really bad a few days ago, and she didn't make it."

"Why didn't somebody call me and tell me she was in the hospital?"

I didn't mean to badger the child, realizing she had just lost her mother. On the other hand, I needed to know.

"I don't know. There was so much talk. People kept saying that you two weren't on good terms."

"What people?"

"I don't know. I guess everybody said it."

"Everybody like who? Have you ever heard your mother say that there was a problem between us?"

"No. You know she didn't talk."

"No, but everybody else *did*. Are your brother and sister there?"

"They're on their way."

"I'll be there this afternoon."

I don't think I said good-bye or offered soothing words of condolence; I just hung up.

One Life, One Spirit

The English word *spirit* comes from the Latin *spiritus*, meaning "breath."

What I know now is that every living thing has a spirit. However, there is only one Spirit. The spirit of a thing or being is connected to the Spirit of life, who is God, the Creator and essence of life. Through breath, God imbues every living thing with its being and its essence. The presence of Spirit is everywhere, at all times, giving life to all things. It is foolish to believe that you are on your own, separate from anything or anyone, or separate from God. The essence of your life is the essence of all life that has come before you and all that will follow you. *We are one* is a reality that many deny, ignore, or resist. Your ancestors are you, and you are the ancestor of those yet to come. We all come from and are connected to the same Spirit, the same essence, the same life.

A family ancestor is anyone you can trace back through your bloodline. A communal ancestor is anyone you knew personally who made a positive or important contribution to your life. A racial ancestor is anyone who has made a positive contribution to the advancement of the race—either your ethnic race or the human race. In essence, any individual whose living contributes to the evolution of humanity, anyone who has left behind positive work—a work that lives beyond him or her—can be considered an ancestor. An ancestor is the spiritual essence of a being that remains alive because others call his or her name, or advance his or her work. My sister had made many powerful and positive contributions to my life. She had made many positive contributions to her community. Like my father, mother, and brother, she was now an ancestor, a spirit, unencumbered by a physical body. What made her a spirit was the memories other living beings would have of her. She, like my parents, was now a friend in a very high place.

On the way to the airport I realized I had to get out of my head, my hurt, and my angry feelings in order to address the needs of the moment. My nieces and nephew needed me. My sister needed me. I took several deep breaths and began to pray. I don't remember what the prayer was, but it certainly had something to do with saving myself from the urge to slap somebody. My sister had been sick and now she was dead. As a spiritual teacher, I understood this meant that she had made her transition from the realm of the physical body to the realm of the spirit. As a human being with a tinge of guilt and remorse, all I could think was, *Oh my God. My sister is dead.*

I had not seen or spoken to my sister for almost three years, and now she was dead. The thought was overwhelming. I was grateful to be sitting in first class with no one on either side of me because the reality was beginning to sink in. My sister, my big sister, was no longer alive. I was trying to remember what had happened, why we stopped speaking. Actually, we had never stopped speaking. We simply didn't speak. Too busy. Moving in different directions. The truth is, neither of us had the courage to say what we needed to say. She had some issues with me, and I certainly had some with her. Rather than deal with our issues, we got busy.

We committed a spiritual bypass. We tried to remain separate from each other.

My sister's name was Ijalu, which translates as "the mother's joy." My big sister had taught me everything I know about what it means to be a woman, and specifically a woman of African descent. I learned that Africa was not a place to be afraid of or ashamed of, but rather a place to be studied and embraced. She was eight years older than I, which meant that when we were growing up, I was the pesky little sister whom she had to drag everywhere she went. I loved hanging out with her. She was a dancer. I got to sit through all of her dance classes. Because of my sister, I met Alfred Perryman, Arthur Mitchell, Chuck Davis, Katherine Dunham, Alvin Ailey, and Michael Babatunde Olatunji. The best thing was that I got to be their little sister, too. I learned about African culture—in particular, Yoruba culture. I learned the meaning and power of being called by an African name. I learned the importance of knowing and practicing African culture and traditions. More important, I learned the power and beauty of knowing yourself as an integral part of a never-ending circle—the circle of life.

My sister also taught me all the "girlie" things I needed to know. She taught me how to put on my stockings, roll them at the top, and tie the little knot to keep them in place. I never did get that knot right, so there were many times when my knots would come undone and my stockings would fall down around my ankles. My sister, mortified, would snatch me into a dark corner, pull my stockings up, then twist them, and tie them so tight that the imprint on my thighs would last for hours after I took the stockings off.

As the eldest, she was also responsible for my hair. Sunday was hair ritual day when she would wash, dry, and braid my hair. I remember sitting on the floor, my back between her legs, as she parted and plaited my hair while we watched *The Ed Sullivan Show* and ate Jell-O. My sister also taught me how to polish my nails and make up my face. She took me to Woolworth's to buy my first Maybelline two-pack eyeliner pencils. She took one and gave the other to me. She taught me how to pull my eye upward and draw the line close to the lash. She was a stickler for a straight line—except when it came to my braids! My sister taught me how to fry chicken, clean fish and get the lumps out of grits. Everything she had ever taught me or told me began to flood my mind as I sat on that flight. It was like having a lump in my throat and a knife in my heart. The hour-long flight seemed to take forever, and I thought it would take me at least that long to accept the reality: My sister was dead.

The Circle of Life

One powerful way to honor our ancestors is to embody the principles they taught and continue the traditions they lived. African people are a "we" people. *We*, in a cultural sense, moves us beyond the shallow consciousness of "my life is only about me." *We* encourages us to remember that everything I do is a reflection on everyone in my line. *We* motivates us to be better for those watching and those coming behind. My sister understood this and lived it. She taught me things that had empowered her as a way of sharing, expanding, and evolving the traditions that sustained her. She taught me what our mother had taught her, what may, in fact, have been taught for generations. Of course, things change, times change; people lose track of stories and the people who passed them on. We can, however, still honor the lives of the ancestors by remembering what we can, practicing and passing on the positive traditions that have been passed on to us. For example, I always washed and combed my daughters' hair on Sunday evenings. I was tickled when I saw one of them had continued that tradition with her own daughter. This is a profound and practical way to elevate the spiritual energy of the ancestors to do as they did in order to sustain the group. Without knowing it, many of us probably do it anyway. When, however, we can remember the name of the one who taught the practice, or lived the principle, we create a more intimate connection.

What I know now is that how I live my life either honors or dishonors my ancestors. I also know it is not important for me to dissect, evaluate, or judge their behaviors and dysfunctions. My job—our job—is to respect the continuum of life. We must embrace and embody with reverence the good/positive qualities that our ancestors demonstrated, because it was this essence of their lives that paved the way for us. They have set the example for how to live in family and community. Dr. Betty Shabazz always invoked a quote attributed to Alex Haley. "We must find the good and praise it." Find the good your ancestors left behind and live your life as an expression of it. We carry the energy of our ancestors in our DNA. Therefore, living the best of who they were, what they taught, and what they believed elevates their essence and advances our growth. What I know now is that every life, every being that ever took a breath in the physical form, is an ancestor.

What I know now is that all things fade into God. All things are neutralized, brought into equality, balanced out in unity with Spirit. My sister is now an ancestor. Not just *my* ancestor, because we do not have the luxury of owning spirits; she is *an* ancestor. In my heart I knew that it didn't matter that we hadn't spoken. It no longer mattered that she had been upset with me or that I had been angry with her. It didn't matter that people had exaggerated the problem with gossip and innuendo. What mattered now was that the ancestors were watching and waiting to see how we, the family, would behave and what I, the next in age order, would do. My sister had taught me what to do when a member of the family made their transition, and it was now my responsibility to make sure it was done with prayerful excellence.

If someone had told me that I would one day voluntarily stand within arm's reach of a dead body, I would have told her she was crazy. Had she told me the dead body would be that of my sister, I probably would have lost my mind. But there I stood, next to my sister, who was dressed in a clear plastic bag, covered by a white sheet. In that moment I did not need to think about what to do. I had to do what I had been taught. My friend Tulani, a master braider, braided my sister's hair. I polished her nails just as she had taught me; one stroke up the middle of the nail, one on the left side, one on the right, two coats. Next, I applied her makeup. I pulled her eyes taut, just as she had taught me. I made a very fine, very straight line of eyeliner across her eyelids. I added just a touch of blue shadow in the corners of the lids. I lined her lips and added just a bit of gloss. I asked my niece to find a small handbag that my sister especially liked. I filled it with coins. In African tradition you never want your family to show up on the other side without coins. I also gave her a small white hankie. She had taught me that a hankie is so much better for dabbing the eyes than paper tissues. I also put a few mints in her purse. It just seemed like the right thing to do.

I dressed my sister in traditional African garb. I wrapped her head in *asoke*—traditional woven cloth—just like she had taught me to do. My sister loved Jean Naté, so I put a dab behind each ear. Finally, I adorned her with traditional beads and bracelets. I placed an *irukere*, the ceremonial horsetail, in her hands so that it lay across her chest. She was now ready for her children and family to view her remains. Holding hands, Tulani and I stepped back while my sister's best friends added their final loving touches. When we were all done, we stood in stillness and silence, gazing upon the woman who, though she stood only five feet four inches tall, had been a monumental influence in so many lives. In that moment I could not remember why we had grown apart, I just wanted to know if she would be proud of what we had done for her. We had prepared her for a traditional burial. We then blessed her to join the ancestors.

I felt regret for having missed the last three years of her life. I felt sad that I would never hear her laugh again. I wondered why she didn't tell me that she was not well. Then I remembered who my sister was. I knew that she probably didn't want to be a burden. She probably thought I was too busy, and she didn't want to bother me. Realizing that that was probably the reason, I felt hurt and angry and sad. More than anything, I was angry with myself. Then I remembered the love and the spirit of love that existed between us, and the anger dissipated. All things fade in Spirit. *All things become love.*

Chapter 2

SPIRITUALITY

I was sleeping, minding my own business, when the first chill went through my body. The scenes began to play out in vivid color. My son Damon was sitting on the floor in a dark room. He wasn't tied up, but I sensed that he couldn't move. I was standing in the room. I called out to him. He seemed not to hear me. I could hear the voices of several men. I knew they were angry and dangerous. I felt the panic flood my mind and body. I ran out of the room calling for Damon to follow me. He didn't move.

I was running down a long hallway screaming my son's name. I looked back over my shoulder to see that the men had entered the room. I stopped running and turned back to face the room. I saw one of the men hit Damon. My heart sank. I started walking back toward the room. I was crying, "Please stop. Please don't." One of the men had a gun. I started running back toward the room. I heard the gun click. I came to a dead halt. The gun clicked again. I screamed. The telephone rang. I sat up in the bed. I was sweating and panting. The telephone rang again. It was 6:30 A.M. on a Saturday.

I grabbed for the telephone, knocking it to the floor. My chest was heaving so hard I couldn't speak. I put the phone to my ear. "Ma?" It was my oldest daughter, Gemmia, calling me from Morgan State University, where she was a freshman.

"Why are you calling me at this time of the morning?" It sounded frightening to hear my own voice.

"Ma, you've got to find Damon." Gemmia then told me about her dream. She and her brother were running from a mob of people. She didn't know why the people were chasing them. Damon kept falling down. She would stop to help him up, and they would run a little farther. Finally, the mob caught up with them and encircled them. Damon was arguing with the people, but she kept pulling him to run away. When they did start running again, they were able to put a great distance between themselves and the mob. Finally, they stopped running to rest. She remembered that she was fine, but Damon was bent over, trying to catch his breath. She was looking right at him when a huge black truck came from nowhere and hit her brother.

I told Gemmia to pack her clothes. I needed a car but I only had $40 in cash and no credit card. I called a friend of mine, Seshmi, and told her I needed to rent a car. She agreed to put up her credit card without ever asking where I was going. She told me to make the arrangements and let her know what time we could pick the car up. I knew I would make it from Philadelphia to Baltimore, Maryland, to pick up Gemmia; and from Maryland to Norfolk, Virginia. What I did not know was where to look for or how to locate my son.

My son had recently been discharged from the Navy. He, his wife, and their baby were living somewhere in Norfolk. They did not have a telephone. I had an address and no idea of where I was going. Seshmi, Gemmia, and I picked up the car about 1 P.M. When I dropped Seshmi back at her home, she put $50 in my hand. I never asked or told her what I needed. She just knew. I pulled up to Gemmia's dorm at Morgan at about 2:30 P.M. It was 6 P.M. when I turned the car off the highway onto Oceanview Road in Norfolk. I told Gemmia that the area looked vaguely familiar. I told her to check the parking lots we passed for her brother's car. We had driven about ten miles when I pulled into a motel parking lot where we had seen several cars with New York license plates. As I turned into the lot and prepared to park, my son Damon ran across the lot on his way to the telephone.

My son was living in a motel on the busiest thoroughfare in Norfolk, selling drugs. He and another young man, about 18 years old, had started their "business" with their tax returns. He estimated that they were making between $5,000 and $7,500 a day. A rival dealer had put a hit out on them. That morning, two of the gunmen cornered my son in the motel. They informed him that they really wanted the other guy but that when they found that other guy, if my son was with him, he, too, would pay the consequences. He said that it had happened about 5:00 A.M. that morning.

Over the course of the next two days, I took the 18-year-old home to his mother, sent his 16-year-old girlfriend home to her mother, dropped two pearl-handled pistols into the ocean, packed my son up, and moved him back to New York. We left my son's wife in Virginia because she had two months left before her discharge from the Navy. I thank God every day that He gave me the opportunity to save my son's life. I believe that God had given both Gemmia and me a preview of things to come. It was a warning that compelled us into action. It was the harvest of our spiritual labor, our spiritual practice. Since that day, when Spirit impresses upon me the need to jump, I simply ask, How high?

Spirit Rises

Spirituality means "of the spirit." It is a oneness within and without. Within the spirit there is a sense of peace, balance, and knowing that you are an integral part of a dynamic whole. That whole is life, expressing itself in many ways and supporting the evolution of all life's expressions. Without, spirituality is a connection to every living force in nature and the universe. This connection provides unlimited resources and a sense of being complete. Spirituality is reliance on your internal universe as the vehicle to carry you through the journey of life. It is a universal connection to everyone and everything. The connection of spirituality means accepting that you are not your sister's keeper. It means knowing that you *are* your sister by the oneness of Spirit.

To live a life guided by Spirit is to live a life of spirituality. It is the result of aligning the conscious mind with the spiritual mind, the inner life with the outer life, all in accordance with spiritual law. Spirituality requires relaxation of the conscious mind, suppression of the ego, and reliance on divine universal energy as the motivating life force. When one relies on spirit—the divine essence of the being—the physical life becomes an expression of well-being.

Spirituality means faith in Self, the divine, and noble expression of the Creator at the core of your being. When used in this way, Self is capitalized in recognition of the presence of God that it represents. Faith in Spirit will serve as a dependable source of guidance in life. Spirituality means viewing life through a Spirit's eye—the third eye, which is not controlled and limited by ego, perception, or intelligence. Spirituality means seeing the truth, value, and beauty in all life forces and dedicating one's self, the physical expression, to the expansion of those lives. When addressing the individualized expression of Spirit, self is presented in lower case. The Self is the presence of the Creator's spirit within. It is the pulse of the universe as it is expressed through your being. Your self refers to how you chose to express your physical world reality.

Spirituality is a journey inward that connects the Self to your self. When you know who you are from the inside out, when you do what you sense is right for you—regardless of what others are saying or doing—when your first point of reference is your own thought, and when your thoughts lead you to actions that serve others as well as make you feel good, then you have encountered spirituality. Spirituality—the alignment of the physical and spiritual minds—creates "a good head." A good head utilizes the divine spark of Spirit as the motivating force of thought, words, and actions. Spirituality is recognition of your connection to the essence of the Creator as the source of your power. Spirituality is not religion, for it does not matter to which church you belong or the religious philosophy you follow. Religion offers a way, the rules and regulations, to approach the concept of God. One advantage of religion is that it ensures consistency and conformity in spiritual practice. It is a process that guides and supports the unlearned and the unbeliever. Spirituality, on the other hand, means that you recognize, accept, and are aligned in your individual connection to the Creator and use that "spiritual connection" as your guiding force. This connection leads to peace, fulfillment, happiness, and abundance because it enables you to overcome the limitations of the physical mind and body by putting you in touch with the true source of power—the spirit of the Creator God.

Spirituality, having a spiritualized consciousness, conquers fear, hate, anger, loneliness, and deprivation. It replaces these ideas with purpose, love, worthiness, understanding, and truth. Spirituality heals the desire to control and dominate, because it fosters greater understanding of life's purpose and your role in life. Consequently, your desire to control events, circumstances, and people is replaced with the knowledge that all we need and want will be provided for us in the perfect time, in the perfect way, as we move through our learning experiences. Life is a learning process. Spirituality is the manner in which we learn and grow.

Another important aspect of spirituality is the recognition and respect of spirit on various levels. Ancestral spirits, nature spirits, and animal spirits must be recognized as they impact our lives. As we develop spiritual intuitiveness, we will be able to communicate and appreciate the impact of these forces. The closer we come to the Spirit life, the less conflicted we become internally and externally, the less stress we create and experience, and the more available we are to receive and follow spiritual guidance. In the beginning, however, it is important simply to acknowledge the existence of Spirit, and to respect the energy around us.

Who's Teaching Whom?

Spiritually, we are all teachers and students at the same time. Once we develop our spirituality, we are able to recognize our role in any given situation. This recognition gives meaning to our life's experiences, beyond what we sense in our mind or through our emotions. Spiritually, in any life experience, we are either teaching a lesson, learning a lesson, or functioning as the object by which a lesson will be taught. Once we understand our role, we know our task. When we know our task, the lesson and the reward come quickly and easily.

Spiritual Teachers

Spiritual teachers realize that everything we think, do, and say will return to us in the mirror of self when the spirit is ready to learn the lesson. A spiritual teacher is also the individual who shares spiritual knowledge with us and assists us on our path to spiritual realization. Often, this can be done without knowledge on the part of either party. The key is to realize that whoever assists us in becoming better, more enlightened individuals is a spiritual teacher. For many adults, their greatest spiritual teachers are their children.

Teaching a Spiritual Lesson

When we are teaching someone a spiritual lesson, we usually have what we call a negative experience. Someone we love or care about a great deal will commit an act against us, which will violate a trust or faith we hold. The person will generally make a choice or decision that seems to be to our detriment. We experience disappointment or emotional pain. As the teacher, our job may be to assist the person in seeing the lack of wisdom in her choice. We can best do this by communicating how we have experienced her actions. When it is not possible to communicate, we must simply let go. When we are functioning as a teacher, spirituality requires that we take action that will benefit everyone involved. Blaming, shaming, or laying guilt on the individual will not assist them in learning the lesson. Communication and letting go will.

Learning a Spiritual Lesson

When you are learning a spiritual lesson, you will usually be faced with a difficult choice or decision. This may occur in a personal relationship or in a worldly experience. The result of the experience, however, will always be the same—you will emerge a more informed person. Some of the more important spiritual lessons we must learn are trust, honesty, forgiveness, and patience. In our relationships and experiences, we will be faced with situations in which we must make a choice to embrace one of these attributes. When we do, we find strength and support. When we do not, we experience or create pain, shame, and guilt.

Functioning as the Object
by Which the Spiritual Lesson Is Taught

When you are the object by which the spiritual lesson is being taught, you will find yourself in a situation that is not of your own making. Usually, two or more people will use you as a pawn, a scapegoat, or the object with which they strike out at one another. Children are often found in this situation, in struggles between their parents. When you are the object by which a lesson is being taught, you must be clear. You must know that the situation is not the result of your choice or your failure to make a choice. You must develop your own relationship with the parties involved, striving to remain neutral. Objects of spiritual lessons must not take sides. They are teaching and learning simultaneously and are, therefore, in a position of power. The power comes with clarity about what you have to contribute to the situation. Spirituality requires you to recognize that all experiences in life are purposeful. What you do today may not have meaning until a later time. However, you must know that nothing happens by chance. You must always seek the deeper meaning to everything that you experience, understanding that the knowledge will bring enlightenment. I once heard a minister say, "If you want to know the purpose of a thing, don't ask the thing, ask the Father of everything!" We have the voice of the Father within us. It is the voice of the Spirit. Spirituality is not "deep" or "mystical," the way most of us might imagine. Instead, it is probably the most simplistic approach to life. For when you have purpose, you are focused. When you are focused, you have clarity. The role Spirit plays in our lives is to make it abundantly clear to us that we have the power to choose, the right to know, and the capacity to be all that we imagine the Creator to be.

Wilt thou be made whole?

— John 5:6 (King James Version)

What I Know Now

*Life is an orderly progress governed and
directed by spiritual laws and principles.
Your spirit is already attuned to the energy
of spiritual law. Your choices direct your path.
Spirituality takes us beyond the physical to the deeper (metaphysical),
more profound experience of alignment with and connection to Spirit.
Spirituality and religion are not the same.
Spirituality is a way of being rather than something you do.*

Connecting the Dots

Before they are disciplined out of their natural inclination to be curious, or educated out of their innocence, children live with a deep and close connection to the voice and presence of Spirit. Children possess a *clear inner vision*, a pure and loving insight about people and environments, and their instincts are generally accurate. In an attempt to make their parents comfortable and conform to the expectations of their environment, children learn how to survive. In the process, they are taught to be afraid of what they see and know. They are trained to be judgmental of themselves

36

and others. They are programmed to be cynical. In an attempt to maintain the status quo of beliefs, to remain acceptable and to promote what matters to them, adults will unwittingly teach children to underestimate themselves, to doubt their instincts, to withhold their gifts or innate talents, and to ignore the truth. Adults are often annoyed by a child's inquisitiveness, challenged by a child's frankness, and embarrassed by a child's untimely revelations.

It is normal in our society for adults to encourage children to be dependent. They also demonstrate how to be co-dependent and ultimately applaud and reward a child's sense of being disempowered. We teach children to *look*, rather than to *see*. We interpret the facts for them and lead them to believe that our interpretations are the gospel truth. As an adult who has raised children, I feel compelled to acknowledge that *it is not our fault*. The simple truth is that we were given inaccurate and incomplete information by adults who had inaccurate and incomplete information. As a result, we continue to live in a world of interpretations rather than learning how to live in alignment with the truth, the laws of the universe. Alignment with spiritual law is the foundation of our spiritual nature, what we know as spirituality. It is this childlike joy, innocence, curiosity, and instinctual wisdom that we abandon in an attempt to make and keep others comfortable with whom they are not, and comfortable with who we are. *Fast-forward to adult disconnection.*

Spiritual Integrity: Acknowledging the Whole Truth

He was a beautiful man: a delight to look at and a pleasure to be around. Gentle, yet strong. Present in all of his masculinity, yet not overbearing. He was a man's man, and the jury is still out on whether or not he was truly a ladies' man. He knew all of the lingo, the spiritual platitudes that he shared at will or upon request. He was very cultural and promoted the advancement of ancient African culture as a foundation for living. He was a vegetarian chef who ate only raw food. He was a martial arts master and teacher. Some say he was the picture-perfect man, living the will of God, sharing his gifts with the world to facilitate spiritual growth and healing. Others say he had a dark side. They say he was emotionally and sexually abusive. These others—all women—stress that he was not at all what he seemed, but that it was hard to prove just who and what he was because he did what he did with such finesse. Who would ever believe that the "perfect man" had such a profoundly destructive shadow? Who?

I recently saw a greeting card that read: "I pray. I meditate. I practice yoga. And I still want to slap somebody." That card speaks to the power and the dilemma of spirituality. It is about the practice, the daily spiritual practices that will take us deeper into the realization and experience of our union with God. The sentiment of the card speaks to the innate contradictions that exist in human consciousness. Spiritual practices are designed to minimize these contradictions, and in the long run, eliminate them. Having the urge to slap someone and admitting that you have that urge is a spiritual practice. It is the practice of acknowledging truth. Truth is a spiritual principle that, if practiced consciously and embraced wholeheartedly, will eliminate the dark, negative thoughts that we, as physical beings, are prone to have. Allowing spiritual principles to govern and direct our behavior is a spiritual practice that establishes integrity. Spiritual integrity. The depth of our spiritual integrity will guide us with regard to which thoughts to surrender and which to act upon. Spirituality is about having one's mind, heart, and behavior in alignment. This alignment is a function of a consciousness that promotes the harmonious interaction between our mental, emotional, and spiritual essence. It is our spiritual essence that is innately aware of, attuned to, and aligned with the creative causes, the universal law to which we are all held accountable.

Spiritualizing Your Consciousness

Spirituality boils down to the following:

- Conscious acknowledgment of who you are as a unique expression of God.

- Conscious awareness that you are connected to God and all things created by God at all times. There are no exceptions.

- Conscious alignment with the principles, qualities, and nature that represent the universal truths about God.

- Conscious acceptance that you choose moment by moment whether to, and how to, experience and express your authentic identity.

- Conscious experience and expression of universal spiritual principles until they are so ingrained that they ultimately govern your every thought and subsequent actions.

When Spirit Calls

It was after 11 P.M. when the call came in. Despite caller ID, I always take a long, deep breath when my telephone rings after 11 P.M. What I heard left me with my mouth hanging open and my head shaking in disbelief. I knew that my goddaughter and this man had been dating. In fact, that is how I had met him. I also thought they had separated as lovers and were working on being just friends again. According to my caller, however, I was mistaken. They had been together for the past two days. During that time, something ugly had transpired between them. I was told that my goddaughter had allegedly shot and killed her lover. One shot to the chest, and two beautiful lives were destroyed. After several more telephone calls I discovered that she was being held in a hospital. Something about a rape kit and a suicide watch.

When I got to the hospital, no one could tell me anything, and I wasn't allowed to see her. I decided to go to the police station. On my way there, I was on my cell phone frantically trying to locate a good criminal lawyer. It is really challenging to find a lawyer by telephone at 2 A.M. Perhaps the police could help me? They couldn't because, as they informed me, "She is grown. If she wants you to know where she is and what to do, she will call you." By 3 A.M. I decided to stop driving up and down the roads like a lunatic, go back home, and surrender to the process. I wanted to believe that everything would unfold as it needed to at the right time, but doing so was a real struggle.

I was awakened at 7:20 A.M. by the gentle voice of Spirit instructing me: *Call now.* Swinging my legs over the side of the bed, I could not figure out who to call. The hospital? The police? A lawyer? Which lawyer? The court? It was time to practice what I knew. I took several long, deep breaths. I waited for the beating of my heart to grow stronger and slower within me. I prayed my favorite prayer, the 23rd Psalm, and I listened. At 8:10 A.M., I picked up the telephone and called the court. A lovely woman told me that she did not see my goddaughter's name on the arraignment court's docket.

"Hold on," she said. "Let me check one other place." In my mind, I kept praying.

When the angel court clerk returned, she gave me the case number and the list of charges, and she told me that my goddaughter would be appearing in court at 8:45 A.M. that same morning.

It's called a bird bath. You rinse out your mouth, scrub the tight places of your body that could emit an odor, and spray a light fragrance all over. That's what I did. I threw on what I had worn the day before, a coat, a wide-brimmed hat, and jumped in my car. The blessing was that I live seven minutes from the court where she was to appear. I got there in six minutes. As I attempted to find my way around the court building, some people stared and others pointed at me, but they weren't quite sure. I whispered to the woman at the information desk, knowing that once my voice was heard, I would be mobbed. The clerk told me just where to go and how to get there. I walked into the busy courtroom and didn't see my goddaughter. The court officer instructed me to remove my hat. I knew then that it was all over. Even though my hair was not combed, he recognized me. I turned away before he could say another word. As I walked out of the courtroom, people began to gasp.

One woman spoke aloud: "Hello, Miss Vanzant. How are you?"

Without stopping, I responded with a smile, "I am fine, thank you."

I made a beeline for the door, trying to figure out where I could hide until I had more information about the exact time my goddaughter would appear.

The woman followed me out of the courtroom. She caught up to me and said, "I just realized that you have never seen me. I'm Pamela."

Pamela was a friend of my son's. I had spoken to her many times by telephone regarding business matters, but we had never met face-to-face. Pamela was an attorney. She was in that courtroom waiting to represent a client on a criminal matter. I shook my head and prayed, "Thank you." I told her my story and asked if she would be willing to represent my goddaughter; she took it from there. Spirit always knows and will respond appropriately when we are in alignment.

To Be or Not!

When you violate spiritual laws, whether you do it consciously or unconsciously, the effects of the violation will manifest in your life, somehow, someway, someday. For example, if you are prone to gossiping about people or betraying the confidence others place in you, rest assured that one day, someone will gossip about you or betray your confidence. If you cheat on your taxes or accept too much change at the supermarket, you may consider it a windfall in the moment; however, one day someone will swindle you out of your resources. The law is the law, and it works impersonally. What you create and cause to happen today will be returned in kind at some later date.

For many of us, we do not realize when it is happening because it comes from or through another, unexpected source. And because so many of us are unaware that spiritual laws exist and are always in operation, we sing the somebody-done-me-wrong song. In the moment of our seemingly normal human reactions to life, we may not realize that there will be consequences for our spiritually illegal actions and thoughts. Yes! Thoughts are creative energies that have consequences. What I know now is that a fundamental requirement of enhancing our spiritual nature, of becoming a spiritual being, is to know and live within the boundaries of spiritual law. Every religion and spiritual community teaches and/or promotes spiritual law, even though it may not be identified as such.

The Spiritual Laws

A few of the spiritual laws that operate in our lives include the law of cause and effect, also known as "reaping and sowing"; the law of vibration, commonly referred to "as birds of a feather flock together"; the law of correspondence, which your mother probably quoted as "what you give, you get"; and the law of polarity, which you may recognize as "what goes up must come down." Each of the laws requires that we cleanse our thoughts and our hearts in order to become greater demonstrations of the wholeness and holiness of the one Spirit of life. Then there is the supreme law of love. Love is the foundation of the universe. It is the reason we come to life and the reason for living. Love is also the creative energy of life. God is love and what God creates can never be destroyed. Each of us was created by love for love's sake. We are here to give and receive love, to demonstrate and exemplify love, to create and re-create love. Love is the food of the spirit. In essence, it is *soul* food. We need it. We want it. We seek it. And for reasons most of us know well, we have a distorted meaning of how it must operate in our lives. Spirituality is the process and practice that restores our consciousness to the fullness of the meaning and demonstration of love.

My goddaughter is one of the sweetest, most gentle and spiritually grounded people I know. Apparently, in many aspects, so was her lover. Yet, like us all, they were both consciously and unconsciously influenced by the human frailties, emotional challenges, and spiritual hurdles that they had yet to overcome. Neither his behavior nor her response to it negates the fact that they were spiritually directed people. Since I did not have firsthand knowledge of all that transpired between them, it was not for me to judge or speculate. I made a great effort not to demonize either of them. My responsibility to spiritual law, as an elder and a godmother, was to support the soul who, for many years, relied on me for spiritual support. Thinking back on some of the foolish things I had done in the name of love, I thought it best to surrender my opinions.

React or Respond—Acknowledgment or Enlightenment

What I know now is that "the law" is a metaphor for "Lord." The law rules, and it will attract to us whatever is required for us to learn what we need to learn and to fulfill the spiritual curriculum designed for us in the spiritual realm. How we respond to the experiences and challenges with which we are confronted in life does not raise the question of whether or not we are spiritual. How we respond to life addresses the issue of whether or not our spiritual consciousness and spiritual integrity have developed deeply enough to sustain us in our moment of need. It is about whether or not our state of being was advanced and enhanced by the nature and depth of our spiritual practices. Whether we "react" or "respond" in any given situation will be determined by whether we actually do the healing, learning work required to be consciously aware of and connected to Spirit, or whether we did a "spiritual bypass"—learning the words, feigning the practices, and creating what we thought we needed without the guidance of Spirit. How can you tell? How will you know if your spirituality will sustain you? Look at the quality of your mind, heart, and life. If you think the same, feel the same, and live the same as you did five years ago, chances are the Spirit is calling you to come closer and dig deeper.

The bad news is: *You will never be more spiritual than you are right now.* This means that no matter how much you pray, how long you meditate, how pious or astute you may deem yourself to be about things of a spiritual nature, you will never have any more *spirit* than you have in this moment. The good news is: *You will never be more spiritual than you are in this moment.* This means that you already possess everything you need to have an authentic, fulfilling, connection to and relationship with the full Spirit of God.

The difference between the good news and the bad news is *acknowledgment* and *alignment.* Like anyone with whom you are in relationship, the Holy Spirit of God within you requires time, energy, attention, and affirmation if it is to deepen and mature in its expression through you. Spending the time to engage in prayer, meditation, and the study of things of a spiritual nature; expending energy to study, learn, and practice how to be a more loving, grateful, forgiving, compassionate individual; focusing your attention on what is *within* rather than what you can accomplish outside of yourself; affirming the truth about yourself, about God, and about life are the essential requirements for growing and maturing your spiritual nature. This is the path to a spiritualized way of being.

Spirituality is not about *what* you know. It is about growing, deepening, evolving, and becoming a living reflection of your spiritual identity. It is about bringing your human nature into alignment with the essence of light and love and God. Light is a principle. It means the absence or overshadowing of darkness. Love is a principle. It is the presence of God active in our consciousness in such a way that it creates more of itself through each of us.

Growing up in a dysfunctional and abusive environment, I considered myself the first runner-up for the Wretched of the Earth door prize. What I know now is that there is a seed of peace, joy, love, and wisdom in each of us. My seeds had been trampled upon by the bad behavior of the big people, the adults in my life. Bless their pointed heads! It would be a spiritual bypass for me to say that they did the best they could, because the truth is, we can all be better if we choose to. Your adults were probably like my adults, they did the best they could, what they knew how to do, and they didn't realize that, spiritually, they were capable of being and doing more. More peace, more joy, and more love is available to every living being when:

- They acknowledge that it is possible to know and live a God-filled life.

- They accept that their life does not belong to them. It belongs to God and the Spirit of God for a high calling.

- They align themselves with the nature, essence, and energy of God as the foundation for all human activity and interactions.

And it ain't easy!

Don't Get It Twisted!

As a child I was taught that spirituality meant going to church, being washed in the blood of Jesus, and being saved. What I know now is that my father would not have gone to church if his last supper were being served there on a platter of thousand-dollar bills. My grandmother, who raised me from age three until age five, went to church almost every day and twice on Sunday; she was still as mean as a wet cat! So what happened? How did my father finally line up and live according to the laws of the universe while my grandmother ended up old and alone in a nursing home without the comfort and support of her grandchildren and great-grandchildren? It came down to religion versus spirituality, and principles versus dogmatism.

My father eventually embraced the teachings of Paramahansa Yogananda, the founder of the Self-Realization Fellowship. Through Yogananda's teachings, he was inspired to develop a close, intimate, and personal relationship with God, which altered his behavior and perspective of life. He changed his diet, embracing the belief that eating was meant to sustain the temple of the body, rather than to satisfy the desires of the physical senses. He learned and practiced spiritual principles such as compassion, gentleness, meekness, and selfless service. What I know now is that the man I saw caring for my children, sitting peacefully in a lotus position, or dressing in a suit and tie even though he was just a foot messenger, was not the same man who was barely around when I was growing up. His spiritual practice had altered who he was at the core of his being. He was definitely a new creature. He tried desperately to share with me what he had learned, but I had yet to heal my childhood wounds. I rejected him and his newfound philosophy hands down. Today I know enough about forgiveness to recognize that he and I would be best buddies. Could be. Maybe. Maybe not. Who knows? Everything is always as it should be in the realm of Spirit.

My grandmother chose another route. She was a devout Pentecostal parishioner. She embraced the strict teachings of a brand of Christianity that saw evil in most things, which she took upon herself to stamp out at all costs. In my case, as the child of a forbidden relationship between her married son, my father, and a single woman, my mother (who was a loud, cussing alcoholic), my grandmother believed I was born wretched and sinful. Grandma believed it was her God-given responsibility to save me from myself. Her intention was to wash the devil out of me with a scrub brush and lye soap. She endeavored to beat the devil out of me with an ironing cord, a razor strap, or whatever else was available.

Her mission was to pray the devil out of me by dragging me to every church she could find between Kingston Avenue in Brooklyn, New York, and Lenox Avenue in Harlem. My grandmother knew the tenets of religion, but had no idea about the principles of Spirit. She believed you had to use the rod to control the child, and preach the word but not live it. Like many, she had a relationship with religion rather than a relationship with the spirit of God. The sad thing was that she knew her behavior was inappropriate because she hid it and forced me to hide it, also. Her threats of what would happen if I told my father or anyone else were deliberately issued. Some would say, based on her behavior, that my grandmother wasn't a Christian. It matters not what people say, what matters is what she believed. And what she believed was based on her interpretation of what Christianity required of her.

True Spirituality

What I know now about spirituality is that you cannot make it up as you go along. The principles must be embodied, embraced, and lived. There must be accountability for the development of spiritual integrity. Whether you receive your guidance from a sacred text, a minister, or a spiritual teacher, everyone must be held accountable for the spiritual beliefs that manifest as behavior. In ancient African and Native American traditions, ceremonies and rituals are one level of accountability. Whether you dance in a circle or before a fire, whether you spend days alone in the woods or sit alone in a room until you have a revelation, spirituality is developed through self-discipline and study under the watchful eye of an elder. In today's world, things are not so structured and guarded. We are free to develop our own brand of spirituality and to promote it as "how I've been guided by spirit." Few know whether the spirit that is guiding is a spirit of light or one we made up. If left unexamined, unchecked, and unconfirmed, these loosey-goosey beliefs and practices can get us into trouble. In the worst-case scenario, they can prove to be not effective enough to sustain us in crisis before we actually do slap somebody. In the best-case scenario, we preach them and even teach them, but fail to grow in awareness or alignment with the creative energies of life. Whether you embrace a specific religion or some philosophy of spirituality, there must be order in your practices, your philosophy, and how both manifest as your behavior.

When I acknowledge to others that I am a Yoruba priestess, a cultural custodian in an ancient African tradition, I have seen expressions raging from shock and horror to awe and wonder. Some are innocent or courageous enough to ask what it means. Others, those who do not ask, I believe, walk away with a preconceived notion that labels me as something or everything between being a pagan devil worshiper, a witch or the anti-Christ.

I am aware that many people still experience what I refer to as *"Afro-phobia"*: the fear of all things African. In today's world it has become fashionable to embrace African art and artifacts, to visit Africa armed with an expensive point-and-shoot camera and to wear imported African garb. When it comes to embracing the depth and richness of the cultural and spiritual philosophies of ancient African traditions, fear is more often than not the first response. Many people—more specifically, many African Americans and most Christians—are still committed to the belief that things African are dark, magical, dangerous, and Godless. The cultural supremacy of modern Western cultures and the proliferation of Christian religious principles as, *"the only way"* have rendered traditional African spiritual philosophies and practices as wrong, bad, and outside of the will of God. In the modern world where God and State are separate entities, where the so-called rational mind is advanced and elevated over the inherent spiritual nature of life, control and domination are the goals.

In Yoruba and many other indigenous African and native traditions where God, a Supreme Being, is regarded as an integral aspect of all life, surrendered cooperation for the good of the whole is the way to evolution and survival. Reverent respect of God must be extended to all things and people for the purpose they serve in God's plan. In Yoruba tradition, there is no separation between man and God. God is life. As such, all life is a representation of God. As a Yoruba, it is my duty to live my life in such a manner that I represent to the world, that I believe in and am aligned with the Spirit of God. It is this Spirit that expresses Itself through my behavior.

Spirituality is not something we can do to get or stay out of trouble. It is a *breathing* essence that must be carried out in our lives. Living in the modern world, where almost anything goes, many of us don't have the first clue about where to start the inner development process that will enhance our spiritual nature. I stumbled into the process during my own healing and development. Because I was on my own in many ways, I took copious notes. It began as a series of questions I asked myself in order to understand my responsibility in the difficult experiences of my life. I understood that in order to actualize my God-given ability to create and re-create the conditions of my physical world reality, I had to know and demonstrate my authentic identity. Most of what I did in my life was what I learned from the adults in my environment. I had very few, if any, original thoughts or beliefs, including the ones I held about myself and God. I realized that my behavior was the key. If I could understand why I did what I did, the way that I did it, I would be on my way to total transformation. I could more consciously choose how to bring my behavior into alignment with my spiritual nature and the principles that governed it.

Core Questions

The core questions I examined were these:

- What am I doing?

- Why am I doing it?

- What are the results I am achieving?

- How does what I do move me toward the results
  I desire?

- Is what I do self-supporting? Self-nurturing?
  Self-loving?

- Is what I do kind and loving to others?

- Am I willing to change what I do?

For more than two years my life became a ruthless, vigilant investigation of my own beliefs, intentions, judgments, projections, expectations (of myself and others), choices, perceptions, and the resulting behaviors. In the process, I discovered that the overwhelming majority of my behaviors and most of my choices were a function of anger, fear, habit, and the misdiagnosis of what I thought was going on. I realized that for most of my life, I was alone in my head without adult supervision, making up stories about myself and other people, as I did everything possible to avoid what I thought might be a painful outcome. I lived in survival mode trying to avoid what had happened before, but with no vision of the many possibilities that were equally valid. By answering these questions within myself and for myself, and then presenting my responses to a trusted spiritual elder, I became aware of the misalignment between my consciousness and universal law.

Trust me when I say that *it was horrific!* I was out of order! My thinking was out of order! My behavior was out of order! My life was out of order! Worst of all, I discovered that *I* was the cause of most of it. My reactions were habitual. My future projections were grounded in past failures. My interpretations of the physical-world realities I faced were self-defeating, self-debasing, and self-destructive. With the help of a few teachers and a few great books, I discovered how to apply universal laws and spiritual principles to every thought, every word, and every action. In doing so, my consciousness was healed from the emotional imbalances and misinterpretations of my life lessons, which I had mislabeled as: *It's hard out here for a black girl!* I share with you now the fruits of that investigation—what I call the "Seven-Level Healing Paradigm."

The Seven-Level Healing Paradigm: Feeling Leads to Healing

Unfortunately, we all too often get so caught up in what *others tell us* about who we are that we fail to do our own independent investigation. Self-investigation is an elementary step toward spirituality, and it is an inner process rather than an outer destination. We can get so stuck in our interpretations of the facts others have given us that we stop seeking the truth for ourselves. Our lives are the vehicles that teach us how to fly. Yet, we can be so sidetracked by the facts of our lives that we forget we have wings. We are grounded by our stories. Each story represents a set of beliefs that are etched into our consciousness by experience. We are not told that beliefs are the foundation upon which we build our lives. Rarely, if ever, are we informed that as we change our beliefs, we alter our perception, our vision of reality. In fact, we are encouraged to believe that our experiences justify our beliefs. The truth is that our beliefs, although programmed and conditioned into our consciousness, are what create our experiences. The Seven Level Healing Paradigm will support you in recognizing and embracing the truth of who you are in the eyes of God.

Know Yourself!

This is the level of acknowledgment. Acknowledgment is the door to healing and growth. Until we are willing to acknowledge what we do, we have no power to choose or change our behavior. Acknowledgment does not require explanation or defense. It is simply a process of recognition. Only through willingness to become *aware,* to acknowledge and accept all aspects of who you are, can you *know* your Self, your unique, divine, authentic identity. It is human nature to accept, often without question, what we are told about who we are. We oftentimes embrace the concepts, roles, prescriptions, and judgments of race consciousness, gender, and class as the foundation for developing self-identity. To truly know yourself means to become fully aware of both your divine and human nature and to utilize that knowledge as a basis of choice in all aspects of life.

See Yourself!

This is the level of awareness. It takes acknowledgment to a deeper level. Through awareness you become attuned to your moment-by-moment responses and reactions called "triggers." When you are aware of which triggers are present, you are empowered to heal wounds and make new choices. The goals of awareness are these:

- Right thought
- Right action
- Right response (rather than reaction)

This level of development and growth requires a willingness to engage in a process of introspection and self-reflection. In doing so, we allow ourselves to become familiar with and explore our internal landscape. Self-exploration and reflection is the precursor to the ability to know yourself. It is the process by which we become familiar with the aspects of our divine and human nature that makes us uniquely who we are as individual expressions of life.

Be Yourself!

This is the level of inner personal integrity where thought, feeling, and action are congruent. In order to be yourself, you must have inner cooperation on all levels of existence (mental, emotional, physical, and spiritual). This level also requires a willingness to live beyond external expectations and habitual responses. Once there is an awareness, and an unconditional acceptance of your true identity, the need for pretenses and defenses is eliminated. To be yourself means to accept and stand for the authentic Self, and to live a life of conscious choice from that level of internal and external reality.

Accept Yourself!

This level requires diligent and compassionate self-forgiveness of all of the judgments you hold about past behaviors and experiences. It is the loving and self-support required to learn from previous actions in order to take corrective steps. Acceptance cannot be facilitated without acknowledgment and awareness. This level of personal growth, development, and healing requires an acknowledgment that we are spiritual beings having a *human* experience, and gives us the courage to accept our human frailties. In order to do so, we must resist the temptation to judge ourselves as needing to be perfect, and resist the temptation to seek perfection. The truth of our experience is that we are always exactly where we need to be, doing exactly what we need to do, in order to experience a deeper level of self-acceptance.

Trust Yourself!

This level requires the willingness to live beyond past errors, unconscious choices, and self-judgments. Knowing that you are authorized by the universe to re-create yourself and your experiences—moment by moment—supports the development of trust. This is also the level of commitment to following inner guidance and directives without fear or hesitation.

Trust is a principle and an acknowledgment of the truth of your divine identity. It is the recognition that, at the core of your being, you have a connection to the divine intelligence of life, Spirit, God. Because of this connection, you will always make the right choice for yourself based on your unique spiritual curriculum. It is this curriculum, the learning plan for your life, that governs your choices. It is always your choices that lead you to *what* you must learn and determine *how* you will learn.

Honor Yourself!

At this level we are each called to live in a state of radical honesty with regard to our thoughts and emotions. While being yourself requires integrity, honoring yourself requires that you act in your physical world reality in a way that is self-supportive and self-nurturing. Honor is another principle. It is the internal impetus not to discount or deny who you are, what you know, or what you feel at any given time. To honor is to take a stand *for* yourself, *within* yourself, and to stand for what you know to be true for you, regardless of any opposition. It is also a demonstration of your willingness to take a stand for yourself in all aspects of your life's experience. It is through honoring yourself that you build your own value and worth.

Appreciate Yourself!

At this level we become willing to give ourselves credit for the small, although seemingly insignificant steps we take to practice each of the other six levels. Self-appreciation builds a greater awareness of inner and outer healing and progress. It also opens the heart to experience and express more compassion toward self and others. Appreciation is a function of the principle of gratitude. It is the way in which you demonstrate to yourself that you are worthy of your own time, energy, and attention. It is a statement to life that you are willing to continue growing, learning, and healing, and that you are grateful for the efforts you make on your own behalf. Appreciation is a form of gratitude that conveys support and recognition.

Awareness of and willingness to embrace each level of the Seven-Level Healing Paradigm facilitates the activity of our "internal committee members." These members control our internal dialogue, or *self-talk*. A deficit at one or more of the levels of the paradigm invites critical, judgmental, and often abusive members to sit on, and possibly run, the committee. When this occurs, our internal dialogue incites fear, worry, judgment, and mental and emotional confusion. This often results in abandonment of, or resistance to, the presence and energy of the inherently divine nature within each of us. By consciously choosing to acknowledge and heal at all levels of the paradigm, we redirect the energy of the committee. As a result, the content and essence of the internal dialogue becomes self-supportive and nurturing, leading to a more elegant creation of reality.

Chapter 3

BLESSING
YOUR HEAD

As a child, I remember being told that I would never amount to anything. I was constantly reminded about the "bad" things I did. I was always being compared to cousin so-and-so, or to the kid next door, and to people I didn't even know. I grew up trying to be like everybody else, anybody other than myself. After all, I was told that I was ugly. I was reminded daily that I was bad. At first, I wanted to be like Penny, the young cowgirl on the *Sky King* television show. She had long, blonde hair and a horse, and everybody liked her. I made myself pigtails like Penny's by pinning yellow knee socks to my sparse pieces of hair. I would flip them around my head and tell myself how beautiful I was. When they canceled *Sky King,* I decided to be like Veronica in the *Archie* comic books. Veronica was beautiful and rich, but when I realized that nobody liked her, I changed my identity again. I decided I was going to be like Mary. No one would dare dislike the mother of Christ. As luck would have it, there was a big Baptist church directly across the street from my house. I thought Mary would be in all of her glory in that church. I was wrong. The only time she was ever mentioned was at Christmas. I had to find another medium if I was to learn about my mentor. I found it in the Catholic church.

I had my first contact with Mary at St. Matthew's Catholic Church in Brooklyn, New York. She stood as a 12-foot statue with spotlights at the base of her feet! She was positioned in a way that made her eyes follow you everywhere. I was convinced that Mary was looking directly at me! Whether she was or not didn't matter; I knew she would one day speak to me, and I took every opportunity to stop by the church to see her. I would go to St. Matthew's every day after school since it was on my way home. I would also sneak by to see Mary on my way to any store that took me near the church. I stopped playing with the other children. I spent many afternoons in long conversations with Mother Mary, moving around from seat to seat just to see if her eyes would follow me. If she could see me, I thought it meant she could also hear me. My words were always the same: "Show me how to be like you. Please help me be somebody better." When winter came, I stopped going to church because it was too cold to walk the extra two blocks, but I continued my prayer. I also wrote letters to Mary, and I wrote about her in my diary every day.

One day my older brother and I were having one of our sibling wars. He was screaming that I was weird and ugly. As I cowered in the corner, waiting for him to pounce on me, I took my hands from my face for a moment, to see how close he was to me. When I looked up, I didn't see my brother, I saw Mary! She was standing between my brother and me. Her face was as beautiful as it appeared to be in the church, except she was darker. I realized that Mary, the mother of Christ, was a black woman. She was wrapped in flowing blue cloth. Her head was draped in a white cloth that fell across her shoulders. She had a very serious look on her face. I could hear my brother screaming at me, "You make me sick! That's all you ever do! Stop copying what I do!" Then his voice stopped, and Mary stared right into my eyes. I felt the touch of her hand on my head, and I heard her say, *Just be yourself. Keep your head clear and be yourself. I will always be with you, in your mind.* Then she was gone. My brother was back. I could hear him saying, "Stop trying to be like everybody else!" I just stared at him and started crying.

The Head Rules the Body

Ori, or the head, is the seat of spiritual consciousness. As such, we must begin to pay close attention and give great care to our head. We must be conscious and cautious of what we put on and in our head, as well as where we put and what we do with our head. It is through the head, the base of thought, that we are guided. Understanding spirit as the key to our destiny, we want to keep its house, the head, clear and clean. One way to achieve this is to begin the day by blessing our head.

In Yoruba culture, we are taught that "the head rules the body." We know, with all of the miracle transplants medical science can perform, there is nothing they can do to replace your head. In the New Age movement, this theory is represented by the philosophy that whatever is going on in your mind will manifest itself in your life. You give issues, fears, and ideas power by virtue of your thoughts. African culture teaches that one must be careful not to speak or think about those things you do not want to see or experience. As you strive to become a spiritual being, taking time to pray and meditate is the perfect way to keep your head and mind clear.

Your head represents a universe within itself. It is round, representing the 360 degrees of knowledge. It is ruled by the astrological sign of Aries. Aries is the concept of "I Am." "I Am" is the creative power and consciousness of God. Your head is like a laboratory through which you take in information and elements and then transform them to another state. Your thoughts are processed in a way similar to how you take in food: You chew food to prepare it for digestion by mixing it with enzymes in your mouth and stomach, and it is then transformed into nourishment, which sustains your life. Similarly, every experience you have is absorbed by one or more of your physical senses. When you see or hear things, they enter your head and are meshed with your pre-existing knowledge and memories of past experiences. This information is then transformed into a perception or aligned with an existing belief that holds meaning for you. That meaning is then interpreted by your mind and serves as the motivation for your very next thought, spoken word or behavior. The head also encases your face, which represents your universal identity.

In many ancient traditions, people were taught to cover their heads to protect the sacred knowledge they received. In many African cultures, covering your head during a spiritual ceremony is considered disrespectful. Africans believe that the spirit enters and leaves the body through the head. Therefore, if the head is covered, you cannot give or receive the blessings of spirit. Today we have lost touch with the value and meaning of protecting, blessing, and guarding our head. Somehow during the American socialization process, the head has become an item to be adorned rather than an element to be adored. It is through the head that spiritual enrichment takes place. For unless your head and heart are aligned with righteousness, you can never hope to achieve spiritual purification. As a Yoruba, I have been taught about the sacredness of the head. My godparents, those who initiated me, stressed the importance of following my head, my destiny. My grandmother taught me always to "follow my first thought," but it was not until I was initiated that I realized the importance of that simple act. What comes into my head is what I need to know.

No one else can do or learn what I need to know. Each of us must learn to master and manage our thoughts. This is accomplished as we cleanse our hearts of toxic emotions and bless our heads with loving sincerity. The greatest resistance to honoring and following our own thoughts is fear. We fear being wrong. We fear being hurt or harmed. More than anything, we fear losing the love of others. This, we believe, will happen if we dare to be different and think outside of the box our loved ones have given us. Fear engenders self-doubt and second-guessing of our first thought, which is usually our most accurate thought. We are taught not to trust ourselves, which leads to a fear of change, a fear of failure, a fear of the unknown and—the big kahuna—a fear of isolation. Fear and self-doubt are common human conditions that lead us to deny, resist, and ignore the very thoughts that lead to actions that are essential for our personal growth and spiritual evolution. One simple way to overcome this challenge is to perform the sacred ceremony of blessing our heads daily, or, at the very least, weekly.

Blessing your head develops and
strengthens your consciousness and character.
Blessing your head accelerates spiritual
development and facilitates learning.
Blessing your head diminishes limited perceptions of reality.
As you learn your unique life lessons, your behavior changes.

Blessing the Head

- You will need a small glass or clay vessel with a cover that has not been used for any other purpose. Fill the vessel with spring water. (If you have a personal altar or sacred space, you may keep the vessel of water there.)

- Upon arising, before speaking to anyone or beginning daily activities, bless your head with the water in the following manner:

- Sit or stand in a secluded and quiet area. Place two fingers of each hand into the water.

- Place fingers in the middle of forehead; draw them from the center of your forehead, across the top, and down the back of your head to the base of your neck. *Prayer:* "I bless the spirit of my head." Repeat this motion three times.

- Dip your fingers again. Place your fingers at the top center of your head (the crown). Draw your fingers across your head to your ears (draw right hand down to right ear, left hand down to left ear). *Prayer:* "I bless the spiritual energy of my head."

- You will now bless each part of your head in the following order with the appropriate prayer. Dip your fingers before each blessing.

Forehead [Third Eye]

Draw fingers from center of forehead out to each side.
Prayer: "I bless my spiritual vision that I may see my way clearly."

Eyes

Simultaneously stroke each eye gently outward. Right hand, right eye; left hand, left eye.
Prayer: "I bless my eyes that I may see truth in my life."

Nose

Stroke each nostril from top to bottom.
Prayer: "I bless my breath that my life may be sustained by spirit."

Ears

Stroke each ear with fingertips.
Prayer: "I bless my ears that I may recognize and follow the guidance of my spirit."

Mouth

Stroke lips from center outward.

Prayer: "I bless my ability to speak the truth of spirit, to affirm the guidance of spirit, to give thanks for the blessings of spirit."

Face

Stroke the circular outline of your face from the center of the forehead around to your chin.
Prayer: "I bless my unique identity as an expression of God, my Creator, and I ask to be an expression of divine light and divine love."

Bless your head again, from the center of your forehead, across the top, and down to the base of your neck.
Prayer: "I bless the spirit of my head to guide me throughout this day."

Bless your head from the crown to either ear.
Prayer: "I bless the spirit of my head to protect me through this day."

Another way to reinforce the power of this ceremony is to recite your favorite psalm or prayer over the water when you first fill your vessel. You may also place your covered vessel of water in places where it may be exposed to sunlight. Change the water weekly. Feel free to add an essential oil to the water:

- Sage for wisdom
- Frankincense for clarity
- Myrrh for purification
- Lavender for peace
- Rose or rosewood for joy

Blessing your head will allow you to begin your day by contacting your own spirit, the guiding force in your life.

Hard Is Hardly It!

Many women like things to be hard. A lot of people get turned on by the dramatic frenzy of running here and there, trying to find this or that in order to get something or learn something else at the last possible moment. Life does not have to be hard! There was a time in my own life when I had a tendency to make my life experience much harder than was required or necessary. In fact, the "last minute" was my drug of choice. Then, as I matured and my memory ceased to be as cooperative as it had once been, I had to abandon the "last minute" and focus on where I had put my glasses! Now I watch in total amazement as the young women around me, drama queens and divas, push the envelope of the important things in their lives to 15 minutes *after* they are due. What I know now is that making life harder than it needs to be does not make you more valuable, worthy, or stronger. In fact, it gives you wrinkles!

One of my favorite Bible verses is Proverbs 3:5-6 which says: "Trust in the Lord with all your heart, do not depend on your own understanding. Seek His will in all you do, and he will show you which path to take" (New Living Translation).

I consider this the absolute mandate for blessing your head daily. Understanding that it is not the physical head we are addressing, but rather the spiritual head, or consciousness, this proverb clearly indicates that if we want to know what to do, we must honor the Creator of our head. If we want to know how to do it, we must seek guidance and direction. We must be obedient to our inner voice, and we must stop believing that we are out here in the world alone.

There have been many times in my life when I have been totally lost and confused but would not admit it. I thought my life had to be hard; after all, I was *ugly* and *bad*. Because I had watched the adults in my life do it with such finesse, I believed that struggle was necessary for the development of an all-around personality. I tell you, *I really knew how to struggle!* I struggled to make ends meet. I struggled to raise my children, attempting to teach them how not to struggle. I struggled through one relationship after another, one *bad* relationship after another. I struggled to manage my life rather than live it. It felt as though I had been beaten up so badly, and for so long, *in* life and *by* life, that I believed struggle, hurt, and pain were the natural order. I knew how to take a punch in life, and I was *determined* not to be knocked down even when I was on my knees, crawling, with my tongue hanging out. I would survive!

I now realize that just because you can take a punch does not mean you must stand in front of a fist, particularly not when the fist is your own. *It is like self-flagellation!* With my extremely negative internal self-dialogue, I would beat myself up for who and what I was and was not, what I had and had not done, what I did and did not own. Externally, I tried to prove to myself and the world that I was more than I actually believed I could ever be. It was *crazy-making behavior,* and I was doing it to myself. I had a very limited perception of reality and myself based on the many things I had been told during childhood. I had also created enough drama on my own to make my life a hotbed of difficulty.

If you live long enough, life will humble you. Life will level your defenses, expose your bad habits, and reveal self-deception, all in an attempt to push you beyond your self-inflicted nonsense and self-imposed unworthiness. When you are paying attention, you will get the point. When you are not, *you will be humbled.* Life can and will bring you to the stark realization that your thinking and feeling nature—in essence, your level of consciousness—controls what you can and cannot do or be. If you allow yourself to think and believe that *being human sucks,* you will find yourself in a perpetual state of being puckered up. We all become a slave of sorts to what we believe. Each of us has a set of *core beliefs* that compete with our divinity and attract the very things we try so desperately to avoid.

Understanding Doesn't Happen Overnight—
"What Happened to You and Oprah?"

Over the years many people have asked me, "What happened to you and Oprah?" There has been a lot of speculative innuendo. I think that the time has come to address the matter openly and honestly. What happened? *I leaned on my own understanding!* I asked for guidance *after* I took action, rather than before, as suggested in Proverbs. Let me explain: My opportunity to spend time and space with Oprah Winfrey came along when there was a lot going on in my life. I had recently been married to my lifelong love. All of my children were grown and leaving home. My career was moving faster than I could keep up, and I stopped doing the things that had sustained me for so long. I prayed when it was convenient. I meditated when I had time. I continued to buy beautiful journals, but I had stopped writing in them with any regularity. I was moving through life on the fumes of what I had learned and mastered rather doing what I knew was required to stay spiritually strong and grounded. I stopped blessing my head. I allowed all that I was *doing* to take precedence over honoring my *being*.

One unsuspecting day when I was minding my business *doing* a million things at once, I received a handwritten note card from the vice president of a major television network. I read the card in total amazement. The vice president praised my work and wished me continued good luck. She provided me with a telephone number and invited me to lunch at any time. Because I was raised to have manners and I knew that it was good business to have the private telephone number of a television executive, I called her to say thank you. To my surprise, she answered the telephone on the second ring, and when I introduced myself, she squealed and thanked me for calling. In a brief conversation she informed me that she had been trying to contact me for some time but had been told that I had a six-figure deal with Harpo, Oprah's production company. Because I was thinking rather than being, I explained that while I had a wonderful working relationship with Harpo, I did not have a six-figure deal. She simply said, "Oh, really?" After a few more well wishes, she reaffirmed her lunch offer. I was flattered, and I told her so. With that, we ended the call.

A few days later, I received a telephone call from the same executive. She informed me that her boss had an idea for a television show that she thought I could help her develop. She indicated that what they really wanted was advice on how to execute a show focusing on relationships. Her boss had seen my work on Oprah and thought I may be able to point them in the right direction. She assured me that all they wanted to do was pick my brain. When she told me her boss's name, my mouth dropped open in shock. Why in the world would *this* person need my advice? They had been trying to get this show off the ground for a while and were getting nowhere because, her boss felt, they were taking the wrong approach. She shared the idea for the show with me and asked what I thought. It was in that moment that my ego took control. This is me, I thought, a poor, ugly girl from Brooklyn, New York, being asked her opinion by an executive of a major television network. *Lordy, Lordy, I must be hot stuff!* I thought it, but somewhere deep inside, I did not believe it. In fact, there was another voice screaming in my head at the same time, *Girl you better shut up and go somewhere and pray! These people are getting ready to find you out!* I didn't know what they might find out, but I know it did not feel good in my gut.

Life will humble you! Had I been grounded, had I been clear, had I been handling my *spiritual business,* I probably would have been unfazed by her request. Instead, despite the disquiet in my spirit, I thought I could help, I thought I could be of assistance to a major network executive. This is the exact moment that my understanding kicked in, and I made the first misstep. *I said yes without asking for guidance.* I was invited to dinner. I was given a plane ticket and a hotel room at The Plaza on Central Park. I was driven to a secluded, private restaurant on the Upper East Side. When I arrived there were four people at the table, Executive #1, Executive #2, Executive #3, and the boss, the Executive #4, who would eventually back my television show. I was impressed. I was scared to death. *What the heck do they want with me?* I had a lovely meal of food that I could not spell, and then it began: the stroking of my ego, the plucking of my brain, the schmoozing, and the subtle—very subtle—setup.

When you do not have a good relationship with your head, people can know more about you than you realize about yourself. Because there is only one Spirit that connects us all, it is almost impossible to hide or disown your insecurities and fears completely. People pick up subtle clues about you from what you say, what you do, and how you present yourself at any moment. When people are well versed in and/or trained to recognize human nature, they will follow the clues you offer straight to your weak spots. And if there is something they need or want from you, they can exploit your weaknesses to their advantage. It is an aspect of human nature—the animal part of us that leans toward the survival of the fittest—that the bigger, stronger one conquers the weaker one. In this case, my case, the strong-conquering-the-weak analogy had nothing to do with our physical bodies. It had to do with knowing who you are and what you want. The executives knew who they were, what they wanted, and how they could get it. I had become so busy, so self-directed, that I was losing touch with my inner voice. My life had become about working it, making it happen, and getting it done. The "it" I am referring to is about the external world—external validation and affirmation. Internally, I was still working to silence and heal the poor, dysfunctional, ugly, bad girl who was still trying to prove to herself that she was worthy of the time, energy, and attention she was receiving.

Hungry All the Time

In the next few weeks, there were a series of telephone calls from the network asking that I consider an offer to host a new television show. My response was, "No, thank you. I am happy where I am." The executive *said* she understood, but thought she would ask in case I had changed my mind. She wanted me to think about it because they were running out of time. There were some changes going on at the network, she said, and they needed to make some decisions real soon. If I changed my mind within the next week or so, I could call her. She gave me her home telephone number. That bothered me, but it was also intriguing. *Why are these people so hot on my tail? What do they want from me? What do I have that they want?* Based on my understanding, I thought I needed answers to these questions when in the spiritual reality I did not.

Until and unless you know that you are enough just the way you are, you will continue to look for more. You will sell off pieces and parts of yourself in an attempt to get more and do more, hoping it will help you feel like more. Knowing that you are enough is a function of consciousness. Your *enough-ness* unfolds and develops in direct proportion to the relationship you have with your head, your authentic identity. Until you wholeheartedly believe in your own value, worth, and worthiness, in spite of your accomplishments and possessions, or lack thereof, there will be a void in your spirit. Think of it as feeling hungry all of the time. Anyone who is really hungry cannot think properly. You will eat food that you do not actually enjoy, or food that does not nourish the body. You will eat things that are too cold or things that burn the roof of your mouth. You are also prone to stuffing the food into your mouth. You shove it in and gobble it down. In doing so, you miss out on the flavor, the wonderful blend of ingredients and spices turn a good meal into a great meal. Hungry people chew fast and swallow hard. In fact, you may chew so fast that you don't crush and grind the food effectively, which means what you have ingested will not be properly digested.

When you are the kind of hungry that feels like being on the verge of starvation, you can lose your sense of dignity and self-respect. You will fight your children or lie to your best friend to get something, anything, into your mouth and stomach. A deep painful hunger will even make you lose your grip on reality. Eating whatever is available will fill and sustain you if you are on the verge of starvation. However, when your palate desires a *specific* thing, eating what is available is a waste of time, energy, and food. You can eat until you are so full you cannot move, but you will not be satisfied. You are left with a hunger, an incomprehensible yearning.

I was appearing weekly on national television with Oprah Winfrey. My books were flying off the shelves. I was in love with and married to a man whom I absolutely adored, and still I was hungry. I had a purpose and I loved my work. I had a clear and honorable intention to serve and support people, and I was good at what I did. Still, I was hungry. No. I was *starving*. There was an internal battle between the parts of me that had healed and grown and the parts of me that had not. That really can happen. You can do the work, the spiritual healing work to move your consciousness beyond the wounded places, yet still be plagued by unconscious core beliefs. A core belief is a persistent or habitual thought that sets up the framework for how we respond to the world. More often than not, core beliefs are fueled by toxic emotions—such as fear, shame, guilt, or remorse—that were established in response to our interpretation of childhood experiences. As they function in consciousness, core beliefs influence and motivate our current choices and decisions because the mind will attempt to avoid today the same hurt, pain, or upset that we experienced in the past. My core belief was: *I'm not good enough, and I will never be good enough to deserve this kind of attention.* When your core belief is running the show, it will encourage, inspire, motivate, or drive you. I call it a "TNT"—Terrifying Neurotic Tension—on the inner parts of you that will ultimately blow up in your life, because the TNT premise from which you are operating has very little, if anything, to do with your current reality.

After the third frantic telephone call from the executive, I concluded that the offer warranted my attention. I knew there was a lesson I needed to learn, but I had no clue what it was, and the human, self-directed part of me wanted to know. I decided to engage my spiritual practice of prayer and fasting. My prayer partner joined me. We committed to pray and fast for seven days or until I got the direction I needed. The issue at hand was whether to stay at Harpo or leave and begin my own show. My preference was to stay put, but I had a hunger that was not being satisfied.

On the sixth morning I awakened with the thought, *The time is now.* I shot straight up in my bed and spoke aloud, "I am not leaving Harpo." As if someone were whispering in my ear, I heard it again, *The time is now!* Time for what? I concluded the message I was hearing meant that it was time for me to stand on my own. I came face-to-face with the belief that I was not good enough to stand on my own, and that I was avoiding the offer because fear was driving my choice. But I *really* didn't want to leave Harpo; it was the opportunity of a lifetime, and there were even discussions about my future association with Harpo under way. Why would I walk away from a blessing as huge as the one on my plate? Then I made a fatal mistake. I had one little thought that I could have ignored but did not, because I had not been blessing my head regularly, which meant I was knee-deep in my own understanding with very little influence from my Higher Self. The thought was: *Tell Oprah what is going on and ask her if she would be willing to back my show.* When you are starving and do not take the time to satisfy the hunger, the internal hunger, you are prone to eat something that will burn you.

I followed the thought, with a few minor though devastating adjustments: I did not reveal to Oprah who had made the offer. I shared what I thought was my honest experience and asked for what I thought would be the most appropriate next step. Oprah received my request with gracious consideration. I was told that I would hear from Harpo soon, but what I heard a week later was that I should accept the offer because it was evident that I was not moving in the same direction as Harpo. They wished me well but provided no other information as to why they had made the decision to drop me suddenly from Oprah's show. I was shocked! Did this mean I was not to report for my next scheduled appearance? My attorney got a call that revealed to him the same limited information that was given to me. He, too, was shocked and confused since I did not actually have a firm offer from the network executive who'd been pursuing me. Yes, there had been inquiries, but we had dismissed them, consistently saying that I was happy with my association with Harpo. We received no further information from Harpo. Nothing!

For the next two weeks I rarely ate or slept. Suddenly, the hunger was gone, and what I was left with was drama, hysteria, and devastation. I waited and I prayed, but there was no more information forthcoming. Not a word, a note, a card from Harpo, and not one single thought from my own mind. I got a call from a national gossip paper that wanted to do a story on my sudden disappearance from the airwaves. They had a lead and some speculation that they wanted me to confirm. They also had an inside track on certain animosity between Ms. Winfrey and one of the executives—the boss—with whom I went to dinner. They wanted to know if I was aware of these issues. I made it clear that Ms. Winfrey had been nothing but gracious to me and that my departure was linked to my writing career and certainly not any sort of difficulty. They informed me that they were going to proceed with the story without my input, but later decided to change the direction of the story. All I knew to do was pray.

Fast-forward! Six months later, I received another call from the network executive. They were now ready to move forward. Was I available? I was and accepted their offer, only to discover that everything that glitters isn't gold! Sometimes what looks like gold is really a reflective mirror shined directly into your eyes so that you cannot see. You know the kind of mirror I am referring to; it distorts your image and throws you off balance. It makes things look bigger than they actually are, and it can make you think you see things that aren't there. This time, I didn't think about it. I just sat down at the buffet table and began to stuff my face with things that could never, would never, satisfy my hunger. Whatever was served, I ate. With the loving support and help of some dear friends, I made it through six months of the most grueling experience of my life. It wasn't that I didn't enjoy the work. It wasn't that my dream was not coming true. It was, but now I was working with people who did not have spiritual integrity and who did not support the vision I held of myself or for myself. I knew I needed to push back from the table, and that is exactly what I did.

Let Eyes That Can . . . See!

In the midst of what can be an incredibly enlightening experience, we sometimes fail to realize that the conditions and experiences of our lives speak to us constantly. They tell us where our
strengths lie, and what areas our lives are crying out for intensive
care. Finances, relationships, and the quality of our interactions
with others tell us a great deal about the way we are treating ourselves. The condition of our home, the environment in which we
live and work, the floor of our closets, even the crumbled slips of
paper we keep in our pockets or purses communicate important
messages. They are screaming at us, saying that there is something
amiss in our hearts and minds. Each and every experience, condition, and situation in our lives is telling us what we need to do.
Life will do everything it can to get your attention. What I, like
so many people, had to realize is that it is not necessary to experience pain in the process of hearing what life has to say. Mental or
emotional pain of any kind is an indication that there is a hunger
within us that must be addressed. Blessing your head is a way to
stave off hunger attacks.

September 2001, dealt the first injurious blow to the *Iyanla*
show. This fatal blow came shortly after I asked for what I had
been promised: a show that represented my work in the world.
That was followed by a mindless comment that revealed to me
that most of what I had been told in the beginning was simply
not true. It took only four days to dismantle 17 years of my life's
work. The show was not renewed. My reputation as "a newcomer,
sure to succeed," was over. I packed up my one-bedroom corpo-
rate apartment and moved back to my 14-room home and a husband who now had become emotionally disconnected. I spent
six weeks between the bed and the refrigerator, trying to figure
out what had happened and why. When I had done everything
I knew how to do, I embarked upon a two-year healing process
that included prayer, forgiveness, and blessing my head daily. I
discovered a great deal about myself and my motivations. In the
end, the answer was so simple I almost missed it. In fact, I tried to

talk myself out of it, but it would not go away. What I discovered was that in leaning on my own understanding, I could not see all of the consequences. I did not know all of the players, and I did not know the rules of the game. I was trying to navigate the world of television, about which I knew very little. And I discovered that I had not learned how to fully, masterfully navigate my own internal world. I was looking, but I could not see. I was trying to stand on my own without fully trusting that I could lean on God. Quite simply, I made a mistake that began with a thought, fueled by a core belief that I did not even know was present in my mind.

For those of us who are serious about making lasting changes in our lives, there comes the moment of truth. That is the moment when we become willing to look at our lives and ourselves. It is the moment when we know we must do something about what we see. You can hold a pot-gut in for only so long before you have to exhale and release it. You can make only so many piles of paper before you ultimately discover that you have no more space to make another pile. You can be unhappy in a relationship or without cash for only so long before you are forced to acknowledge that it's not them, it's you! *You* are the common denominator! Knowing or realizing the truth about yourself evokes fear, guilt, shame, and resistance in the hearts and minds of the best of us. More often than not, it is also in that moment, that we will find the strength, courage, and resolve to make *lasting* changes. Without change, we will continue running in circles without realizing that we haven't even made it onto the track.

The mistake had been mine. I didn't understand Oprah's position then, or why she had cut me off so abruptly. Later, someone suggested to me that the other network had let Oprah know that they were courting me but never told her that I had consistently turned them down in favor of staying with Harpo. And because I choose not to tell Oprah the name of the network executive who had made me the offer, it looked like I was playing both ends against the middle, jockeying for the best deal. While the network was playing me, it looked to Oprah like I was playing her.

Oh! Life will humble you! I called Oprah and apologized.

What you believe precedes all experiences. The process of blessing your head will eventually bring to your consciousness an awareness of the beliefs you have that either hinder or support you. Most of us inherit our core beliefs. We are taught or told what to believe by well-meaning adults in authority. We adopt other core beliefs from our culture, customs, and traditions. Once a core belief is implanted, we hold on to it despite the fact that it may not serve a positive function in our lives. In fact, the core beliefs we inherit and adopt become our truths. Rarely do we question them; less often do we recognize how they influence our choices and our responses to life experiences. When you bless your head daily and develop a more affirming relationship with yourself, you become aware of and begin to recognize that some of what you think and believe is actually working against you. You will discover that certain beliefs have a payoff that may serve a limited view of yourself and the possibilities of your life. Other beliefs may poison your energy, making it impossible to move beyond the aspects of your life that are infected by the beliefs you have held. In some cases, you will discover that you have been imprisoned by beliefs that have no factual basis. These are the stories you have made up in the process of denying, dismissing, avoiding, or resisting your true feelings.

Blessing your head is a powerful, self-honoring, self-supportive, and self-affirming step toward connecting with and learning to trust God. God speaks to each of us through our inner voice. That inner voice will never force itself into your awareness. It waits to be invited. Blessing your head is an invitation to the Spirit of your head, your Ori, your highest and Most Holy Self, to guide you, protect you, and teach you. In order to grow spiritually and learn a new way of being, it is necessary to identify and eliminate the core beliefs that can, and most likely do, influence your ability to make conscious choices. In order to live the truth of your being, to align with your purpose, to realize the deepest desires of your heart, it will be necessary to align your thoughts and core beliefs with the spiritual principles.

Conscious Alignment

Blessing your head is one way to realize conscious alignment. I suggest:

- Bless your head daily, followed by a minimum of five minutes of silent contemplation or inner listening.

- Read one chapter of Proverbs daily for an entire year. By the end of the year, you will have read the book of Proverbs 12 times. If you are not familiar with the Bible, start with the New Living Translation or the Message Bible. They are both written in plain English.

- Find a good daily inspirational book and read it every day. There are many books that offer daily spiritual inspiration.

If I could leave you with anything, it would be that you must honor and bless your head consistently, because not doing so is the only thing that stands between you and your blessings.

Chapter 4

BREATHING

I was 21 when I first died. My youngest daughter was six weeks old. My husband had promised that we would move into a better apartment. We had found a nice little two-bedroom place in a beautiful neighborhood. The rent was affordable, and transportation was very accessible. He said he would make all the arrangements. I started packing. I washed all the laundry, threw away all the broken dishes, unhooked the washing machine, and promised my children a better life. On the day we were supposed to move, my husband went to the store for bread at 8 A.M. He returned after midnight.

It was a bright, Saturday morning. Everything was packed. My husband told me that the moving van would arrive somewhere between 9 A.M. and 10 A.M. that morning. At 2 P.M., when he had not returned and the truck had not come, I got nervous. I wanted to call, but I didn't know what moving company he had chosen. I wanted to call the superintendent of the new apartment building, but I didn't have his number. My mind kept telling me my husband had lied, but I couldn't accept that. *Why would he do this to me?* He had taken all the money out of the bank. I had seen him call the super's number. He told me he'd signed the lease. This couldn't be happening. By 6 P.M., I was in a panic. The baby was crying. The sterilizer was packed. My other children wanted their toys. I couldn't get the box open. The telephone was already turned off. My head was spinning. I couldn't breathe.

I dressed the children, and we went to the corner telephone booth. I knew the superintendent's last name and the address of the apartment building. He wasn't listed. I kept looking. I found a "Winston" listed at that address. I called. A woman answered. I babbled my story to her. She gave me the super's number. I called.

"My name is . . . We're supposed to move in today . . . My husband is working . . . The truck hasn't come yet . . . What should I do . . . ?"

"Lady, I don't know what you are talking about . . . Your husband never came back . . . I rented the apartment last week to someone else . . . Lady? Miss? Hello . . . ?"

It was too late. I was dead.

I kept hearing someone say, *Keep breathing. Just keep breathing.* I couldn't breathe. I was dead. My entire body was numb. I don't know how I got back home. I just sat in the middle of the floor staring at the boxes. I don't know what was happening with the baby or the children. I kept struggling to breathe. Then I saw the box marked "bathroom." I opened it. I removed all the pills. One by one I took them all. Tylenol. Aspirin. Phenobarbital. My husband's asthma medication. Vitamins. Water pills. Nytol. I washed it all down with Listerine.

A quiet peace fell over me very slowly. At first, I saw brilliant colors. Then I heard music. I saw a man walking toward me. It was my husband. I lashed out at him, biting, kicking, screaming. He pushed me away. I could feel my chest heaving up and down. The voice was back, *Keep breathing. Just keep breathing.* I heard the baby crying, but I couldn't see her. Then it hit me, panic. "I'm not breathing! I want to breathe! Oh God, please help me. I want to breathe!" Then I saw Mary. She reached out to me. I ran to her and fell into her arms. At first, I just screamed. Then I cried. When I woke up in the hospital, I was still crying, and I was breathing.

Every Good-bye Is Good

Breathing is the life-sustaining exercise that brings the spirit into balance. In the quest for spiritual empowerment and evolution, breathing must become a conscious function. As we breathe, we strengthen our link to the life force of the Creator. That force provides the means by which we can tap into the very essence of our spiritual nature. The more conscious we become of our breathing, the more conscious we will be of our connection to the Spirit of the Creator. When we have a conscious contact, we can receive enlightenment and guidance from the depths of our being. Every *inhalation* is an invitation for God to come into our lives. Every *exhalation* is the release of anything that stands between us and the full realization of God's presence in our lives.

No matter what the circumstances, the moment of death is the same for everyone. We stop breathing! It doesn't matter if we are shot, stabbed, or suffer with a disease. We are alive in the physical body until we stop breathing. It is through the breath that we stay connected to God while in the physical body. Breath is the gift of God's grace, for, at any time, we can exhale and never inhale again. Without breath in the body, the conscious and physical connection to the Creator is broken; the grace of life is taken away and we move back into a spiritual reality. In our conscious, awakened state, we remain connected to the Creator through our breath. As we learn to focus on breath, regulate breath, and channel breath, we can focus, regulate, and channel the energy of the Creator in our life. It will manifest differently for everyone, and it will empower the Spirit (Ori) to bring forth whatever you need at a given time.

Breath calms the emotions, because the emotions we experience do not exist in the Creator. Fear, anger, impatience, and hate are not characteristics of the Creator. When we experience these emotions, we are actually relating to our own human experiences and perceptions. We usually feel out of control and in some way threatened. What we usually do is talk, cry, or lash out, but what we need to do is breathe! With breath, we can draw on the grace of the Creator and the strength of Spirit to guide us. Breath connects the thinking part of us (the masculine energy) to the feeling part of us (the feminine energy). The connection symbolizes a holy union, a force of completion, an experience of joy. Through breath, we are made whole and complete.

When a man and woman come together, it is an opportunity to create new life. When we connect with our breath, we have the opportunity to create whatever we may need at the moment. We can create strength, peace, power, and stillness. We can draw on the presence of the divine energy within us at any time. When we breathe deeply and consciously, the mind and heart become one. In the process we become a new being, a spiritually grounded and directed being. Breath brings forward new life. Breath is the key that unlocks the power of our spiritual identity. When the spirit within is enlivened with breath, we are aligned with and connected to our ability to transform any experience into something new.

The following exercises are designed to maximize the effects of breath in spiritual development. Whether we are having a negative experience or consciously making contact with Spirit, the key is to breathe.

Deep Breaths

Deep breathing aids in the circulation of blood and fosters spiritual cleansing. It also opens A'se, the power of the crown and third eye, while regulating the heart.

1. Sit or stand with your back straight.

2. Inhale as much air as possible through your nose.

3. Exhale all of the air through your nose.

4. After exhaling, count to three before inhaling again. This practice should be repeated five to seven times in

succession, several times throughout the day, particularly before making a decision or responding to an emotional situation.

5. Once you have completed the practice, sit quietly for three to five minutes.

Cleansing Breaths

Cleansing Breath increases blood flow to the brain and the heart. It can accelerate the elimination of toxins in the bloodstream.

1. Sit or stand in a comfortable position.

2. Inhale slowly as much air as possible through your nose.

3. Exhale slowly through your mouth, with your lips puckered.

4. Relax for a few seconds by breathing at a regular pace.

5. Repeat steps 2, 3, and 4 four to eight times.

6. Once you have completed the practice, sit quietly for three to five minutes.

You can use Cleansing Breaths throughout the day to keep our minds clear and our emotions balanced. We should also use Cleansing Breaths when we feel especially stressed or upset in response to our moment-by-moment experiences and interactions with others.

Balancing Breaths

Balancing Breath maintains the equilibrium of the right and left sides of the brain. Clears toxic emotional energy, and cleanses the lymph glands. Strengthens spiritual vision. Opens the heart center (emotional core) and solar plexus (core or center of being).

1. Sit with your back straight and supported, if necessary.

2. Cover your right nostril with your left forefinger.

3. Inhale slowly through your left nostril, to the count of four.

4. Hold your breath for the count of four.

5. Release the right nostril, cover the left nostril with your left thumb.

6. Sit or stand in a comfortable position.

7. Rest to the count of four.

8. Repeat the exercise four times.

9. Switch hands, covering your left nostril with your right forefinger.

10. Inhale slowly through your right nostril, to the count of four.

11. Hold your breath for the count of four.

12. Release the left nostril, cover the right nostril with your right thumb.

13. Exhale slowly to the count of four through the left nostril.

14. Rest to the count of four.

15. Repeat the exercise four times.

16. Once you have completed the practice, sit quietly for three to five minutes.

After two weeks of consistent practice, increase all counts to eight, and increase the practice to twice a day.

Conscious Connected Breaths

Conscious Connected Breath brings to the surface and dissolves suppressed emotions and memories; increases mental and emotional stamina; balances all physical body functions. (This technique is also known as Rebirthing Breathwork. It is advisable to practice this process with the support of a trained Breath Technician.)

1. Sit in a comfortable position.

2. Inhale as much air as possible through your mouth.

3. Without resting, exhale all air through your mouth.

4. Without resting, inhale again and exhale continuously without stopping.

There should be no pause between inhaling and exhaling. You can expect yawning, coughing, and sleepiness when practicing this process. You may also experience coldness in the hands and feet. Do not be alarmed! As the body begins to be filled with oxygen, these are the most common reactions.

It is best to do this type of breathing when you have no other demands on your time, perhaps at night, right before bedtime.

Meditative Breaths

Meditative breathing stills the chatter of the mind; opens the A'se of the crown, throat, heart, and solar plexus.

1. Sit with back straight, feet flat, and palms facing upward on thighs with eyes closed.

2. Beginning at your feet, working all the way up to your head, issue a gentle mental command to every part of your body to relax. *Example:* My feet are relaxed. My ankles are relaxed. My calves are relaxed. Do not worry if you miss a part or two, they will get the message.

3. Drop your head so that your chin is resting on your chest.

4. Allow your body to relax for three to five seconds.

5. While your head is forward, begin to inhale slowly, and, while doing so, roll your head up and backward slowly until your head is dangling. If you are counting mentally, it should take 8 counts to get your head up and back.

6. While your head is dangling backward, inhale slowly to the count of 4, then exhale slowly to the count of 4.

7. On the next inhale, slowly begin to roll your head forward again, mentally counting from 1 to 8, until your chin is resting on you chest again.

8. Rest for three to five seconds.

9. Repeat the process four times.

You will find that your mind and body are now still and you are ready for a longer meditation practice. This would be an excellent opportunity to pray silently or aloud, to repeat affirmations, or to ask questions of your Highest Most Holy Self. Sit quietly for five to ten minutes. This is an excellent breathing technique to do just before you begin a practice of meditation. Breathing is the key to quieting your mind for meditation. The deeper you breathe, the more energy you provide your spiritual Self. When you begin the meditation process, it will be difficult to keep still and to still the mind initially. There is nothing wrong with you! Try listening to some music (flute or piano are particularly soothing). Listen intently to the music. Breathe to the rhythm. When the thoughts come into your mind, simply think—*Peace!*

Each of these breathing exercises should be done consciously and consistently, which means you will need to make an effort to do them. In any breathing practice, be mindful to keep your back as straight as possible and your shoulders relaxed. Always breathe slowly, and breathe from the center of your body (your stomach), not your chest.

It is important to remain conscious of how you are breathing at all times. However, if you need a plan that will support you in practicing any or all of the methods presented here, I would suggest the following: Practice Deep Breaths, Cleansing Breaths, or Balancing Breaths immediately upon rising in the morning. Try each one for a week to see which one has the greatest impact for you.

Practice Meditative Breaths before you sit for any practice of meditation.

Practice Conscious Connected Breaths once a week to clear your consciousness of any and all residue of upsetting or stressful experiences.

What I Know Now

Conscious breathing nurtures and nourishes the mind, body, and spirit.
Breath is how we remain conscious of and connected to God.
When the mind or emotions are stressed,
breathing becomes shallow and restricted.
If you breathe, you will feel and know what to do next.
We hold our breath unconsciously to avoid our feelings.

Last One Standing

Nothing could have prepared me for the reality of what I would see when I walked into the church. I knew my brother would be there. And I knew he would not be breathing. I had seen him earlier in the day at the funeral home, yet this was different.

The sun was setting, its broad rays streaming through the stained-glass windows of the church. The wooden casket seemed to be glowing as the sun's light fell gracefully, elegantly, on my brother's face. In that moment, I could hear someone whispering to me, *You are the last one standing.* I wasn't sure if anyone else heard those words. I didn't know if anyone else saw what I saw. My eyes were locked on his face. I was trying not to say good-bye, resisting the awareness and acknowledgment that my big brother had left me, that I was indeed the last one standing. Feelings of loneliness and sadness overwhelmed me, and for the first time in a long time, I had no need to be strong, nor present.

My husband held me on one side, and my angels, the Inner Vision team, surrounded me. Gail, my sister-in-law, was talking, making last-minute arrangements. She tried to get me to sit in the front row. That would mean sitting directly in the stream of sunlight that was bathing my brother's face. I pretended not to hear her. Maybe I didn't hear her. Maybe I was making it all up in my mind. Maybe I was having a nervous breakdown and these people were psychiatric workers trying to put me in a straitjacket so I wouldn't hurt myself or anyone else.

I really wanted to hurt somebody! I wanted to hurt Ray, my dead brother. I wanted to slap him. Kick him. I wanted to rip his heavily starched shirt to pieces. I wanted to spit and scream and thrash around on the floor like a raving lunatic. But the light was too beautiful, and too warm, and too final. No, I wasn't crazy. My brother was dead. I was surrounded and supported by the people who loved me most, the people I loved with all of my heart. I sat and held my husband's hand, rested my head on my son's shoulder. I knew I couldn't stand, move, or speak. I could not be strong. I didn't know what to do. The minister entered the church. My brother's lifelong friends were starting to arrive. I refused to think about what was going to happen. Then, as if it were all a dream, I heard people talking. The sunlight was gone. The lights in the church were beaming. The service was about to begin, and the hopes I had for my brother and the vision I held for him were about to end. My brother would never breathe again.

How do two people who grow up in the same house, eat the same food, sometimes even sleep in the same bed, turn out to be so dramatically different? I have witnessed it with my own children, and I certainly lived it with my own brother. Our heads were shaped identically. We had the same deep voices and throaty laughter. He had much better legs than I did, but we both had quick, active minds. We lost our mother when we were at a young and tender age. I was two when she died. People chose not to tell me about it, so I was oblivious to the fact that I was a motherless child. Ray, on the other hand, suffered the silent, numbing pain of her death. He felt the aloneness that results from losing your mother in the company of an emotionally unavailable father. When it came to our father, my brother and I saw things eye to eye. We both grew up in a love/hate relationship with him that impacted many of our later choices and relationships. Our feelings about our father are where the similarities between my brother and me ended.

My brother grew up to be a sullen man. He was angry and resentful. He acted out his inner turmoil and conflict with drinking and drugs. He was brilliant but felt inferior. He was capable yet seemed unable. I, on the other hand, have a wicked sense of humor. I have always been an up-in-your-face kind of person. When we were children, Ray called me "Mighty Mouth." I had a need to be seen and heard. As a child, that need often got me into trouble. As I grew into adulthood, I had an uncanny way of attracting negative attention and criticism. When it came to something I wanted, I would not give up. In fact, I acknowledge that I came frighteningly close to being obsessive and compulsive. I am now aware that my saving grace has been that, despite two suicide attempts, I love life! I love the colors, the aromas, the feeling, and the excitement of life. I believe it has been my love of life that taught me to breathe deeply moment by moment.

My brother Ray had a take-it-or-leave-it attitude, and when you took it, whatever "it" was at the moment, he would be terribly upset with you. Nothing seemed to matter to him, yet at the same time he cared very deeply. If you didn't know him, you might be fooled into thinking that he was detached. I have very little tolerance for pain or hurt or foolishness, but Ray seemed to thrive on it. I also know that he hurt too badly not to take some kind of action to ease the pain. I used fantasy and seemingly mindless chatter the way he used cocaine and alcohol. Knowing, as we did that our mother was an alcoholic, it seemed foolish to me to drink the way my brother did. From what I knew about him, he had been so wounded for so long, he had hurt so long and so hard, that his spirit ultimately bled to death.

My brother also suffered from severe asthma most of his life. I still have vivid memories of his being rushed off to the hospital, gasping for every breath, tears streaming down his face, his legs barely able to carry him. He had been on the verge of death many times in his life and always for the same reason: he could not breathe. What I know now is that that is how he lived his life, as well. In her classic book *You Can Heal Your Life*, master teacher and author Louise Hay states that asthma represents "the inability to breathe for one's self. Feeling stifled, and suppressed crying." My brother was also cross-addicted. According to Ms. Hay, addictions are: "Running away from Self. Not knowing how to love the self."

When I think about the sadness and pain I often saw in Ray's eyes, when I remember how he was so afraid to do so many things because he might have an asthma attack, it makes perfect sense to me that he would take mind-altering substances to help him forget that he simply did not know how to live beyond the fear.

There is pain, sometimes guilt, associated with my knowing how to help and serve others yet being unable to help family members in the same fundamental ways. I have learned how to surrender the guilt, but there are days when I feel just a tinge of the pain. Had I understood the healing power of breath much sooner, I would have suggested, encouraged—no, demanded—that my brother practice Conscious Connected Breathing. Even with his asthma, this form of breathing would have helped him in healing the painful memories of his childhood. It would have brought to the surface of his consciousness his limited interpretations of reality and the wounds associated with them. Had I truly recognized the depth of his pain, I would have somehow convinced my brother that he needed to learn and consistently practice Balancing Breathing. This breathing practice would have brought his left brain—the logical, analytical, practical part of his mind—into alignment and harmony with his right brain—the intuitive symbolic, philosophical part of his mind. Maybe, just maybe—who knows for sure—had my brother learned how to breathe consciously, he would have known the joy of living fully. In the end, I do know whether the choice to breathe or not, to live fully and pain-free or not, was his alone to make.

When we were children, I was always making stuff up and trying to get Ray to play along. I would tell him about things that could happen, things that might happen, on the rare occasions when Daddy came home. I would pretend as if they had already happened. I would dance around and have conversations with one dead parent and another absent one. Ray said I was "a nut," "a liar," "a pain in the butt." My grandmother who raised us said that my imagination was "too wild for my own good." But everybody needs a coping mechanism, and I used storytelling and daydreaming as a way to live beyond the immediate experiences of pain and dysfunction in my childhood.

As an adult, I was often told that I lived in denial, or that I refused to see things and people for who and what they were. I now realize that before I even knew what it was called, I was aware that breath expanded the mind beyond the limitations of the moment. The fact is that most children, when they are daydreaming, are also engaged in a very slow, rhythmic breathing pattern that is akin to the Meditative Breath. When children are telling someone a good story, even if they have made it up in their own mind, they will naturally breathe in through the nose and exhale through the mouth as they tell the punch line or the conclusion. This breathing pattern is closely related to the one used for Cleansing Breaths. Conscious breathing leads to expanded vision, an inner vision: a way of seeing things that are not, as if they were. I could see who I wanted to be and what I wanted my life to be like, when there was absolutely no evidence that it was possible. Breath was my ticket.

The Midnight Train to Mindfulness

Conscious breathing, deep breathing, can take you into a profound understanding that grows from the core of your being. Often, it comes to you as a brief glimpse of your true self. It pops into your head as snatches of where you are going in your life. These snatches of reality may be difficult to believe, even frightening. More important, it is your breath—not another degree, or a different relationship, or more money—that opens your mind so that you will always know where you are going and what you must do to get there. Conscious breathing is a beam of light in an often-dark world. Like a laser, it will support you as you move through obstacles enabling you to remain steady, strong, and powerful. You eventually come to realize that everything in your life must be aligned with your breath. No matter where you are, you got there through your ability to remain connected to and conscious of your breathing. Breath is your source and your strength. It is the eternal beacon of light that beckons you and guides you home. Breath is the place in which you meet God, the I Am-ness of our nature where you are not too afraid, stressed out, or freaked out to take a look.

Nothing happens in life that does not begin with breath. Once you learn how to do it, and do it consciously, you begin to understand what the philosopher Nietzsche said: "If you have a strong enough what, the how will be presented." The how of breathing means doing it slowly and deeply from the belly, not from the chest. Believe it or not, most people do not know how to breathe. As a result, they breathe in the chest when real breath must come from the center of the body. With every inhalation, the belly should expand. With every exhalation, it should deflate. This will not only strengthen your stomach muscles, it will bring oxygen to every part of your being. In addition, each breath must be full, a complete inhale and total exhale. If not, we are simply circulating toxins and killing off our brain cells. True breath requires an investment—of time, energy, and faith. When you make the investment in learning how to breathe properly and practice it vigilantly, it will wake you up from a sound sleep. Then, and only then, will you dare to invest your entire self in your life.

What I know now is that when you are fully breathing, you outgrow self-doubt and needless self-sacrifice. The incessant nagging of the have-to-do's and need-to-do's for others? Gone! Breath gives birth to readiness. You become ready to move, ready to jump, swim, fall, survive, drown, thrive, flourish—taking no prisoners, hangers-on, or leeches in the process. The neediness, the desire for approval and acceptance, the hesitancy that kept you in the desperate despair of wishing and hoping? Gone! You are about the serious business of making a dream into a reality. You have moved beyond the practice of mere goal setting. You have become a vessel for what you know and feel must and is happening through you because you are breathing. It is just that simple!

On March 30, 2002, the eve of Easter Sunday, one day before his 50th birthday, my brother Ray died of a heart attack. His body—filled with heroin, cocaine, and alcohol—succumbed to the effects of holding his breath in fear, of his taking in only little sips of air rather than taking long deep breaths that would have supported his life. His life was consumed by anger. He was angry about who he was and who he was not as defined by our father. He was angry that he grew up without a mother. He was angry that he could not rise above the fear that filled his heart and mind. He was angry because he believed that no one, not even God, understood his pain or his needs. Fear and anger were the cornerstones of his personality. His I Am-ness, his personage, had ceased to be many years before his spirit actually left his body. There was only a dark vacuum where there should have been light and alignment. I saw it coming. I felt it coming. Yet I continued to hold an elegant vision of the truth I knew him to be. You can hold a vision for someone else; however, it is up to that person to make the vision a reality. Ray's life had no focus, no direction. Pain, anger, and fear had taken his breath away long before he actually died.

I wanted to convince my brother that we/he did not have to hurt. I wanted to create the place, the school that we both needed—a school for motherless and fatherless children. A school where we could learn how to live in grace and peace without the pain and struggle we believed was normal. From the very essence of my DNA, I knew that it was not normal to suffer through life. I watched many people in my family and community do it until they died. I watched my father do it until he embraced the teachings of Yogananda. I heard stories of how my mother did it until she died. I actively participated in and, on many days, financed my brother's struggle in and through pain.

So many of the visions and images Ray and I had been given about life were distorted. I learned in a very difficult way what my brother never seemed able to grasp: *God has a plan for my life. My job is to breathe my way to it and through it moment by moment.* God's plan is the essence and the energy that lives within each of us. Unfortunately for my brother, and for many of us, the physical events and circumstances of our lives put us in a choke hold. We are strangled by the pain of what we believe are disappointments, abandonment, and rejection. Then we unconsciously hold our mental and emotional connection to breath and life, waiting for the next indignity to befall us. In doing so, we engage in a sort of unconscious suicide: where there is no conscious breath, there can be no conscious life. What I know now is that when we are not living every breath to the fullest, we cannot see our way out of the very circumstances that cause us the greatest amount of pain.

What I know now is that most of us simply never received the tools or the information that we need to create the lives we dream of living. In addition, the challenges and hardships we face in life—more often than not—cause us to lose faith in ourselves, in our abilities, and in our dreams. Suffering, struggling, barely making it from one day to the next *is not normal!* Living in pain, dysfunction, limitation, and discord is not what God intended for us. In all of the years of my traveling, lecturing, and writing, I have met far too many people who live below their potential. They live a life of accommodation. We are taught to accommodate conditions and experiences that are in conflict with the truth of who and what we are born to be in this world. Most of us lose our way in life because we play small games for small prizes. The meager rewards we seek are not satisfying enough to keep our attention, so we get sidetracked, distracted by what we call "problems." Breath can and will eliminate accommodation and prevent distraction. Learning how to do it so that every moment is filled with the power, majesty, goodness, and grace of God is not an easy process, but it is well worth your effort.

Remaining conscious of our breathing moment by moment takes willingness and practice. It requires that we mentally check in with ourselves in order to monitor the intake and output of breath. Try it right now. As your eyes are gliding over these words, notice the depth or shallowness of your breath. Is your chest or your belly expanding? Is your mind calm, or racing? Take a moment right now to regulate your breathing. Take it deeper. Breathe consciously and enjoy your life in this moment and in those that follow.

Chapter 5

MEDITATION

I saw very little of my father when I was growing up. On those rare occasions when he spent two or three consecutive days in our household, I came to realize that I was better off with him gone. By the time I was seven years old, I concluded that my father was the meanest person alive! No matter what I did or said, my father always addressed me with the same six words: "Sit down! Shut up and listen!" At that point, he would give me a ten-minute to two-hour lecture on the deeper meaning of life, or tooth brushing, or shirt ironing, or floor sweeping, or whatever the issue was at the time.

By the time I was 13, I vowed not to speak to my father except for the obligatory daily greeting. It didn't matter. If I tried to creep past the living room or bedroom door, he would call me in and give the command, "Sit down! Shut up and listen!" He would then tell me about the birds and the bees, the birds and the dogs, the bird's mother and the bird's father. Ninety-nine percent of the time I had absolutely no idea what my father was saying. It was so philosophical, very intellectual, and totally off the wall! Whenever I had a question or offered my childish opinion, he would ignore me and continue his rambling. I would be half asleep when he dismissed me. I knew when the end was near, because he always finished up the same way: "One day, you'll understand what I'm talking about." That day took 25 years to come!

I was 30 years old when my father made his transition from life. I took it very well, because my newfound sense of spirituality helped me to understand that life does not end with death. I was 33 years old and well on my way down the path of spiritual enlightenment when I truly understood the gift my father had given me; those six words would change my life forever. Unfortunately, my understanding did not come until my world had fallen apart—for the 99th time!

Quieting the Monkey Mind

There comes a time in everyone's life when your spiritual philosophy just doesn't seem to answer the questions. This is a desperate moment. You search for answers that do not seem to come forth. You may read books. They will not make sense. You may ask questions of elders. Their ramblings will annoy you. My day came when I was verbally attacked by a devout Christian who told me I was going to burn in hell because I had not given my soul to the Lord!

Under normal circumstances, this would not have bothered me, but on this particular day, something the woman said rubbed me the wrong way. I prayed for clarity and guidance. What I got was Jehovah's Witnesses ringing my doorbell for three days in a row, Robert Tilton screaming and pointing his finger at me on late-night television, a barrage of religious mail from sources I had never communicated with, and a migraine headache! I went walking in the park to think. Sitting on a bench to watch the birds, I noticed an abandoned paper bag on the bench, begging me to look inside it. I did. It was a Bible and a crucifix. I was staring at the book in total disbelief when a voice called out to me, "Oh, thank God, you found it! I thought someone would steal it. You know there are so many evil people on their way to burn in hell." I handed the bag over, realizing that my headache had just gotten worse.

This went on for two weeks! A myriad of questions kept popping in my mind. Am I doing the right thing? How did the Yoruba faith survive without the Bible? Is there a heaven? Is there a hell? Are African people really condemned to hell because they are black? What do I believe? I couldn't find the answer! I couldn't sleep at night! I became increasingly irritable. I tried reading my Tarot cards, thinking I could get a gauge of my emotional level. I pulled the Hanged Man, Death, and Fool cards. I checked the calendar to see if the moon was full! There was a new moon in the sign of Sagittarius, representing expansion and growth. I was desperate! I took out all my crystals. I lay on the floor and placed the crystals on various parts of my body. They got hot. I felt as though I was on fire. Nothing seemed to work!

Finally, I screamed out, "Oh God, please help me! I'm confused! Please tell me what to do! I was on my knees rocking and crying when the answer came: *Sit down! Shut up and listen!* Those words jarred me back to reality! They came again. *Sit down! Shut up and listen!* I scrambled to a chair, dried my eyes, and waited. Within a few moments, my mind was clear. My hands had stopped shaking and I was very focused. Each of us vibrates to what our soul inherently knows. An old soul, an expression of Spirit that has taken on many forms and life experiences, has more experience and a deeper recollection than a young soul, an expression of Spirit that has not incarnated in many forms. What we spiritually believe is only a reflection of what the soul already recognizes from its previous forms of expression. No one can tell you what is right for your soul, because your soul never forgets what it has been or can be with the guidance of Spirit. Be still and know. What you know in your soul will bring you peace. Be still and listen.

I had spent hundreds of hours and thousands of dollars buying books, attending workshops and seminars. I had been initiated into orders, societies, and faiths. I had slept in the woods, floated in tanks, talked to rocks, and stood in fire—all in a search to find what the Father and my father had given me for free! I was convinced that I wasn't good enough, that I couldn't do "it" right! That there was something I was missing, something wrong with me! In the end, I discovered that all I needed to do was shut up and listen. I had to learn how to listen to the quiet voice that spoke from the center of my being. I had to learn that when I didn't know what to say, it was best to say nothing. I had to learn that it did not matter what anyone else was doing or saying, I had to be comfortable within myself. I had to learn that no one can give you what you don't already have! What I had was a soul's experience.

I made it through that growth experience and the many others that followed by taking my father's simple advice. When I don't know what to do, I don't do anything! When I can't figure out what to say, I don't say anything. I stopped letting my ego, the opinions of others, and the trend of the times dictate my moods. It took 33 years for me to discover how brilliant my father was! I only hope that he can see how brilliant I have become.

Meditation—the Key to Enlightenment

Meditation, while not strictly African, is absolutely spiritual. It is the process of stilling the body and mind to align the physical and spiritual being. The root word *medi*, the same as in *medicine*, means "to heal." Meditation brings mental, emotional, and spiritual balance, which is the key to enlightenment. It is the process that enables you to contact the true Self, eliminating all external interruptions.

Meditation is a process of taking time to do nothing. It is an opportunity to make contact with your spirit and soul. Many of us believe that we don't have time to meditate. The truth is, unless you meditate, you won't have enough time to do what you set out to do! Some of us think we must always be busy doing something. What we fail to realize is that the busier we are, the less we accomplish. Without meditation, we move about frantically and hastily, totally out of control! We are not clear about where we are going, why we are going there, and how we are going to get there! Meditation stills the mind, aligns the mind and the heart, and allows us to transcend time and space.

Meditation should not, cannot, be forced. It must be a relaxed, conscious, disciplined effort to focus inward. There are no set rules or procedures that must be followed. However, the meditative process should be consistent and purposeful. You should declare to yourself that you want to meditate and that your goal is either peace, relaxation, enlightenment, and so on. You should pick a location in which you feel comfortable, and a time at which you will not be disturbed. The key is to practice meditation on a regular basis. As you develop the ability, your spirit will guide your next steps.

Meditation Made Simple

The meditative breathing exercise or the simple relaxation meditation is a good place to start. Seated in a comfortable chair, with your back straight, your feet flat on the floor, your hands on your thighs, and palms facing upward, take a deep breath. Close your eyes and relax. If you have trouble relaxing, begin by talking to your body. "My feet are relaxed. My ankles are relaxed. My legs are relaxed..." and so on. Talk to every limb and organ, from your toes to your head. Believe it or not, that's enough for the first day. Any more will be forcing it. You have just spent four to seven minutes talking to your body. For many of us, this is a first!

The next day try it again. You will probably find it much easier to relax, so move on to breathing. Listen to yourself breathing. Monitor how long it takes you to inhale and exhale. Next, try to regulate your breathing as follows:

- Inhale through your nose for four counts.
- Exhale through your nose for four counts.
- Repeat four counts.
- Next, inhale through your nose for four counts.
- Hold the breath for two counts.
- Exhale through your nose for four counts.

The counting occurs *mentally*. If you speak aloud, you are engaging your mind in counting, rather than focusing on the breath. Five minutes of practice should be enough.

On the next day, your goal should be silence. Relax yourself. Regulate your breathing and listen to your thoughts. You may find that a number of things will run through your mind: things you need to do, things you want to do, things you forgot to do. You may hear a familiar song or voice. Let these thoughts flow. Your mind is clearing. Your job is to keep negative, disruptive thoughts out. The best way to do this is to not engage them. When and if they crop up, simply think, *Peace.* Try this process over three to four days, for short intervals of time, until you find that by using the words *Peace, Silence,* or *Be still,* you can stop the negative thought.

Finally, you will reach a truly meditative readiness. Your goal is to achieve silence. What you will probably hear in your thoughts is the beating of your heart. You may feel light-headed. This is normal. With practice, you will discover that you are able to sit for longer periods. You may even nod off. It's all fine. You may ask yourself a question and find thoughts answering it. Trust those thoughts—your spirit is speaking to you. You may get ideas or thoughts about things that seem totally impossible. Act on what you are told and see how it will manifest. You may see things, people, or places. This is fine. Once you master quieting your mind, you will find you can meditate while walking or even washing the dishes.

Meditation is the process by which you can set aside and let go of the burdens or challenges of your life. It removes you from the past by focusing your attention on now. You cannot realize the calming stillness of the meditative state if you are worrying about the future. Meditate on where you are now. Now means that you must turn your attention within, to the true essence of you. You are divine, and meditation permits you to experience your divinity. In your meditative exercises, strive to give yourself time and energy. For it is in this state that your spirit gains A'se (power). Always know that Spirit is with you, guiding you, and protecting you. Simply relax and let go. Let Spirit heal.

My destiny has been fulfilled, fulfilled by you, oh, God.
My search is over and I rest in Thee.

— *I Rest in Thee* by Rickie Byars Beckwith

What I Know Now

Meditation is a process and practice that
will reveal the wisdom of the soul.
Meditation is an excellent way to train the mind and nurture the spirit.
Meditation will bring to your awareness aspects of your self
that go unnoticed because of the chatter and activity of the mind.
Meditation is a practice that will bring into word and
action that which is known at the level of the soul.

The Sacred Journey Home

The images were black and faceless. They appeared one at a time through a haze of bluish-white smoke, dressed in white garments that reminded me of choir robes. Some were taller than others; I sensed that they were also older. Although they had no faces, I knew that some were crying, others were laughing. Some stood starkly staring into space. One of the small images was clutching the leg of a taller, older one. I could feel the terror of the smaller one in the pit of my stomach. With my eyes tightly shut, I felt warm tears roll across my cheeks. My heart began to race. I took a deep breath.

They're all coming home.

The vision came to me in the midst of our weekly coaching session.

"Who? Who is it, Iyanla?" Norm Frye, my instructor from the University of Santa Monica, was whispering into the telephone.

All the pieces of me. The pieces I lost. The pieces I gave away. They want to come home.

Norm was silent. My heart slowed to its normal rate as the tears continued to flow. Flashes of my past came into my mind. I recalled memories of my childhood, adolescence, and adult life. Snapshots of my life flashed and flickered, each one attaching itself to one of the figures I could see standing on the hilltop. *There's one missing. A little one.*

As if he did not want to interrupt the process, Norm whispered, "Where is she?"

Immediately my mind shifted to another time and experience in my past. *She's under the table. She's hiding. She's crying.*

"How old is she?" Norm asked.

I think she's three. She's very little.

"Do you know what she wants, Iyanla?"

She wants her mommy. She's crying for her mommy.

Knowing that, I began to weep. Norm became silent again. We both knew that our prayer was being answered. We both recognized that the intentions we had set during our weekly sessions were culminating in the experience of my vision.

On this particular evening, I had set an intention to heal the aspects of myself that were not ready to move forward, bringing them into alignment with the aspects of myself that were ready. This, I believed, was at the heart of the difficulty I was experiencing in making certain decisions. I would make decisions with great sincerity, only to experience severe difficulty in following them through to completion. No matter how hard I tried or how much I terrorized or brutalized myself in the process, there was a part of me that would give up on the very thing I desired. I tried really hard to convince myself that this was natural and normal. I told myself that it was okay simply to lose interest in certain projects or pursuits. Yet there was a part of me that *knew* something else was going on. Somewhere on my internal landscape there was conflict and confusion. I was fighting with myself, within myself, and against myself. I set a clear intention to discover what I needed to know: to bring balance and harmony to my inner life in a way that would alter my outer experiences. Guided meditation and visualization was the process I used to facilitate the healing I desired to experience.

I watched as one of the taller figures crawled under the table and scooped up the little one. At first she struggled as if she were trying to get away. My heart began to race again. I felt the familiar terror I had grown to know in my childhood. That terror had resulted from my mother's death, my grandmother's anger and abuse, and my father's absence. I felt alone. I felt confused. The larger figure held on to the little one until suddenly my heart was beating normally again. I could see that the little one had rested her head on the shoulder of the larger figure, who turned its head slightly to look directly at me. My terror was gone. Slowly, all of the images disappeared from my mind. I sat silently until I heard Norm's voice again.

"I could see them also, Iyanla. They were beautiful. I could see them and feel them. Where did she go?"

I can't explain how I knew, but somehow I did know. I shared my thoughts with Norm. *She's with my mother.*

I had had visions in the past, but never anything like this. This was different. This was sacred. My body felt depleted yet totally peaceful. I could barely open my eyes or my mouth. Norm and I agreed to end our session so that I could integrate this experience of spontaneous healing with my intention to experience inner alignment. It was one of the most powerful meditations I have ever experienced, although some would not consider it a meditation at all because I was speaking. What I know now is that any process or practice that stills the chatter of the mind and allows you to tap into the core of your being in a sacred manner can be considered a meditation.

The process of meditation can be a process of exploration, examination, and evaluation that will establish or reestablish your desire and ability to make conscious contact with your Highest Most Holy Self, your soul, and the presence of God. When I first began a practice of daily meditation, I was not aware of how difficult it can be actually to meditate. The mind is such a powerful and creative tool, but it is also very busy. The mind loves to be engaged in activity. Listening, interpreting, analyzing, and other activities of the mind take place with rapid-fire speed, second by second. Meditation—the act of stilling or quieting the conscious mind—can take years to master. However, once you master it, it can take you deep within your consciousness and reveal things you never thought were possible.

Training the Mind

What I know now is that there have been many things that have occurred in my life for which I have not been present. I was there. I heard everything, saw everyone, but *I* was not present. I was lost in thought, mentally tripping, out in space somewhere, making up stories about what I thought was going on rather than actually paying attention to the reality of what was happening. I call this "being alone in your head without adult supervision!" When my uncle sexually molested me, I lost my mind. When my first husband physically abused me, I left my mind. When I was stressed or frightened, or trying to figure out how to get out of some mess I had put myself in, I would take leave of my good senses and retreat inside my mind. As a result, my mind became a cesspool of bad memories, bad experiences, misperceptions, and, quite frankly, confusion. My mind was working against me. It would dredge up old scenarios in my present-day experiences, and I would race to the finish line of conclusion in the middle of what was actually going on. Nowhere was this more apparent to me than in my relationships with men. I would have relationships with them *all by myself* in my own mind, despite evidence to the contrary in reality. It was not until they behaved badly or left me that I realized something was not right with my thinking.

I had heard about meditation, but I had no clue what it actually meant or how to do it. The truth is that growing up in the Pentecostal church, I was taught *not* to meditate on anything except God's word. As a recovering Pentecostal, I wasn't quite sure what to do because I had moved away from the Bible as the foundation for my spiritual growth and evolution. But I was in trouble, and I knew it. My choices had become self-defeating. Making a decision was like pulling wisdom teeth from a raging bull. There were times I could not sleep at night because my mind was racing so fast the thoughts would keep me awake. I had to risk going straight to hell. I got my Bible. I took a long, deep breath. I put the Bible up to my forehead and I prayed, "Help!" I opened the Bible to Psalm 77. The entire chapter spoke to my experience, but it was verse 6 that caught my attention: "I call to remembrance my song in the night; I meditate within my heart, And my spirit makes diligent search." Searches where? Where am I to look for my answers? Once again my father's words rang loudly in my ears, "Sit down! Shut up and listen!" The question was not *what* to do. The question was *how* to do it.

The mind must be trained to be still. Meditation is a process that stills the mind in order to facilitate sacred healing and growth. In order to make self-supportive choices and effective decisions and to take productive actions, you must have a well-ordered mind. Meditation can and will order your thinking and therefore your mind. As we heal the broken and wounded places that exist in our hearts and minds, we grow mentally and emotionally. Meditation is, therefore, a tool for growth. Mental and emotional growth is a requirement of spiritual maturation. Until we are mentally sound (able to create clear intentions), emotionally balanced (able to integrate and embrace all aspects of self), and spiritually mature (teachable and available at the soul level), we are consistently unable to create the reality we desire. We are spiritually immature. Establishing and maintaining a meditation practice is a bold declaration of what you are choosing to be, what you are choosing to experience, and how willing you are to surrender to divine will. It is a progressive step toward training your mind.

Moving through the experiences of life, it is quite easy to lose track of the essence of who we are at the deepest level of our being, at a soul level. As children, we deny and bury these aspects of ourselves that our parents and caregivers do not approve of or accept. As adolescents, we avoid the feelings, questions, and private experiences that occur within ourselves, the things that we believe or are taught to believe are *not normal*. As teenagers, we stop asking questions. We make up stories. We accept the opinions and suggestions of those we believe are smarter and wiser. As we cross the threshold into adulthood, we deny our instincts and hide our fears in an effort to avoid what may appear to be selfish, greedy, aggressive, or inappropriate. We deny ourselves in order to fit in, to be accepted and acceptable. We learn what to do and how to do it to keep ourselves safe from perceived dangers and to make others comfortable in our presence. We want to eliminate the possibility and pain of rejection and abandonment while we increase our pleasurable experiences. In this process of living and growing, we deny and avoid aspects of our life force and personality that make us each unique. As a result, our minds become like wayward children, flitting from pillar to post, making up what we think is necessary to gain acceptance, validation, or approval from others.

In addition to the aspects of ourselves that we deny, avoid, and suppress, there are emotions we are not taught to express or understand. How do we as children learn to process or express the experiences of grief, rage, and terror? We may learn what to do to satisfy the adults, to allow them to believe those feelings have passed, yet in doing so we do not erase their imprint from the fibers of our consciousness. How does a three- or four-year-old express loneliness, shame, and confusion when she does not have the verbal skills to convey the magnitude of the experience? A new toy or a cookie may satisfy her for a moment. However, the thoughts and emotions that evolve from the inner experience do not disappear. What becomes of our latent talents that are unnoticed and undeveloped during childhood? Quite often they emerge as a burning passion later in life—a passion that may drive or haunt us, a passion we are quite often afraid to pursue.

Some people believe that unexpressed thoughts and emotions of childhood become stumbling blocks in our adult lives. "Not doing it" in the past often becomes "can't do it" in the present. The "don't do it" of childhood become the "will never do it" that so many of us struggle with as adults. Remembering what was *not* nice to think or feel as children may cloud or steal our creative energy and voice today. The aspects and elements of childhood experiences plant the seeds of the successes and challenges we experience as adults. You must call all of the aspects of your self home in order to be centered and grounded in your present-day experiences. You must recognize and embrace all of who you are in order to experience your authentic self, your inner truth. You must align your consciousness with the truth of your being, which is anchored in your soul in order to create and experience inner peace. You must reclaim all parts of your self, no matter how broken, bad, or inappropriate you may believe they are, in order to be fulfilled and live a full life. Meditation is one way to call your pieces home. Meditation facilitates and supports you in answering the higher calling of your soul. And, yes, you can teach children to meditate.

Sit Down! Shut Up and Listen!

In today's world of drive-through spirituality, you will find that there are many varying methods and practices of meditation. What I know now is that it is always best to stick with the basics: Sit down! Shut up and listen! Listen first to your breath. Any of the breathing practices listed in Chapter 4 will provide you with a good place to start. Or listen for your heartbeat. By practicing the Meditative Breath, you can still the mind and turn your attention inward. It may take some time of serious practice, but as the mind becomes calm, you will first feel and then hear the beating of your own heart. It is amazing and calming.

Guided Meditation

If your mind is exceptionally active or if you have never seriously practiced any form of meditation, you may want to start with a Guided Meditation. There are simply hundreds on the market. I have always found the meditations by Lazaris (www.Lazaris.com) to be particularly uncomplicated and easy to follow. The

AM/PM Meditation taught by Lazaris has helped me to gain or restore peace to my mind during many difficult experiences. If you are truly serious about learning how to meditate effectively, get a digital recorder, find a meditation you like in any self-help book, and record it in your own voice. You can then download it directly into your MP3 player and listen to it. I have found this to be particularly effective since the mind knows the sound of its owner's voice. While these practices do engage the mind, they also serve to bring thoughts into focus.

Mantra Meditation

Many Eastern traditions use mantras to induce a meditative state. A mantra is a word or phrase, repeated silently or aloud, that focuses the mind and leads it into a meditative state. The works of Thomas Ashley-Farrand (whose spiritual name is Namadeva) provide detailed instructions on how to empower yourself using the mantra techniques of the ancient sages. After many years of teaching and sharing, he has created a beautiful series of books and recordings that will guide you through the techniques of using mantras. Additionally, he shares some of the moving experiences that he has had with spiritually advanced beings, as well as the lessons that he learned from each encounter. I have found that his works are offered in a spirit of service to both the novice and the advanced student. Farrand's works are offered in Sanskrit, an ancient Eastern dialect, however, you can just as easily and effectively use a single word such as *Peace, Love, Wisdom,* or a scripture from the Bible. The science of mantra is that the repetition and the rhythm at which you speak lulls the mind into silence. At any time you can stop the mantra and simply listen.

Consistency Is the Key

The key to receiving the benefits of a meditation practice is consistency. This is not always easy for working or single parents. When my grandson was younger, I would make him some tea, give him a few crackers, and sit him in front of the television telling him to have his snack while I was doing my meditation. I would sit for 15 to 20 minutes, knowing that his program would be over in 30 minutes. When I was finished, he and I would go for a walk or read. Even at the tender age of three, he must have sensed the calming effects of my meditation practice. One day I was particularly frazzled and had very little patience with him. He must have noticed. He put his hands on my knee, looked me in the eye, and said, "Yeye, make me some tea, please, because you need to go do your medication." I had to laugh because it was so true. *Meditation is medication!*

Chapter 6

LOOKING
IN THE MIRROR
OF SELF

There is an old saying: "What you draw to you is what you are." For most of us, this is a difficult concept to accept or appreciate. We spend most of our time trying to fix what we see. We try to change people, conditions, and situations outside of ourselves because we don't realize that what we are seeing is actually a reflection of who we are. Think of it this way: When you look in the mirror and decide to fix your hair, you don't brush the reflection! You brush the hair on your head! In other words, we have to learn to fix ourselves, not what we see.

A very dear friend of mine taught me this lesson. Over a span of two years we worked together, confided in each other, and endeavored to bring our lives into order. At one point, our relationship changed, and I became her spiritual teacher. At first, it felt really great; we had what I thought was a good, honest foundation. However, as her teacher, my focus shifted. My priority became assisting this woman to grow spiritually. This often meant I had to tell her things that she was resistant to hearing. It also meant that I had to tell her things that I had not yet mastered myself.

A spiritual brother once told me, "We teach what we most need to learn." Unfortunately, we do not realize we need to learn it, and our students have egos that make it difficult for them to accept the teacher's weaknesses and flaws. This was the case with my friend. I had revealed to her many of my shortcomings, my fears, and a past that was not strewn with lilies! She offered support, encouragement, and usually tremendous insight. I respected her and her opinion, because, as her teacher, I knew this woman had great potential. As her friend, I understood what her challenges and issues were. What I had not fully come to understand was that the people in our world reflect who we believe we are, even when we are unaware that the belief exists. The things I saw lacking in her were the very things I lacked myself.

In *A Course in Miracles*, we read: "When your brother (sister) acts insanely, it is an opportunity for you to bless him (her). You need the blessing you can offer. There is no way to have it except by giving it. Your brother is the mirror in which you see the image of yourself." As usual, I did not understand this statement when I read it. Like most of us, I allowed my ego to convince me that I had it all together. After all, I was a spiritual teacher and counselor. I had helped so many people come to grips with their issues that I was convinced I had mastered many of the challenges most people struggle to overcome. I had not yet realized that we never stop learning, and that a lesson will repeat itself over and over until we recognize it and make better or different choices. My friend taught me the lesson I needed to learn in a most unpleasant way.

One day, in a spiritual ceremony, my friend acted out. As her teacher, I was forced to take a position. I released her as my student. Her reaction to this was insane. She began writing a series of letters to me. She sent a copy of one letter to everyone whom she and I both knew. She sent the letter to all of my students, my former students, my supervisor at work, and the producer of a documentary I had been working on for two years. In the letter, she accused me of being a liar, a thief, and a con artist. She accused me of taking advantage of her, ruining her health, and destroying her home. Then, as justification for her attack on me, she wrote about everything I had ever told her in confidence as a friend. My first reaction was to ignore her. My lack of reaction infuriated her, so she started calling people and telling them the story. People then began to question me. I continued to ignore her, but somewhere inside of me, I knew she was showing me something.

Fears and Shadows

Almost everyone is afraid of something. This is the thing that we will go to great lengths to avoid. What we fear usually involves a perception of danger or harm and is usually associated with a particular incident or situation. Some people fear animals. Others fear heights or feathers. My fear was I would not be liked and that I was being talked about by other people. Like Job, my greatest fear had come upon me. People were talking about me, thinking bad things about me, questioning me about the validity of my friend's statements. Some people chose to ignore her. Others came to my support and defense. Others assumed it was true because she and I had been so close. I couldn't figure out what to do, so I did nothing. I was hurt. I was angry. I was scared to death! Yet something inside of me was very still. A quiet voice in the back of my mind said, "Just wait for the final outcome and watch who is here when the dust settles." I stopped reading the letters. I stopped answering the telephone. I just watched and waited. I knew the answer would come.

When the thing you fear comes upon you, it is like a sharp pain in the pit of your stomach. It causes you to double over. You can't move. And then it's over. When you don't face your fear, you have a constant ache. You don't know where it comes from or when it is going to stop. You just live with it. Perhaps I'm a masochist, but I will take the sharp pain. From one day to the next, my world as I knew it was falling apart. People doubted the validity of the work I was doing. They began to tell others about their own experiences with me. Most stories were embellished to fit the tale being told. Others told downright lies! I wondered what else people were saying about me. What were they thinking? How was I going to straighten this out? Were people going to like me? The hysteria continued for three weeks. I knew there was a lesson looming somewhere, but I couldn't see it. Finally, I decided to pray. I asked Spirit to show me what was going on. A passage from *A Course in Miracles* came to me: ". . . your brother is your mirror." It was too painful to look at myself, so I had looked at my friend.

113

My friend feared being abandoned, my own fear as a child. She did not want to take responsibility for herself, so she blamed others for everything that happened in her life. My friend had low self-esteem and a poor self-image. She resented criticism almost as much as I did. My friend was brilliant, intelligent, and beautiful, yet she behaved irrationally, self-destructively, and irresponsibly. She did things based on emotions and then, after thinking about what she had done, berated herself. My friend was lonely. She wanted love but was afraid of being hurt or abandoned. She had many painful issues surrounding her worth. She believed people were taking advantage of her. My friend would volunteer to do things for people. When they did not respond in a certain way or pay her what she thought her efforts were worth, she lashed out. My friend said yes when she meant no. She wanted to be liked, needed, and accepted. She was, however, convinced that there was something wrong with her. She thought that she wasn't good enough or smart enough, that she did not deserve good things. I knew these things about my friend, but I had not accepted them about myself. I was fixing the mirror. My friend cracked the mirror for me.

Spirit will always give you what you need when you need it. Unfortunately, we don't usually want what we need. We fight tooth and nail by blaming others and refusing to accept the truth about ourselves. We create our own experiences because we need to grow. It was time for me to grow. I had to move to a new level of awareness about myself and my work. It was time for me to let go of the thoughts, habits, attitudes, and people who were causing me harm. I had prayed for it. I had asked for it, and it came in the only way I was able to accept it at that time—painfully.

The things my friend wrote and said about me were things I had said to myself, about myself. I doubted myself! I questioned myself! I beat up on myself! I believed that my past, my family, and my mistakes made me unworthy. Yet I projected another image to the world. I spent my time fixing other people—people whom I thought did not have it together. I was fixing the mirror! This experience taught me that whatever we see in others is a reflection of ourselves. It was time for me to learn that just because we are defective does not mean we cannot see defects in another! Further, because we are defective does not mean we are not worthy! It simply means that we have to work a little harder to learn a little more. In order to be whole, complete, and beautiful beings, we have to put the lipstick on our lips, not on the mirror! My friend taught me this lesson in her first letter when she wrote: ". . . heal yourself and leave the rest of us alone!"

The Mirror of Self

The most important step toward the power of Spirit is knowing, accepting, and loving self. This is a vital process for women. We are the composite of past teachings, past experiences, life pressures, and external values. Consequently, it is often difficult to distinguish who we are from what we have been *told* we are, or what we have been *taught* to be. We are told that we are incapable of making our own decisions. We are taught to be dependent. We are socialized by generalizations. We are molded through external expectations that are primarily focused on the way we look, the environment from which we come, and the degree by which we attempt to appease the expectations. Since we are taught to respond to life's *external* stimuli, self is generally the last place we look to find answers, seek guidance, or resolve conflict.

Self—your true, authentic self—is the gentle, knowing, powerful essence of the Creator. Self is without judgment, without societal prejudice, without expectation. Self is the keeper of information and the promoter of revelations. Self is the witness and the judge. Self is the storehouse of guidance necessary to fulfill life's mission. Self is a student of life who has studied all that is required to pass life's tests and overcome life's obstacles successfully.

When we look in the Mirror of Self, we are asking to see all that we are, all that we have been, and all that we can be. It is a painful process, a loving step toward maximum growth, and the only way to develop self-acceptance. Looking in the Mirror of Self

115

opens our eyes to our self-destructive, counterproductive ideas, attitudes, and habits. It is the only way to accept responsibility for our actions and gain an understanding of our experiences. Because it crystallizes the quality of our intent, looking in the Mirror of Self opens the door to accepting our mistakes and weaknesses. When we can accept what we have done with an understanding of why we acted, we can no longer be persecuted. Looking in the Mirror of Self reveals the strengths we can rely on to guide us through challenges. When we know who we are, accept why we are, and understand what we are living to learn, self becomes a constant source of encouragement.

Mirror of Self Exercise

You will need the following:

- A four- to five-foot-long mirror
- Two white candles, preferably encased in glass
- A white sheet or towel
- A straight-backed chair or floor pillow

You may sit in the chair or in a lotus position on the floor pillow. Make sure you are comfortable because you will need to sit as still as possible for at least 20 minutes. The room should be completely dark, except for the candlelight.

- Place the mirror against the wall, so that it is straight.

- Position the chair or pillow three to four feet away from and directly opposite the mirror.

- Place one candle on either side of the chair or pillow so that the reflection of the candles can be seen in the mirror.

- Sit with your back flat against the back of the chair or in the lotus position on the pillow with your back straight.

- Rest your hands on your knees, palms up.

- Focus your eyes on a place on the floor between you and the mirror.

- Take eight deep Cleansing Breaths.

- Sit quietly and listen to your breath for a minute or two.

- Silently affirm in your mind, "I am willing to see my true self."

- When you can hear your heartbeat in your ears or feel throbbing throughout your body, slowly raise your eyes to the mirror.

- Continue repeating the affirmation until your head is lifted and you are focused directly on your eyes in the mirror.

- Take eight more deep Cleansing Breaths while gazing into the reflection of your eyes in the mirror.

- Silently affirm in your mind, "Show me my true self." When you feel ready, stop the affirmation and concentrate on your breathing. Keep your eyes focused on your reflection until your eyelids feel heavy. When they do, allow them to close.

What You Can Expect:

- You may see nothing at all the first few times you do the exercise. Do not be alarmed. This is normal.

- You may see something or someone in the mirror that you do not recognize. If this happens, close your eyelids and take Cleansing Breaths. Refocus your eyes on the floor and raise them slowly again. If the same thing reappears, remain focused on it. Spirit will clarify what it means to you.

- You may begin to remember an incident or experience from the past. If this happens, close your eyelids and let it play out. Silently ask for understanding and clarity.

- You may cry for no apparent reason. Close your eyelids and give yourself permission to have the experience even if you don't know why you are crying. Listen carefully to your thoughts and silently ask any important questions.

- You may see nothing except the reflection of self. If so, silently ask, Who am I? and listen to your thoughts.

- You may see colors. Check the Color Reference Chart in Chapter 13 for clarification.

- If at any time you experience fear, lower your gaze to the floor and listen to your breath.

- When you feel ready to get up, take a few deep breaths, lower your eyes to the floor, stretch your body, and move slowly away from the mirror. Use a journal to write down what you have seen or experienced.

- You can repeat this exercise once a week.

- Spend a minimum of 20 minutes, a maximum of 45 minutes for each session.

- This is also an excellent exercise to resolve and gain clarity when you have a conflict with another person. While looking in the mirror, ask Spirit for clarity and understanding about what the person is revealing to you about yourself.

Speaking in the Mirror of Self

Speaking in the Mirror of Self is an excellent process for developing positive thoughts, which will manifest as experiences in your life. When you are speaking to yourself in the mirror, you are opening your mind and spirit to different, more expansive, more self-honoring experiences. To speak in the mirror, stand directly in front of the mirror, look directly into your own eyes, and talk to yourself. By doing this you are sending commands to the essence of your being. Your spirit is ready and willing to follow your instructions and commands. The key is to surrender to the energy of Spirit as it guides you.

Speaking in the Mirror Exercise

Stand before the bathroom mirror in a relaxed posture. Look directly into the reflection of your eyes. Take three to five deep Cleansing Breaths. In a firm but loving voice, instruct your spirit. Be mindful not to yell at yourself. The following examples can be used. Feel comfortable to create your own statements.

To Create Wanted Conditions

Repeat each statement nine times.

- "I am open and willing to change."

- "I am releasing all excess weight easily and effortlessly."

- "I am attracting abundantly positive conditions and people into my life."

- "I am creating positive conditions/relationships/ situations in my life."

- "I am all that God created me to be, and I am experiencing and expressing that truth moment by moment."

To Create Self-Acceptance

Repeat each statement nine times.

- "I am beautiful/peaceful/confident/powerful."

- "I am enough."

- "I am worthy just the way I am."

- "I am that I am."

- "I am attuned to and aligned with the presence of God in my life."

What I Know Now

*Every person, situation, circumstances, and experience in your life
is a reflection of some aspect of who you believe yourself to be.
All difficult, challenging, painful experiences and relationships
provide us with an opportunity to heal some part of our consciousness.
We focus on the weaknesses and shortcomings of others as a function
of the shame, guilt, and fear buried in our own internal landscape.
No matter how painful an experience is at any
moment, you must know that you will be okay.*

Me, Myself, and the Other People

There comes a moment for each of us, a definitive moment, when we are compelled to assess where we are, and where we are going. In that moment, we must come clean with ourselves about what we say, what we do, and whether or not the two are aligned. Depending upon our internal response to this experience, we will either volunteer or be forced to take a long hard look at how we are showing up in the world. Looking at ourselves can be frightening at worst, and nerve-wracking at best. To see ourselves for all that we are or are not, to tell the absolute truth about what you see, is possibly one of the most challenging experiences we face as human beings. When done with humility and integrity, self-examination and self-reflection lead us to the brink of greatness. Once on the brink, we are called forth to jump, to make the necessary changes that will ultimately transform our state of being.

On the other hand, if you jump before you are ready, before you take a good look at yourself, you could fall face-first into self-brutalization and really hurt yourself. No one can beat up on you with the same intensity and severity that you use against yourself. No one can become more fixated on what's wrong with you with the same level of scrutiny as you use in the privacy of your own mind. It is what I often call "self-terrorization." We brutalize ourselves for feeling afraid, ashamed, or guilty about all that we

121

believe is wrong with us, and we invite others to participate. It is very, very painful. On the other hand, it is the way we learn our most empowering lessons.

I had just buckled my seat belt and turned the key in the ignition when the telephone rang. I can't say I was surprised. At the height of my career as a writer and speaker, I was emerging from seclusion at a four-day staff retreat. I knew that my message box was full and that there would be quite a few hysterical people trying to reach me. Losing most of your privacy is a part of living a public life that I find difficult to accept. To my surprise, the call was from my daughter, Gemmia. She wanted to give me a heads-up to lessen the likelihood that I would lose what little hair I had left after cutting off my 12-year-old locks. I was glad that she called, but dumbfounded by her news.

A major national magazine, one with which I had enjoyed what I thought was a good relationship, was running a cover story on me. So far, so good. They had lifted a candid photo of me in which I was making a mocking gesture. In context, I was probably talking to someone and trying to make a point. Taken out of context on the cover of the magazine, it appeared to reflect my genuine attitude. The headline was something about a wolf in sheep's clothing taking Christians off the path of righteousness.

Driving down a winding road in the hills of West Virginia, I did not dare slam on my brakes. Instead, I screamed, "What?!" which scared the bejesus out of the three passengers in my car. Gemmia informed me that it got worse. They had interviewed some of my neighbors who attended the church directly across the street from my facility. The neighbors indicated that they didn't know who I was or what I did, but if it had anything to do with Yoruba, it was against the Bible and against Christians. They interviewed prominent women speakers who had appeared with me on various panels. One recounted a story of my calling up ancestors at a luncheon that left women wailing and screaming. She went on to denounce me and ancestor worship, and particularly warned Christian women to be leery of me. I had absolutely no recollection of what luncheon she was talking about.

For three pages, the author of the article questioned, challenged, and twisted my work, my character, and my motives as she interviewed ministers, educators, and everyday people. The stated purpose of the story was to discover why my work had struck a chord with so many people. In essence, they wanted to know if I was successful because I was good, or if I was promoting something evil in order to make myself successful. And did unsuspecting people, particularly Christians, know the difference? The one saving grace in the article was an interview of a prominent minister from Chicago who stated simply: "They are jealous of who Iyanla is and what Iyanla stands for: the freedom of people's minds and hearts outside of the boundaries of the Judeo-Christian community."

I stopped at every 7-Eleven and newsstand I could find between Jefferson County, West Virginia; and Alexandria, Virginia. I found two copies of the magazine. I bought them both. I called Gemmia back and told her to go out and buy every copy of the magazine she could find. She told me she had started to do that, but realized she would probably run out of money before she got to the Delaware border.

"Breathe, Ma. Just breathe. Nobody is going to believe this crap. It is too disgusting and ridiculous."

"That's not the point," I told her. "I don't want anybody to see it."

"Well, it's too late for that. This is a national publication and people have already seen it. The telephone is ringing off the hook, and the e-mails are up to about 50 a day."

"Oh my Lord! Who's calling? What are they saying?"

"Breathe, Ma. People are outraged for you and with you, not *about* you. This is just another lesson."

I knew she was right, but it didn't stop my hands from shaking and my stomach from churning. Why? Why in the world would they do something like this? I had recently invited the editor of the magazine to my book-release party and he had come. He ate my food, talked to my guests, smiled in my face, and then *this?* It just didn't make any sense. What about my family, my husband, my children, my grandchildren? Don't people know there are real people attached to an attack of this magnitude? Any attack, for that matter, is a form of violence. I couldn't figure out what I had done to warrant this from the publication that had dubbed me "one of the foremost African American speakers in the country" just a year earlier. I was hurt and angry and embarrassed; I was about to learn one of the most difficult lessons of my life.

What I know now is that looking in the Mirror of Self boils down to being responsible and accountable for the creation of our experiences. It also demands that we unlearn certain things in order to learn what really *is* required to live authentically in the world. Our lives mirror back to us what we need to know about our being that is *in* or *out* of alignment with our doing.

I am willing to acknowledge that I have joined a gym at least ten times and never attended a single class. I have bought dozens of cases of Slim Fast that I never drank. I have at least four books that I started and never completed. There have been those times when I believed that any disagreement or misunderstanding between myself and someone else was absolutely *the other person's* fault. I am better now! I acknowledge that as a human being, with weaknesses and foibles, it is so much easier to see *out there* than it is to acknowledge that I am the only one who gets to say what goes on in my life. I am creating my experiences moment by moment, thought by thought, word by word, action by action. For most of us humans, it is difficult to acknowledge that we have bad habits. We make promises that we fail to honor. We speak loosely, saying we will commit our time, energy, and resources to people and circumstances that we then conveniently *forget*. We forget because many of the things we commit ourselves to have no meaning to us. We forget because we have not been taught good *spiritual hygiene.*

Lights! Cameras! Healing!

Good spiritual hygiene requires a willingness to do what my brother-friend Rev. Dr. Michael Beckwith, calls "being in God's darkroom." It is when we are in the darkness that God impresses divine information into our hearts, minds, and souls—information that will become the picture of how we live. We don't like the difficult times; we don't like things we cannot control, or things we really don't want others to know about us. We retreat from that place of not knowing, that place of being found out. It's cold, and it's frightening. In fact, as soon as the darkness of difficulty hits, most of us will run in the other direction. What Rev. Michael helped me to see was that being in difficult places in life offers an opportunity to be reproduced as a clearer vision of how God sees us and wants us to be. I find it very interesting that people are using disposable cameras. We don't want to focus anymore. We don't want to carry the heavy equipment or figure out the right distance, angle, or position required to get just the right shot of life. We want to point, shoot, and record the image instantly. *Life simply is not like that!* To get a really great picture, we must do the work. We must take the film into the darkroom. We must apply the chemicals to the negative. We must stand watch over the negatives, checking to ensure that they receive just the right amount of exposure to the chemicals and light. Finally, we must hang the prints up to dry.

Many great photographers still develop their own pictures. It takes time, energy, and patience to develop the image you desire. I don't think God has embraced the concept of advanced technology in "photography." What I know now is that God still does it the old-fashioned way. He takes us, the images of God's divinity, into the dark places in life where He works in us, with us, and through us, until we become a mirror reflection of who God created us to be. We are God's film. We can be redeveloped as many times as required to get a clear picture of ourselves and our focus in life. Sometimes we are hung up to dry. God will shut down everything and lock everyone out of our lives so that He can do the work required for us to live beyond the demands of instant gratification. When we emerge, we have a new idea about our identity and our purpose for living. We are a new image, with a new focus. *In the darkness, we become the vision, the I-am-ness God created us to be from the inside out.*

There was nothing, absolutely nothing, I could do to erase what had been written about me. I did not know how to respond to the people who wanted to know, Why? I did not have a response to the speculation about the veracity of the article. And I could not answer the questions I had within myself. I wept for days about what I thought was going on and why it was happening to me. I was being attacked for no reason. I was being maligned without provocation. I was being destroyed because of my desire to serve people. Then, as will happen when you are learning a lesson and wallowing in self-pity, the light came on and I asked myself, *What is it that they are actually saying about you?* The thought hit me like a bolt of lightening. Hey! Wait a minute! Why *am* I so hysterical about this?

I went back and read the article slowly, word by word, line by line. I made notes in the margins. In the process I remembered what one of my teachers had told me, "When God gives you something to do, you can't just do the parts you like. You have to do the grunt work in order to get the glory." I believed with all my heart that my work—the writing, speaking, teaching—is my purpose, the reason God placed me on the planet at this time. My intentions to support the evolution of human consciousness were clear. My desire to end human suffering was pure. Why, then, was I giving the publication all that power? The reason became as clear as the hysteria I was feeling: There was something going on that I was refusing to see about myself. *My goodness! Stick me in the eye with a fork!*

Hidden Core Beliefs

Reviewing the article revealed to me that there were elements of truth mixed with opinion and innuendo. People have a right to think what they think and do what they do, and we each get to choose how we respond. I was teaching people about Yoruba culture. I wanted to share with the world the beauty and power I had discovered in my heritage. I was also revealing the similarities between Western spiritual culture and ancient African traditions. In a world that often dismissed and discounted both, the blending of the two had served me well. It had helped me to find my own beauty, voice, and power as a woman of African descent, raised with a Christian theology. I had discovered a way to embrace and honor both the ancient and modern traditions and cultures in a practical manner for those who had lost touch with either.

The article attempted to make my work about the right and wrong of religion. It was an age-old argument in which I could choose to participate or not. I was sharing my personal experiences about culture, Spirit, and spirituality in ways that many people had not heard before, and it resonated with those who were reading my books. The information wasn't new, but it was honest. It was empowering for some and threatening for others. I was writing about what many had wondered about. I was giving voice and validation to things that had been denounced as sinful, bad, and just plain old wrong. I was bringing African spirituality to the table with a universal flavor, and I had not gotten permission or approval from anyone, including myself.

With a closer read of the article, I could see how my core beliefs were coloring my perception of what was really going on. *I wasn't good enough* to have so much attention. *I was wrong* to stand up and speak out about anything, much less God. *I was bad* for doing the *wrong thing,* and now people were upset with me. It was the script of the six-year-old part of me playing things out in living color, and it was now time for me to rewrite that script. What I know now is that the article revealed publicly the secret and private thoughts and conversations I had with myself. There had been moments in my career when I wondered if I knew enough, if I had learned enough, if I was doing the right thing. At the time, I still battled with my own doubts and fears about simultaneously being Yoruba and Native American, and loving Christ as I did. The article said that my message wasn't clear. It was true! *I* wasn't clear. Life is about seeking, searching, and discovering. In order to grow we must question, challenge, and ultimately find solid ground in our spiritual quest. I had found what I thought was a viable alternative for many. It had certainly worked in my own life, and I wanted to share it with others. That is my path. That is my purpose. *I am better now!*

Shortly after I was initiated as a Yoruba priestess, my godfather gave me an instruction that changed my life forever. He told me to read and study every sacred text I could find. That was a lot of information to take in, let alone process, but I did. I read the Torah and the Kabbalah. I studied the Qur'an and the Bhagavad Gita. I went back to *A Course in Miracles* and the Bible. Twenty-five years ago, before I had ever written a book or delivered a lecture, I discovered what I believe God wants us all to know: There are many paths that lead to one road, and that is the road of love and forgiveness as the foundation for and the outgrowth of an intimate relationship with God. The sacred text that I read only confirmed what some part of me already knew: The biggest obstacle we must overcome on the spiritual path is our own mind. The beliefs we hold, and the choices and decisions we make in response to our judgments and projections that are grounded in fear, are the blueprints we use to pave our spiritual path. Our interpretation of who God is and what God requires of us is a matter of faith and belief. No one can give you faith and no one can choose for you what you believe. What I know now is that our experiences become the blueprint we use to build our spiritual lives.

The next issue of that publication was its last issue. What I know now is that my photo on the cover and that lead story featuring me in the next-to-last issue was a desperate attempt by the magazine to stay afloat, to attract readers. I made it about me because my inner landscape needed tilling. Today I am grateful for the experience. It helped me to gain a clarity and strength that has served me well. What I know now is that when we resist or avoid looking at ourselves, the universe will hold up a mirror, making denial impossible.

Do you hear me calling you?
The voice of a mother and a father and a child.
Would you recognize the truth?

Do you feel the love that's falling from my eyes?
Take just a minute.
Come and rest here by my side.
Let me tell you your own story,
Let me walk you through your lies.

— *One Hundred Thousand Angels* by Bliss

Begin Within!

The following exercise is designed to assist you in surveying your internal landscape, the core of your self, in order to identify the core beliefs that may limit or restrict your ability to create the life you desire. This exercise requires that you spend approximately 30 minutes a day for 7 consecutive days, responding to a set of inquiries. Remember, we are not rushing through a self-help exercise. We are creating a spiritually grounded and centered life, a life worthy of your time, energy, and attention. You are powerful and divine, and, as such, anything that interferes with your experience and expression of your authentic self must be addressed and eliminated. Looking in the Mirror of Self in this way is a self-honoring process that reveals a truth that you need to know if you are to experience life at a deeper level.

Your daily supplies for this exercise will be your journal or a sheet of paper and a pen. That's it! It's that simple. You will need a place to work where you will not be disturbed for the prescribed amount of time. If you take this as seriously as I pray you will, go ahead and create an environment that will help you relax. Music. Candles. Incense. No wine or other mind-altering substances! This is sacred work.

Before you begin, take several deep Cleansing Breaths. Allow your body to relax. Align yourself with the rhythm of your breath by focusing on your inhale and your exhale. Allow your eyelids to close for a moment as you focus your attention on your breath. Relax the base of your tongue in your mouth, and allow your shoulders to relax. Set an intention to know the truth. Remain in the stillness until you are ready to begin.

Core Beliefs Exercise

The following is a list of core belief phrases that have a strong and prevailing influence on our lives:

- God is:
- Life is:
- Men are:
- Women are:
- Money is:
- Work is:
- Time is:
- People are:
- Sex is:
- I am:
- Children are:

Complete each of the phrases listed with your most authentic response, *the first thought that comes to mind as soon as you read the phrase.* I encourage you to resist the temptation to write what you *think* you should feel. This is a healing opportunity to do your best to tell the absolute truth. If you have no response to a particular phrase, take a deep breath and respond to the next phrase. When you have responded to all phrases the first time, go back and fill in those that you skipped. If, on the second go-round, nothing comes to mind when you read a particular phrase, close your eyelids, focus on the rhythm of your breath, sit in stillness until you feel ready, and then address the phrase again. When you have completed each phrase, resist the temptation to reread or correct them. If you are not writing in a journal, place your responses in a safe place where they can be easily retrieved. Repeat this exercise for six days. Your responses may be the same each day, or they may differ each day. On the seventh day, the exercise will shift slightly.

Have your responses from the past six days available. At the top of a sheet of paper, write a brief description of the most pressing challenge or need currently present in your life. This description should be no more than 50 words. Under the description, write a brief statement of no more than 25 words that indicates why you believe this experience is present in your life. Beneath this statement provide a list of all people other than yourself who are involved. For example: husband, wife, son, daughter, mother, father, etc. If a person involved is not a family member (that is, mate, co-worker, friend), you must also indicate the individual's gender. For example: best friend—male.

Once you have completed your list, indicating the gender of those involved, match your list against your core belief sheets from the six previous days in order to identify the beliefs you see present. Undoubtedly you will discover that many of the beliefs you hold at the core of your being are present in the experience described. Pay close attention to the responses that came forward repeatedly during the six days of writing. These indicate your most deeply held beliefs, which are influencing your experiences. Most often we think that our experiences dictate our beliefs, when the truth is, our beliefs dictate our experience. When we are not aware that core beliefs exist, we become victims of what happens to us rather than being creators of what we desire. Once we become aware we are empowered to choose a new belief. This Looking in the Mirror of Self exercise will support you in identifying and eliminating beliefs you have inherited, adopted, and made up that have been playing out in your experiences.

Looking in the Mirror of Self is not a process to be taken lightly. You must be serious about healing, committed to growing, and willing to love yourself no matter what you see in your mirror. It is best to approach the process seeking your good, your strengths, and your power with an intention to eliminate anything that may be blocking or obstructing the expression of your authentic self. No good will come from the process if you are afraid that there is really something wrong with you or if you are searching for proof of how lowly or unworthy you may be. In her book *The Sacred Yes: Letters from the Infinite*, Rev. Deborah L. Johnson writes that we must all "Feel, deal, and heal!" This process is about feeling the emotions you have deemed as unacceptable, dealing with the dark, ugly sides of your personality, and healing the unproductive images that have been impressed or implanted in your mind. If you hold in your heart a true desire for transformation rather than merely an end to your current problems, the Mirror of Self is a good place to begin.

Chapter 7

PRAYER

One of my spiritual teachers once told me, "When you get tired of struggling, you stop. Then things change." I had become fed up with struggling, suffering, and feeling bad. I was truly ready to find out why my life wasn't working. I was extremely talented, but working bored me. I was making money hand over fist, yet I was still broke! All my relationships ended violently and painfully. I had friends who weren't progressing, talents I wasn't using. I was in debt, brokenhearted, depressed, and angry. Both of my parents were deceased, so I couldn't turn to them. I was forced, by the luck of the draw, to take a hard, long look at myself!

One of my students recommended that I participate in a Native American purification ceremony called a "sweat." At the time I had no idea what it was, but she assured me it would help me get in touch with myself. So, off I went to the woods to look at myself and get purified!

A sweat is a process of detoxifying the body, mind, and spirit. You are taught how to connect and commune with the earth. Rocks that have been heated on a sacred fire are placed in a pit. The pit is located inside a sacred tent structure, a lodge, which is built to resemble the womb. There were about 20 women "sweating" this day. We filed, in one by one, and took a seat on the cold, bare earth. When the structure is sealed off, it is pitch-dark and airtight. Water is then placed on the rocks and steam rises, creating a sauna-like effect in the tent. Sitting with your feet toward the pit of rocks, you pray and sing, allowing the earth to absorb the toxins you are releasing.

My prayer was to release everything that was making my life unhappy. I closed my eyes and began praying. I estimate that it was about 120 degrees in the tent. The heat had a drugging effect. The louder people prayed and sang, the lighter my head became. My eyes were closed, but I could see myself. I saw myself exactly as I was dressed, sitting on the earth with hundreds of worms crawling on me. I jumped, and my eyes flew open. I looked down at my hands and legs. There were no worms. I closed my eyes again. This time, I was myself as a little girl. It was then that the memories began to flood my mind. The abuse. The neglect. The rape. The tears. The loneliness. Scene after scene. I could feel the pain of those past experiences. I was crying, but I couldn't get my eyes open! The scenes kept coming. The tears were flowing. It was my turn to pray aloud.

After my prayer, everybody was crying. The heat was rising. Somebody wanted to leave, so we prayed for her. When we began singing the healing songs, a cool breeze entered the lodge. I was finally able to open my eyes. Everyone was asked to pray again. This time, we all gave thanks for the healing we had received. No one knew exactly what that was, but I, for one, felt much better. When I looked down at the pit of rocks, they all had faces. The faces were smiling at me. The lodge was opened, and we began filing out. When the sunlight came into the lodge, I became aware of the hundreds of little pebbles around me. I looked down to see if I had been sitting on any. It was then I saw the piles of dead worms in the exact spot where I had been sitting.

To the African people, prayer is an essential part of each day. The Yoruba believe that it is our duty to begin each day in prayer. Prayer is communion (contact) with the Creator, through Spirit. It is a method of positive programming of the mind, body, and spirit as you seek and give thanks for life and guidance. Daily prayer means that your first contact for the day is with your own

Ori (spirit), and the Creator of your Ori. Prayer releases your life force into the universe to produce the right attitudes, reactions, and results as you go about your day. Prayer sets into motion the higher laws of mind and spirit.

Everything Is a Prayer

Every thought you think, every word you speak, is a form of prayer. Why? Thoughts and words are an expression of your life force. When this force is released into the universe, your environment, it will take shape and form. How many times have you said, "You make me sick?" Notice that by the end of the day you have a headache, are nauseated, or feel exhausted. How many times have you prayed for something good for yourself—realizing, hoping, sometimes wishing something negative for someone else? Those negative thoughts and words cancel out the positive energy of prayer. Careful monitoring of your thoughts and words is required to yield positive prayer results.

Frustration, fear, disappointment, unworthiness, hate, greed, jealousy, and self stand in the way of your prayers. Very often when we pray for something, evidence that we cannot or will not get it will manifest in our lives. My grandmother always told me, "Don't believe your lying eyes." If it's good for you, if it will not cause harm to you or anyone else, if you believe, then it is yours! If you pray for it today, don't pray for the same thing tomorrow. Just give thanks, deny all evidence to the contrary, and stand firm.

Prayers are always answered. You don't have to beg or make deals with the Creator when you pray. What you get in answer to your prayer is the direct reflection of what you expect, not necessarily what you pray for. You can pray endlessly and never see the manifestation. The challenge is to pray, knowing that you will see results. If you pray, doubting what you want is possible, you are canceling out the request. The key is to pray with faith, knowing and believing that, what you ask for, you already have!

Many people think that they do not know how to pray, or think that because they are not religious, they cannot/should not

135

pray. This is false. Prayer is an internal experience as well as an external expression. The issue is whether or not you acknowledge that there is something/someone to pray to. If we accept that the life force of the Creator exists within our being, prayer can be seen as communication with the divine part of self. Prayer slows you down, focuses your energy, and opens the lines of purification, illumination, and union.

Prayer need not be set or fixed in any way. It can be a ritual/ceremony or a brief conversation. The words you choose can be your own, or they can be those you have been taught. Since prayer is communion, you should pray what you feel and not what you think. You can pray aloud or to yourself. You can pray standing, sitting, lying, or kneeling. The issue is to be humble. You should not fuss or give directions in prayer. You should not express negativity about or toward anything or anyone. You should not make demands or give ultimatums. You should gently express your thoughts or feelings and ask for guidance and clarity about the situation. It does not matter what you have done or whether you consider yourself religious or not—you can still pray! The divine energy of the Creator is within you. When you pray, you are in essence praying to yourself—and you already know what you have thought, said, or done. The Creator knows, too!

Affirmative Prayer

Affirmative prayer is a traditional African concept that has been reaffirmed by the New Age. Among the Yoruba, we give prayer by addressing the Creator and our Orisa (the various aspects attributed to God) by their praise names and by citing the marvels they have brought to our life. We call the names of our ancestors who now sit with the Creator and thank them for what they have left us. We thank the natural elements (air, water, fire, and earth) for the role they play in sustaining us. We praise the Creator for giving us all that we need and have. For those who are not Yoruba, this form of prayer is called praise and worship. While the ancestors and elements are not included in the Western world, the key is to praise, give thanks, and remind ourselves of all the Creator has already done.

Next, we state our request or dilemma. Speaking about it as clearly and precisely as possible without laying blame, drawing conclusions, or making demands. In prayer, it is counterproductive to pray for harm to come to anyone, or to ask for anything that will make someone else unhappy. You must ask for the best outcome and claim it by giving praise and thanksgiving. Do not negate your prayers by thinking negative thoughts about what you've asked for. Prayer is like planting a seed. Don't dig it up to see how it is doing! Pray for it. Release it by giving thanks. Begin acting like you already have it!

Praising, requesting, and giving thanks are the components of affirmative prayer. It is a sign of faith that you know the best will come. Releasing our concerns to higher forces is an act of humility. If you have nothing to ask for, praise and thanksgiving are enough. If you don't know how to express what you feel, state that and do the best you can. Again, there is no need to make promises, cut deals, or make demands! The faith that backs the prayer is the determination of the outcome. There will be occasions when you feel like you just can't pray or meditate. Take two minutes, breathe deeply, sit still, and do it anyway! You can use the Bible, Koran, Bhagavad Gita, or any holy book you choose to get spiritual guidance and support for your prayer practice. Take a few deep breaths, place the book in the center of your forehead, and think about the situation facing you. Using your right hand, open the book to any page. Read the first seven lines on the right-hand page. Your solution will be there!

One caution about prayer: Be specific in what you ask for, and do not pray about the problem. You must pray for the desired solution. A good friend of mine was once without a place to stay. She was sleeping on the floor in a relative's home. Everyday she prayed for *just* a room with a bed because she couldn't afford anything else. After three months, she found a six-by-eight room with *just* enough space for a bed and her suitcase. She called me to tell me the good news. After a few minutes of conversation, she said, "I know prayer works, so I wonder why I didn't ask for a house!"

Prayer is the key, and, with faith, it unlocks the door. Have faith. You deserve the best! Pray for it and expect it! It is yours!

Prayers for Spiritual Strength

To the Creator, whose mercy endureth forever,
I lift my voice in prayer.

To the Father spirits, whose presence
light my path, I lift my mind in prayer.

To the Mother spirits, whose love is the
source of my life, I lift my spirit in prayer.

I am thankful for the enduring and
everlasting mercy, light, and love in my life.

I know I am watched by
protective eyes, so I can never fall!

I know I am surrounded by
unconditional love, so I am never alone!

I know I am guided by clarity and
strength, so I shall never lose my way.

I am Protected.
I am Guided.
I am Loved.
I am Thankful!

Dear God, please untie the *nots* that are
invading my mind, my heart, and my life.
Please remove the have *nots,* can *nots,* and the do *nots.*
Please erase the will *nots,* may *nots,* might *nots.*
Please release me from the could *nots,*
would *nots,* and should *nots.*
Most of all, dear God, I ask that you remove
from my mind, my heart, and my life all of the
am *nots* that I have allowed to hold me back.

— from *Everyday I Pray* by Iyanla Vanzant

What I Know Now

*Prayer is the foundation of an intimate
relationship with the Holy Spirit of God.
Prayer is not a religious activity. It is the daily minimum
requirement for a spiritual connection to the essence of life.
We do not pray to get God to do anything. We pray to
align our consciousness with God's presence in our life.
Every thought, every word spoken, and every action is a prayer.*

Prayer Changes You, Not Things!

Dysfunction was my very first prayer partner. Desperation was my motivation for the long, pleading prayers I whispered under my bedcovers at night. I grew up in a family where nothing was what it seemed to be, and no one was who he was supposed to be. My uncle was my father. My aunt was my mother. My cousin was my sister. But wait a minute! I had a father! I knew who he was, and he frequently drove by the house I lived in with my uncle/ father and aunt/mother. He usually had strange women in his car and rarely stopped to say hello. In fact, he acted as if he did not see me and did not know me. The problem was that he was married to my stepmother who, I was told, was my natural mother. She wasn't. She sent my brother, who actually *was* my brother, and me to live with my aunt and uncle when we were evicted from our apartment. It was confusing then. It is heart-wrenching now. Thinking back, it seems absolutely amazing that I went along with the stories, the lies, when all along I knew the truth.

The stress of my childhood caused my hair to fall out. I am not speaking of short, broken hair that could be camouflaged with creative combing or decorative hair ribbons. I am speaking of *baby-butt bald* at the temples, in the back, and at the top of my head. Every night I desperately prayed for my hair to grow. I was nine years old, with a flat chest, a protruding belly, and mocking-bird-thin legs. My aunt's answer to my prayer was to buy, and convince me to wear, a lovely auburn page-boy wig. The wig was bad enough, but the frequent treatments of Sulphur 8, a hair pomade that was guaranteed to make hair grow, was worse. It emitted a smelly, hot tar odor from beneath my wig. The first day I wore my new hair to school, my classmates snickered and pointed. My teacher, Ms. Cohen, asked me if my mother knew that my hair was red. I told her it wasn't my hair, and she actually seemed surprised. By the end of the week, the older kids were threatening to pull the wig off and beat it with a stick. Some of the kids called my wig a rat, some called it a Davy Crockett hat. It was also the reason my brother had three fights in two days. All I could do was pray: *Dear God, please let my hair grow. Please don't let anyone pull my wig off. Please make my daddy stop and pick me up. Please God, just let me die.*

Desperation is a very common motivator for prayer. We find ourselves in a desperate situation or with an overwhelming need, and we implore God or some other sacred being to save us, help us, make things better. What I know now is that the desperate utterances we issue in pain and fear are not prayers. They are a form of spiritual begging that generally yields little more than temporary relief, only because we have voiced our dismay. Prayer, effective prayer, is not a plea for things or relief from anything. True prayer is heartfelt, honest communication with no strings attached. It is the respectful, reverent recognition of the essence of God that is at all times, in all places, present in its fullness. Prayer is the process and manner in which we make a conscious connection to the essence we know as God or Spirit. When we pray, we are bringing our conscious awareness into alignment with the truth that God is right where we are. God's love, grace, mercy, and divine intelligence surrounds us regardless of appearances to the contrary. In God's presence there are no needs. There is only love. Prayer is the way we remind ourselves that God loves us and stands by our side in all circumstances and situations.

When the pressures of life get the best of us, we turn to prayer. When we reach the limits of our human comprehension and ability, we resort to prayer. When people get on our nerves or trigger our unresolved issues, or when situations appear to be disappointing, frightening, or too difficult, we use prayer as a possible escape route. Many of us ascribe to the belief that there is a being, a "god," sitting somewhere, listening in, and ever ready to respond to our pleas and demands to fix this or do that so that we can bypass taking responsibility for the circumstances in which we find ourselves. We believe this kind of god is at our beck and call to do what we think needs to be done in the way we think it should happen. We use prayer as our calling card to summon divine intervention, to save our butts, and to get others to do what we want them to do. Prayer used in this way, for these purposes, is a sign of spiritual immaturity. It was this type of prayer that I prayed as a wig-wearing nine-year-old, fearful of having her balding head exposed on the streets of Brooklyn, New York. As the other children continued to harass and tease me, I concluded that my prayers were not being heard, and I was really angry with God.

My best good girlfriend in elementary school was Nancy. She lived around the corner from my house, and we walked home together every day. Back then, she was what we would now call a geek. She was quiet, not particularly attractive, with thick glasses and shoulder-length hair. Nancy was considered suspect because of her association with me. She, too, became the object of the vicious taunts by the other children. I was afraid of being de-wigged. Nancy was afraid of her own shadow. Each day as three o'clock rolled around, we would plan our escape, devising creative ways to make it across the school yard and up the three blocks we had to walk to get home. Every day, we would take different routes in our attempts to escape the looming danger of our tormentors. One day, we walked four blocks out of our way, only to run into a group of girls whom my aunt always referred to as "those people from the projects." We saw them and crossed the street. But they saw us and it was on!

Five or six of them surrounded us, reminding us that my brother was not around now to protect us. They circled, calling us names, using words that we "good girls" heard only from drunken relatives and, as my aunt said, "those other kind of people." They began pushing us with their equally flat chests, preparing to do what they had heretofore only threatened—take my wig and break Nancy's glasses. When one of them reached over the other and grabbed my store-bought hair, Nancy completely lost it! I would like to think she was just a good friend protecting me, but the truth was that she was simply afraid she would be next. Nancy let out an ear-piercing scream that frightened everyone. She began to swing wildly, hissing and spitting. A few of the girls swore and started laughing, but most of the others backed up. Nancy would not stop. She swung her book bag at every target in sight. She was kicking and punching into the air so that no one could come within six feet of her. The girl who was dragging me by the hair let go to avoid getting hit, kicked, or spit on. In the midst of this, I realized that my prayers *had been answered: My* wig was still in place, secured by the huge hairpins that my aunt put in every morning.

A crowd had gathered now, their voices drowning out Nancy's screaming. When I got to her, Nancy was on the ground still kicking and screaming, fighting no one but herself. Some of the children were laughing; others stared in amazement. In her frenzy, one of Nancy's kicks landed on my shin, and I fell on top of her. For a minute or two we tussled on the ground until she fell limp. Both of us were crying; when the crowd fell silent, I thought they were feeling sorry for us. But suddenly the circle parted. My brother and a few of his friends were standing over us, yelling and making threatening gestures at the crowd of onlookers. One of my brother's friends reached down and repositioned my skirt so that my panties were no longer exposed. Someone else detangled Nancy and me, helping us to our feet. As we made our way through the crowd, I realized that not only was my wig still in place, Nancy still had her glasses on.

Praying for Answers Is an Answer

Prayer—fervent and effectual prayer—raises the vibration of your mental and emotional energy, making it possible for you to see, know, and do what once may have seemed impossible. Prayer opens your mind to the answers and solutions that have always been present. When we pray, it opens our minds to the divine presence and consciousness of God. We experience a sense of peace and resolve that, more often than not, leads to physical inaction because we gain a sense of knowing that, despite appearances, all is well. This sense of well-being does not come because we expect God to do anything. It is the result of an internal connection to God's presence and the realization that we are not in charge of anything or anyone. The peaceful stillness that results when we pray without fear, expectations, or a predisposition to a specific outcome has nothing to do with God's ability or inclination to save, support, or rescue us. It is a function of alignment. When our consciousness is energetically aligned with the law, principles, and spiritual essence that we refer to as God, all things are possible. Prayer is not the fix-all, do-all practice that many of us have been taught it is. It is a process of communication with the essence of God within each of us; it stills the mind and heart, enabling our internal spiritual authority to control the frantic ranting of the mind. When the mind is still, Spirit prevails.

If you pray for something and you do not see the answer, consider the following: (1) Is what you want good for you? (2) Will you or anyone else be hurt by your having it? (3) Are you ready for the responsibility of having it? If you can answer these questions affirmatively, and the answer to your prayer has not manifested, the issue is probably patience.

What I know now is that for most of my life I prayed according to beliefs about God that were given to me by other people. I had no concept of God as the essence of my being. Instead I prayed to an all-powerful, external God who performed miraculous feats and healed broken people. I wanted that God to fix me, to change circumstances, people, and situations in a manner that would decrease my mental or emotional discomfort, and thereby provide me with a sense of safety and security. I now understand that the spirit of God is within me, and when I pray I am surrendering the demands of my human will to the presence of divine will. The will of God is that we experience and express love. I also realize that because God exists within the very essence of my being, every thought I think, every word I speak, and every action I take is a *prayer*. Prayer is a form of communication. This means that my very living must be a demonstration of what I know and believe to be true about God. My life is an opportunity and a divine calling for me to express, in all of my affairs and interactions, what I know to be the character and nature of God. Because God is within me and everyone else, it is my spiritual responsibility to demonstrate the active presence of God's love to everyone in all situations and under all circumstances. This makes prayer a state of being rather than a situational practice.

I, like you, am human, and I will be the first to say it is not easy to remember that the presence of God is within and that my life is an act of prayer. We all have sensibilities, foibles, and weaknesses that motivate us to speak harshly, behave inappropriately, and fight to resist the urge to slap the taste out of the mouths of others who also have foibles, weaknesses, and bad behaviors. This is where your daily spiritual practice becomes useful. The more you pray, the more you communicate with the divine within, the less likely you are to succumb to the demands of your animal nature. Prayer is the answer that causes you to change on the inside, which in turn governs how you respond to what occurs outside of you.

What I know now is that the people who hurt me, betrayed me, and disappointed me did not change. My prayers for spiritual clarity, peace of mind, and the desire to be pleasing in my service to God changed how I viewed myself, my life, and the others who come to share the experience of living with me. Once I dropped my internal demands, requirements, expectations, and judgments of how things and people should be, the way in which I viewed and interacted with the world around me shifted. I looked for what I could love, rather than what I or someone else lacked. Prayer—constant, consistent communication with the presence of God within you—will open your heart, your mind, and your spiritual eyes to the perfection that already exists. Prayer is the path to the realization that we need not perfect what God has created. On the seventh day of creation, God said, "It is good." It still is. We still are.

Prayer Works Through an Open Heart

With all things in life, we do not get what we ask for, we get what we *expect*. Expectation is a powerful tool of reality creation; it is the essence of our thoughts fueled by emotions, and it manifests as a demonstration of the mental images we project out into the world. Our mental images attract in kind. What we see in our mind, we will experience in our lives. When we expect to be hurt, betrayed, disappointed, denied, abandoned, or rejected, no amount of prayer will circumvent those expectations. Praying that Boo-Boo does not leave you for someone else, or that you get the job you do not believe you are qualified to get, or that you can pay your bills after you have spent your money frivolously will not change the experience. Prayer does not alter a conscious *mis*alignment with your desires. What prayer can and will do is bring your subconscious and conscious mind into alignment with the right thought, right action, and right response to whatever circumstances you face in the moment. Nancy could not see anything loving about the crowd of girls who surrounded us. In our spiritually immature minds, it appeared that God was not present enough or powerful enough to overcome the crowd's desire to embarrass me and cause Nancy harm. We expected to be beaten down and beaten up. Perhaps our many trips to Sunday school and my prayers to the Virgin Mary had some impact. Perhaps not. What we both needed to do was work through our fears. My wig was securely pinned in place, and Nancy was stronger than she ever realized. It wasn't pretty, but I can see how it was the most appropriate response in the moment. We had to go through it in order to realize that we could overcome it. Those girls never approached us again. In fact, one of them became very close to Nancy and me.

Many people pray as a last resort, after their human efforts have failed to yield the desired results. Others pray with a limited expectation that what they desire is possible or even plausible. What I know now is that an overwhelming majority of people pray from an internal experience of shame, guilt, resentment, anger, and fear, bringing God into the process after what they have done is less than successful. They pray, believing they do not deserve what they desire. That belief nullifies the energy of their prayers. People sometimes pray for rescue, relief, or retribution. They pray, believing something or someone is standing in the way of the outcome for which they are praying. Holding on to judgment or blame about anyone eliminates the miraculous possibilities that can unfold as a result of prayer.

Prayer can only be truly effective when we have an open heart, an open mind, and a willingness to move through the circumstances and events with a loving and peaceful essence. An open heart means that we hold no malice or negative expectations of anyone. An open mind means that we are not dictating or demanding how things and people should or must be. Willingness means surrendering control, knowing that no matter the outcome, you will be just fine. By holding on to memories or projecting onto the future expectations that cloud or color the realm of possibility, you short-circuit the essence and impact of your prayers. Remember, God is within, so when you pray with a closed, clouded heart or mind, you will create or re-create what you expect. *You cannot fool Mother Nature*, that loving presence of God within you. She knows everything about you, and she hears you *from the inside out*.

On any given day, in any given city, on any given street or highway, you may pass an automobile accident. Many people slow down and gawk with amazement. When I pass an accident, I pray, "Dear God, let the fullness of your presence be with everyone here. Let them remember your love." I do not remember every prayer I pray, but those that open my heart and mind to the love of God usually leave a lasting impression on me. On September 11, 2001, I was standing half naked in my dressing room at the CBS studios in New York City. As I watched the video feed streaming into the newsroom from the cameras on location, I saw the second plane hit the second tower. Smoke billowed into the sky and I prayed: "Dear God, Your grace is our sufficiency. The power of your love is now moving through every mind, every body, every soul present and watching this experience. Make us all instruments of your peace. Help us, Lord, to remember that you are our light and our salvation."

Then I cried. I cried at the realization of the horror that humans can inflict on one another when we forget our relationship to God. I cried because I knew that God loves everyone, even those who behave horrifically. Very often, when we are faced with experiences and situations in which we feel helpless or hopeless, we fall into the trap of our human limitations. What I know now is that those are the moments in which we must pray. When we are watching the horrors of the nightly news, we must pray. When we hear about or witness any form of human suffering, we must pray. Prayer not only opens our minds to the possibilities and presence of God's grace, it keeps us from falling into the pit of despair. What I know now is that as a human being, prayer is my responsibility to all other human beings. As a woman, mother, and wife, prayer is my commitment to all other women, mothers, and wives. Prayer is my gift to the world as a demonstration and representation of God's presence.

"The Work"—Byron Katie

In recent years I have been blessed and my prayers have been intensified by a process called "The Work," created by a woman named Byron Katie. In her book *Loving What Is: Four Questions That Can Change Your Life*, she teaches a simple process of asking four questions that will engage the consciousness beyond biases, limited expectations, judgments, and expectations bringing the heart and mind to the realization of the presence and love of God in every situation. The first two questions say it all for me: (1) Is that true? (2) Can you absolutely know beyond a reasonable doubt that it is true?

Regardless of the situation or circumstances we face, we must remember the truth. The truth is that God is always present, loving us, and seeking our highest good. Every situation is an opportunity for us to learn and grow in the experience and expression of God's love. When we judge others or ourselves, when we limit the possibilities to what we know and believe, when we lace our prayers with "coulds," "shoulds," and "must bes," we are not broadcasting the truth; we are standing in the way of God's ultimate wisdom and presence. The Work teaches how to disengage from our mental and emotional judgments in order to see, know, and remember the truth. When we pray, we must pray for truth to be known, revealed, and activated, even when the truth is beyond our limited knowledge and expectations.

The remaining two questions of The Work are these: (3) How do you react when you think that thought? (4) Who would you be without that thought? These two questions demonstrate that all thoughts, even when they are not true, have an impact on our state of mind. Without certain thoughts, we are open to seeing and experiencing every situation in a more loving and productive way. Prayer requires that we are willing to see everything and everyone in a different light.

As a student in high school and college, I hated math. It is probably more accurate to say that I was *afraid* of math. I could never seem to get the numbers to do what I thought they should do. Eventually, I came to the understanding that math is a principle-based science. If you learn and apply the correct formulas, you will inevitably arrive at an accurate answer. Prayer is a sort of new math. It requires you to divide your thoughts, emotions, beliefs, habits, judgments, choices, and decisions into two columns: those that are loving, and those that are not. In the process, you will become aware of the thoughts you have adopted that may or may not have anything to do with what is actually going on in a specific situation.

Once we learn the principles of division, we move on to subtraction. The process is simple: Subtract from your thoughts those things that are unnecessary and unproductive; surrender everything that could be harmful to yourself or another; eliminate every thought or emotion that does not bring more peace, joy, or love into the experience. From there you will begin to add useful, productive, and desirable experiences that do not harm or limit anyone else's right to choose the same for themselves. Along the way, you keep a running tally of what is working in your life; what brings you peace, joy, and the exponential increase of your self-value and self-worth. For those things, you pray in gratitude. Focus your thoughts, attention, and intentions on those things. Ask that they be magnified, and that anything in your own heart, mind, and life that blocks, delays, hinders, or denies a fuller experience and expression of your Highest Most Holy Self be eradicated from your mind and heart, easily and gently, while you are asleep.

Act "As If" the Prayer Is Already Answered

What I know now is that life really intends for us to succeed in everything good. I also know that life will lead us to things and people who support our success. Several years ago while shopping in the Dallas airport waiting for a connecting flight, I was literally attacked by a book. I assumed that the book fell off a shelf and hit me in the head. The store clerk was so hysterical, thinking I might sue, that he gave me the book at no cost. The title of the book was

Too Busy Not to Pray by Rev. Dr. Bill Hybels. I devoured the contents of that book on my flight to Los Angeles.

Dr. Hybels wrote about a very simple process of keeping a daily prayer journal, which is something I had always done. He encouraged readers to write just one page of prayer a day, using a very specific formula. He called it "ACTS": Affirmation, Confession, Thanksgiving, and Supplication. Affirmation is the process of stating the truth we know about God and life. Certain spiritual philosophies encourage us to affirm what we want and to deny those things that we do not desire to have or experience. (We will cover this more specifically in Chapter 8.) Think of affirmation as the sacred, reverent, and respectful acknowledgment of God's presence. Confession means acknowledging those things about yourself and your life that you know are not in alignment with the essence and nature of God. Thanksgiving is the heartfelt expression of gratitude for all that you are and have. If you think about it, you will see that the good far outweighs the not so good. Finally, supplication is the act and art of laying your requests before God. It is so much more than asking for things. It means stating your desires and needs and allowing the results to unfold and manifest in the most loving way possible.

The teachings of this book spoke to me in a way that altered my prayer habits and my relationship with the presence of God within me. With the intention of supporting you in reconsidering the role and practice of prayer in your life, I offer you my very first ACTS prayer from the prayer journal I started in 1996.

Affirmative ACTS Prayer

Affirmation

Good Morning, God!
I love you today. I love how You love me and call me each
morning into a state of deeper awakening and knowledge of You.
I love how You allow me to breathe and move and
live without expecting or demanding anything in return.

*I love how You continue to provide me with every breath,
the total functioning of my body, the ability to choose and
change at a moment's notice whatever I think or feel or do.
You are awesome, God, and I love that about You.
I love the sight of You in the trees and flowers. I love the presence of
You in my children's laughter and my sweetie's eyes. I love the joy of
You in my heart, which gives me the courage, the strength, and
the stamina to move through whatever the day may bring.*

Confession

*Now God, I confess that yesterday I ran amuck! I did not demonstrate
love at every opportunity. I allowed myself to be lulled into gossip
and unkind speaking without self-correcting or offering correction to
others. I stood in judgment of my husband, and when I thought he was
getting the upper hand, I told a lie. I confess that I was complaining
about things that I know I need to handle so that my life will be in
order. I confess that there were moments when I was trying to out-God
You, offering my unsolicited advice to others when I have enough of my
own affairs to manage. I confess that yesterday my humanness was in
control and that I eased You out of the process. I confess that to You
now, asking for a closer walk with Your Holy Spirit this day.*

Thanksgiving

*Today, I just want to thank you, God, for being an understanding
and forgiving God. I thank You for reminding me moment by
moment that my only task to is grow in You. This is my purpose,
my joy, my life assignment. Thank you, God, for giving me a healthy
appetite for more peaceful interactions, more joyful activities, and a
greater discernment of what is or is not pleasing to You. Thank you,
God, for my health and my strength and for the health and strength
of my family. Thank you, God, for opening my eyes to see the
places within me that are still broken, wounded, and out of order.*

*Thank you for the courage to acknowledge them, and the willingness
to heal them. Thank you for my home, the people who love me,
and all the ways that demonstrate to me that You are still and
will always be on my side. Thank you, God, for having my
back at all times, in all circumstances and situations.*

Supplication

*Today, God, I ask for a closer walk with You. I ask that You guide
and lead me away from the mistakes I made yesterday. Today,
I ask that at every moment I remain conscious, aware, and aligned
with Your Holy Spirit so that I may demonstrate to others the fruits
of a close relationship with You. Today, I ask for a greater experience
and a deeper expression of Your spiritual authority within me. Bless
my eyes that I may see all things. Bless my ears that I may hear Your
words and desires in every situation. Bless my mind that I may think
about You, Your will, and Your word before I open my mouth. Help
me today, God, so that I may be of greater service to You. For all
I have received and all that is yet to come, I say yea, God!
Thank you, God! Bless me, God, so that I may be a blessing to others.
And so it is!*

Chapter 8

AFFIRMATION

"Death and life are in the power of the tongue" (Proverbs 18:21). Africans call it Afo'se, (pronounced *Ah-Fo-Shay*) the power to bring about occurrence by speech. In essence, an affirmation is a statement that declares a situation to be true. It is the bringing forth of the life energy in a concise and positive way and releasing that energy into the universe. Everything we say is an affirmation. It can be positive or negative. The universe does not censor what we say; it simply creates.

My life affirmation was: "It's not going to work." Throughout childhood, I had many experiences that left me cynical. I didn't believe anything good would ever happen. As a result, it usually didn't. I had a habit of verbalizing what was wrong with everything and everyone. I was always right, because that is what I wanted to see. When I began to consciously seek my spirituality, my words took on a new meaning. I would recognize what I had said almost instantly. Unfortunately, it took me a while to realize what was happening.

My idea of a good relationship was to have a "gorgeous" man! It didn't matter if he was cheap, selfish, confused, or a total egomaniac, as long as he was gorgeous. He could lie, be unfaithful, or be unreceptive, but he had to be gorgeous. I always said, "I want a nice-looking man," and that is what I usually got! Unfortunately, that's all I got! I was stuck on the physical without any consideration of the deeper levels of a person's being. In the process of seeking a physically gorgeous man, I usually found fault with myself. I was too fat. I was dark. My legs were skinny. My hair was short and nappy. I had big lips, a flat butt, and ugly stretch marks. I thought no one would know these things if I had a nice-looking man! Surely, no good-looking man would accept these faults in a woman!

I finally met the gorgeous man! Believe me, he was a traffic stopper! I couldn't figure out what he saw in me, but he seemed genuinely interested. My first thought was, *It's not going to work!* But each time he called, I convinced myself that he accepted me, loved me, wanted me for just being me! I kept struggling with my ideas of inferiority, even when they didn't seem to matter to him. I ignored his shortcomings by telling myself it was the best he could do. I accepted the relationship, even though I was unhappy with it, because I was grateful that this gorgeous man wanted me. What I came to realize was that this man was the instrument being used to bring my words back to me!

A year into the relationship, I decided to express my displeasure with the way things were going. As quietly and gently as I could, I asked this man why we didn't spend more time together. At first, he tried to comfort me, but I pushed on. I gave him ideas about things we could do together, places we could go together. He looked at me as though I had grown horns! When I asked him what was wrong, he said, "What makes you think I want to take you anywhere? Do you realize what it would do to my image to be seen somewhere with you?" I asked him what he meant. He went on to talk about my hair, my legs, my weight. He told me how I had been the first dark-skinned woman he had been with and that I would probably be the last, because "we" had too many hang-ups! In essence, this man repeated to me every negative thing I had ever said to myself!

When we speak, we may not realize that we are creating! If we say something enough times, we will see it manifest! Often, we do not recognize what we have said when it comes to life. If someone else repeats to us the very thing we have said to ourselves, we resist. We feel hurt or angry about the way they have spoken to us. We fail to recognize that they may be repeating the very thing we have said about them, or what we have said to ourselves. The process of speech creates! It brings the essence of our thoughts and emotions into a tangible form. When we believe what we say and focus our mind on it, it will become truth. It may not be reality, but it will be our truth!

From a spiritual perspective, we can create our reality through speech. The process is called "affirmation." It requires that we use our thoughts and emotions to create what we want and then speak the words, which will then manifest as reality. Affirmations uttered repeatedly create the energy of what we desire, and send that energy out to work. They must always be positive, specific, and spoken with conviction. The difference between a prayer and an affirmation is purely structural. While prayers are general requests, i.e., "Spirit/God give me peace," affirmations are about existence, i.e., "I am peaceful." Affirmations are a backup to prayer, since once you request something, the affirmation confirms your belief that it has been given. Affirmations are a positive step toward bringing into your existence all that you need and want.

The language used to develop affirmations determines the effectiveness of the statement. Language that identifies the conditions we do *not* want should be avoided.

Example: "I do not want to be sick." A more effective affirmation would be, "I am whole and healthy."

Example: "I do not want to be alone." A more effective affirmation is: "I am one with all life."

Language is the vibrational key to the universe. Words create energy! The words we use in our affirmations create energy that will influence the tide of our lives. Structured affirmations create forceful energy. Structure your affirmations to create powerful, focused, positive results, without focusing on the unwanted conditions.

Denials

Words that negate the existence of unwanted conditions and beliefs are called "denials." They erase negativity as a reality in our lives. Denials pinpoint negativity and issue the command to extinguish it. They serve as the foundation upon which affirmations are built. However, every empty space must be filled. When you deny that something can or will exist, you must fill the void with something positive.

Denial: "Sickness is not a reality in my life."
Affirmation: "I am whole and healthy."

Effective Denials and Affirmations for Centering Energy:

Denial: "There is no truth in confusion or chaos!"
Affirmation: "I am centered in divine clarity and understanding."
Denial: "I have not given weakness permission to exist in my being or life."
Affirmation: "I am experiencing and expressing my strength, my power, and God's peace!"

To Attract the Things You Want:

Denial: "Lack is an illusion I choose not to entertain."
Affirmation: "I am the center of abundance. I am a magnet of prosperity."

When Facing a Major Decision or Challenge:

Denial: "Fear is not of God or good."
Affirmation: "I am facing all challenges and decisions with courage and faith."

To Neutralize Energy Between People:

Denial: "Discord and disharmony are not welcomed or invited here."
Affirmation: "I am in perfect harmony with all people and things."

What I Know Now

Every word we speak is a prayer.
Your mouth can be your greatest ally or your strongest foe.
What is on your mind will eventually come out of your mouth.
When you have nothing good to say, say nothing.
Every experience in our lives was spoken into existence.

Wash Out Your Mouth Frequently

I thought she was a nut. She was walking from table to table in the food court introducing herself and offering unsolicited mini-lectures. I tried to act as if I were fixated on my french fries, hoping she would move past my table without stopping. The closer she came, the faster I chewed, but when my youngest grandson screamed at his brother for taking the last packet of ketchup, we became the focus of her attention.

"Hello, my sister. Are these your sons?"

I guess the baseball cap made me appear to be younger than I really was. Hoping she would detect the attitude in my voice, I responded without looking up.

"No, these are my grandsons."

"Grandsons! Oh, you must be like me. I was a young mother, too. I've got three sons. Three beautiful sons. They're grown now. They've got kids of their own. They turned out okay. All teenage mothers don't raise thugs and hoodlums. Some of us just start out a little confused. We get clear when the babies come, don't we?"

It was true, but I didn't particularly care to have my history revealed in the food court of the mall. She was talking at a rapid-fire pace. I kept chewing and prayed that my grandsons did not respond to her.

"And what is your name, young brother? Who are you?"

Why is it that children seem to forget everything you have taught them in the precise moment you want them to demonstrate what they know? You teach them to hold their heads up and to speak clearly when they are asked a question. You also teach them not to talk to strangers. Inevitably, when you take them out in public, they act like they have no home training. They can't seem to distinguish who strangers are or when they should speak up. With ketchup all over their lips and cheeks, and their mouths filled with partially chewed food, each of them in turn mumbled something that was incomprehensible.

Before I could open my mouth to respond on their behalf, the woman barked: "Oh, no, little brothers! You must speak up. You must let the world know who you are."

I was not at all pleased with the tone of her voice, but she said what I was going to say before I could give them my own grandmotherly correction. Without batting an eye, the woman slid into the chair next to my eldest grandson and turned her head, focusing her attention on me. Looking so deeply into my eyes that I felt immobilized by her gaze, she started the conversation in midsentence, as if I knew what she was thinking.

"It is important for our children to know who they are. When they are born, we teach them who they are. If we call them Frank, they respond to it. If we call them Pookie or Boo-Boo, they respond to that. They have no idea who they are until we call them a name. Whatever we call them is what they will respond to. It is what they will grow to be. What do you think would happen if we called them Doctor So-and-so or Professor So-and-so? They would respond to it! They would have a very different expectation of themselves. They would grow into those names. When we affirm the very best of and for our children, they have a very different view of their place and position in the world. Don't call them anything you don't want them to be. Speak seeds of greatness in their minds, and they will respond to those seeds. They will grow into strong, sturdy plants. Now you have a good day, my sister."

She was gone before I realized that I had stopped chewing, and my mouth, filled with fried potatoes, was hanging open.

I am always amazed at the things you can learn from seemingly wacky people in the street or, in this case, the food court at the mall. Everything she said made perfect sense. In fact, it made so much sense, I immediately put it into practice with my grandsons. I began to call them Dr. Oluwa and Dr. Adesola. I told them that they were going to Morehouse College to become doctors—doctors of what did not matter. Nor did it matter if they went to Morehouse, Princeton, or Yale. Like the woman in the mall said, I was simply planting the seeds. I was preparing them to pursue a college degree. I was preparing and supporting them with an appropriate way to let the world know who they are by affirming the possibilities of greatness that lie dormant in their minds and souls. Perhaps if my parents had called me a dancer or lawyer or writer when I was a child, I would not have become a teenage mother. Perhaps if they had spoken possibilities rather than problems into my heart and mind, I would not have lost my way and my identity. Maybe, maybe not... who really knows? I do believe, however, that at the very least it is worth the effort to try affirming the best rather than rehearsing the worst.

It's not what you say that matters. It is where you speak from within yourself that counts. It is not what you hear, it is where you listen from within yourself that gives meaning to the message. Many times we create our lives from the place within us that is broken or wounded. We speak into existence more of *what has been* rather than *what could be* because we speak from our pain rather than our power. Like children, the circumstances of our lives respond to what we feed them. Our lives grow into the attributes with which they are saddled and labeled. What we embody in consciousness and character as a result of past experiences becomes what we expect. Since we always get what we expect, we unwittingly limit ourselves with the words we speak that affirm our fears and disappointments.

An affirmation is a statement spoken and proclaimed as truth. In essence, when we speak what we believe, we are making an affirmation. The essence of our individual belief system is a key factor, since many things we believe as a result of the past have absolutely nothing to do with the truth of God or the unlimited possibilities that actually exist. The words we speak reveal the energy of our thought patterns. *Energy follows thought.* Thoughts fueled by emotions are the foundation of an individual belief system. Our beliefs are the raw materials of the reality we expect, the reality we create, and the choices we make moment by moment. It is our choices that determine our experiences. *The energy of our thoughts, fueled by the energy of our emotions, fuel the energy of the words we speak, which results in the actions we take.* When we speak our fears, doubts, and limitations, we are actually *affirming* the things we do not want. In the process, we violate the laws of creation.

Ears May Not Always Hear, But Life Always Does!

My name is Iyanla. It is a Yoruba name that means "Great Mother." It is a name that is easy to mispronounce. I have discovered that many people are intimidated or confused by the configuration of letters in my name; the *I* followed by a *y* is not what people are accustomed to seeing or pronouncing. Quite often they mispronounce my name because they do not believe that they know how to pronounce the sound of the two vowels together. I believe that many people have the same experience when something unfamiliar enters their lives.

People have a tendency to name an experience based upon whatever they've learned from past experiences. In the human mind, the past often gives character and essence to the right-now moment. When you have been hurt, disappointed, or unfulfilled in the past, you may expect to experience more of the same with almost every new experience. Once you give voice to that expectation, you create a 99 percent guarantee that it will happen. By speaking our negative expectations, we give power to the past

and undermine the possibilities for the future. By speaking what we already know, rather than what is true in a spiritual context or what is possible through our creative ability, we give credence and power to an undesirable reality. To speak affirmatively means learning to speak into *where we are headed* rather than *where we came from*.

What is your first response when you encounter an experience that is unfamiliar or uncommon? The greatest temptation is to name it something you have seen before in your past, rather than name/affirm it as something new and exciting. There are positive and negative affirmations. To call a new experience something that is familiar, like "a problem"—or to name it "weird," "strange," "frightening," or "unnecessary"—is a negative affirmation. There are positive and negative affirmations. A negative affirmation recycles the past. When we do not understand the process of creation (thought-feeling-word-action), or when we are without an intimate knowledge of the truth of our identity, we are tempted to name our experiences incorrectly or inappropriately. A positive affirmation calls new possibilities into existence. In the presence of and with a commitment to speaking affirmatively, we learn to name experiences what we *want* them to be. And because our lives are obedient to our consciousness and expectations, whatever we call a thing is what it grows to become. Learning to speak affirmatively requires that we unlearn habitual phrases and declarations.

We all receive a sign when something in our lives is about to change. And the first sign of change is the presentation of your name, whether it is something small or seemingly insignificant that requires your attention, or an emergency that requires your presence. A past-due bill that has been overlooked or avoided comes with your name on it. An appointment that needs to be kept is presented as a telephone message or notice addressed to you. Even a problem in a relationship has a finger pointed toward you, perhaps as an accusation hurled in your direction. When your time, energy, or attention is required, you hear or see your name. The calling of your name puts you on notice that you are being summoned into a potentially new experience. You are being provided with an opportunity to learn something new or rename certain expectations you have held about yourself and your life. How do you respond? What do you affirm when a potential for difficulty comes your way? *How you hear and respond to your name being called is a function of what you think, believe, and know about yourself.*

More often than not, our responses to life are a reflection of our beliefs about and our connection to Spirit. Because we don't know or are unfamiliar with the unlimited possibilities and opportunities Spirit offers, we are prone to respond to name-calling with the limited, unconscious expectations of our belief system. As a result, we affirm the worse possible scenarios rather than speaking the highest vision we can imagine. Within the normal course of human existence, discovering the truth of Self is a journey of many paths and years. Most of us will have changed mates and/or careers several times, parented children, and gained or lost a ton of weight or a fortune in money before we achieve a substantial level of clarity about who we really are. The many trials and errors of my life have led me to believe that every difficulty and challenge I have faced in life has presented the same question: *Who am I?* The experiences of a failed marriage, abusive relationships, and financial destitution present the question in a variety of forms. *Who are you? Who do you be? What are you doing here? What do you want for yourself? Is this experience of your life an accurate statement of who you are?*

Speaking into Your Greatness!

What I know now is that for most of my life, I have been a chameleon, choosing my identity to fit the circumstances in which I have found myself. In many instances, my identity has been a response to what I have seen others do, what I have experienced within myself, and what I have been told about myself. Not only did I believe things about myself that were inaccurate, I made up stuff that affirmed the distortions. I believe that many of us answer to what we are called because we simply don't know anything else. We respond to what is expected because we dare not challenge the figures that we believe exert authority in our lives. We are saddled with names and expectations by people who may not realize *they, too, have issues of belief and expectations that have not been resolved productively!* Until and unless we are conscious and spiritually mature, the issues of others become our issues. We accept them! We affirm them! We live them! Our identity becomes meshed with our circumstances, many of which we inherit. Our true self becomes a shadow of what has been projected onto and into us. Learning how to affirm ourselves and the experiences we desire supports us in emerging from the shadows. However, it also challenges the status quo, which, for many of us, is too frightening to engage.

If your life had a name, what would it be? Broke Again? Left Again? Lost Again? Any of these statements may characterize your current experience, but are probably not the experience you would choose to continue living. In the hundreds of letters I receive from people, I have become aware that we often name our lives without realizing that is what we are doing. *I'm confused. I'm sick and tired. I don't understand why!* These are some of the most common names I encounter. Then there are the more serious names such as *I can't take anymore! I really don't care anymore. I don't think I'll ever get ahead.* These names clearly indicate a loss of identity and a lack of vision, as well as a disempowering disconnect from our spiritual reality.

Self-limiting, self-debasing affirmations come from a place within ourselves that identifies us with our circumstances, thereby affirming them as truth. However, those statements are not the truth of who or what we are created to be; what we affirm is a statement of what we *believe* to be true. Of course, there are those instances when we make dramatic statements simply to get someone's attention. This is both an expected and an accepted practice among human beings; we believe that if people know how much we hurt, they will do something about it. My point is, what you name your life, what you call yourself, is what you will ultimately experience. I also know that, if you call yourself or your life nothing, nothing is exactly what you will receive and experience. It is for this reason that we must endeavor to remain conscious of the nature, energy, and essence with which we speak to ourselves and to others, and conscious of how we apply language to every moment of every experience.

In learning the power of affirmations, you are raising *the vibrational frequency of your life experiences.* Fear has a specific energetic or vibrational frequency. Anger, guilt, and even laziness exist within a certain frequency. By the same token, wealth, health, joy, love, and peace also have a particular frequency. Since all words carry energy, you will want to name your life *within the context of the experiences you desire.* You will need to speak these words often in order to create the energy that will attract them into your life. At the same time, you will need to heal and transform your belief system to match the energy of those things you are affirming. You cannot talk or affirm yourself into a better experience in life until and unless you believe it is possible. You must believe you deserve to have what you are calling forth.

What I know now is that naming your life is a good idea. For example, Mo' Money or Good Loving are names you might consider for your life; however, neither of these names give consideration to the experience you are seeking. Many of us have been taught to thread our experiences *from* the past rather than *into* the future. In this instance, Mo' Money might give rise to or reinforce a belief that "mo' work" is required to get "mo' money," since this is the experience most of us have had throughout our lives. Good Loving may give rise to the fear of more pain, more rejection, more compromise, or to a host of beliefs from past experience. By affirming and focusing on the experience desired, these names would be transformed to a higher vibration. For instance, Mo' Money could be transformed into Clear Guidance to Unlimited Supply, or Overflowing Abundance of All Things Good. Good Loving could be transformed into Loved, Lovable, and Living, That's Me! Remember, we are going for mental, emotional, physical, and spiritual experiences that exist at a higher frequency. We are affirming our destiny and our divinity through our connection to God. Affirmations are not meant to be words that simply pump the ego's need for instant gratification. Powerful and effective affirmations require a belief in your spiritual connection.

Human beings want money, comfort, and pleasure. These things within themselves are not bad. Within a spiritual context, however, they do not take into consideration the lessons we must learn and master in order to live a spiritually grounded and directed life. More money, more comfort, and increased pleasure satisfy the quest for creature comforts that rarely take us beyond the surface of our personality and into the deeper realms of our spiritual being. As spiritual beings, there is a deeper longing, a desire to have all needs provided easily and effortlessly so that we may be of greater service in the world. Identification of the self based upon the limitations of our human perspective leads us to want *things*. As we mature spiritually, we seek satisfaction of our needs, support in our work; and mental, emotional, and spiritual sustenance from our internal source. God is the source of our true and divine nature; affirming that spiritual source and nature is essential to the process of creation.

What I know now is that experience and habit can limit us to the subconscious self-talk, the script we run in our minds, and what we believe we can or cannot do in response to what we have or have not done in the past. When the personality is driven to acquire things, such as money, possessions, acceptance, and validation by others, more often than not, we are attempting to re-create or avoid something we have learned through past experiences. In learning how to affirm, and thereby call forth the *experiences* we desire, we must create a new language and develop a new skill set that supports a new vision *of* ourselves and *for* ourselves. Affirming your life will transform the *nature, energy,* and *essence* of what you call forth. Begin by making a list of the experiences you desire. Peace, for instance, is an experience. Joy, love, clarity, passion, and harmony are experiences. They are also principles. From a spiritual perspective, principles are the acceptable rules, boundaries, guidelines, or methods of living and behaving. On the path of spiritual evolution they are the solid rocks upon which you can stand in the midst of a flood, whether the flood occurs mentally, emotionally, or physically.

In the process of affirming yourself and the experiences you desire, principles must govern your thought patterns and behavioral responses. In essence, when you affirm who you are and what you want, you will also need to be willing and able to embody and practice the underlying principle of the experience. Let us say, for example, you want to experience peace of mind. You can pray about it or meditate on the word *peace,* but chances are the experience will continue to elude you if you pick fights and arguments with family members for what they do that disturbs your peace. I have a personal aversion to the political mantra "No justice! No peace!" Protestors have been chanting it for years without realizing that what they are affirming is *exactly* what they experience: no justice and no peace. Along those same lines, you will not experience joy if your main pastime is complaining. Mantras like "I am broke" or "I can't afford it" rarely lead to wealth. Being a 'fraidy cat who avoids the perceived pain of relationships is not the ticket to love. Fear is an emotion that cancels out or negates the principle of love. The key is to *be* the thing you desire. Be it! Affirm it! Have it!

What I know now is that it is self-loving and self-supportive to focus on and affirm the experiences you desire. I once thought it was selfish or silly, I now know it is essential. When my butt started to spread, I didn't call myself: "I'm getting too fat!" Instead, I affirmed myself: "I am slimming down easily and effortlessly." I particularly worked to remember this affirmation when I was at the dinner table reaching for a second helping. When it seemed as if the balance in my checking account was not sufficient to meet my monthly obligations, I refused to panic. Instead, I affirmed, "God is the source of all supply that always meets my needs." I also learned that when you start to affirm things in the positive, the negative will challenge you. In his book *Conversations with God,* Neale Donald Walsh wrote: "Whenever you call forth a certain thing, everything unlike it will show up." When dealing with money, an overdue notice or a bouncing check will threaten your resolve. Be mindful that your old beliefs will outpicture themselves

as an experience when you attempt to adopt new beliefs. Should this happen, stay focused, keep affirming, and make sure your behavior is in alignment with what you desire.

Think of your life and daily experiences as if they were a newborn baby. *What would you want it to be when it grew up?* How would you want the world to recognize your life? Powerful affirmations are not predicated on what you know, what you have, or what you can do in the present moment. Remember, an affirmation is something you grow into. It is not based on what you know *now.* Like an innocent infant, you must affirm what is possible in your life, and eliminate every belief that is to the contrary. An affirmation has no knowledge and makes no presumptions. The baby will become whatever you call it; it will respond to the nature of the label you give to it. Be daring! Be bold! Call the things you desire into being so that your life will come into alignment with your greatest expectations.

Chapter 9

FORGIVING
AND RELEASING

As a child, I spent my summers on Uncle Jimmy's farm in Smithfield, Virginia. He was a livestock farmer who raised pigs and chickens. During the summer of my eighth birthday, Uncle Jimmy gave me a baby chick. He told me that he would take care of the chick in the winter, and I could care for her on my summer visits. Penny grew up to be a beautiful brown-and-white-speckled hen. Uncle Jimmy built a special coop for her so she wouldn't be sold off as an ordinary chicken!

When I was ten, I made my usual summer journey to Smithfield. I had been there about two weeks when one morning I discovered that Penny was gone! I ran into the house to report the news to Uncle Jimmy, and I found Aunt Mattie in the kitchen plucking a chicken. Aunt Mattie had killed Penny to make soup because, "This cold was killing me, and I just grabbed the first old hen I saw!" Surely, I didn't want a "sick old aunt" over a "fat healthy hen!" When I cried in protest, Aunt Mattie screamed at me, "Don't you dare cry over an ole, stupid chicken! The yard is full of them! Go get another one!" I thought Aunt Mattie didn't like me, and this was all the proof I needed!

Uncle Jimmy made her apologize to me, and he promised to get me a pony. "I'm sure Mattie won't have any use for horse soup!" He gave me a dollar for ice cream. I ate three ice-cream pops that day, and, with each one, I vowed never to forgive Aunt Mattie! It took me 24 years to realize how damaging that day and my commitment to unforgiveness had been to me!

Doing Unto Others Is the Undoing of Self

Why do we hold on to negativity? For some reason, we believe that others are affected by our experience of remaining upset, hurt, or angry. They hurt us, and we want to hurt them back. We want them to experience our pain, so we hold on to it, believing that somehow they are suffering as well. Holding on to pain, anger, guilt, shame, or any other negative experience is the glue that binds us to the situation we want to escape. The longer we hold on, the deeper we hurt. In the meantime, each time we encounter a similar situation, the memory shifts from the unconscious to the conscious mind. We re-create the initial situation and respond, not to the present experience, but to the experience we had 5, 10, 20, or 50 years prior! Holding on to negative experiences burdens the spirit. It is an investment in hate, not healing. Spirit, our life force, knows only the universal law of love. When we hold on to the memory of painful experiences, we violate this law. When we hold on to negative emotions, we are denying our own spirit what it needs to grow and what it needs to help us grow. We limit our creative abilities, and we cause damage to the essence of our authentic being. The key to opening the way of spirit that leads to understanding and healing is forgiveness.

We all are held accountable for what we do and say, and even what we think! The responsibility of this level of accountability, however, is to the Creator. We are held accountable for the energy we create and release in life. Our life force, our spirit, is endowed with the knowledge of universal law, the Creator's law, whether or not we are consciously aware that it exists. Those laws mandate that we strive for and master divine understanding, harmony, peace, and love. When your mind and spirit are burdened with memories of painful experiences, you are emitting and sending a discordant energy into the universe. It is your responsibility to neutralize this energy. Making amends for and neutralizing the initial wrongdoing is the responsibility of the others. That is, they are responsible for their behavior, and you are responsible for your response to that behavior. While the energy of your negative thoughts may reach the intended party, the spiritual burden for sending them remains with you, not the receiver.

By sending out negative energy, you unconsciously re-create the same or similar negative experiences. This is the foundation of *victimization*. As long as you hold on to negative memories, you will create more of the same. You become a victim of the memories, not the person who offended you. Remembering the first betrayal will attract more betrayal. The memory of the hurt or disappointment will attract into your life others who will behave in a similar disappointing manner. The person to whom you have attached the first memory may receive the energy of your anger or upset. She may or may not remember the initial experience. However, as long as *you* remember, you re-create the pain. The other person may hold or remember guilt as it relates to her experience with you. You, on the other hand, remember the anger! Although you may be thousands of miles apart, you are both locked into the energy of the negative situation, and you are not free to move and grow. Forgiveness is the foundation of freedom.

The Creator brings us to the world as unique individuals. We come to this life to learn our own lessons and to complete our unique mission. This process is what is known as *your spiritual curriculum*. Your unique curriculum will lead you onto the path of others who have similar lessons to learn. All spiritual lessons are taught through experiences. How we face, respond to, and come through those experiences determines the depth and breadth of our spiritual growth. In every situation, positive or negative, we must discover: *Am I learning a lesson? Am I teaching a lesson? Am I functioning as the object through which a lesson is being taught?* Once we understand our role in any given situation, we can accept our lesson and move on!

A *Course in Miracles* teaches us that we are all teaching and learning at the same time. It encourages us to remain open to the voice and presence of the Holy Spirit so that the required learning, growth, and healing may occur. The universe may use you to demonstrate to another something about herself that she could not see without your participation. You are teaching, and inevitably, in the process, you will learn something about your consciousness, your behavior, and your level of development. By the same token, life will bring others into your experience who will behave in ways that trigger memories within your conscious or subconscious mind that require healing. As difficult as it may be to accept, you are the student and the other person is your teacher. Their behavior, as dysfunctional or neurotic as it may seem to you, is designed by life to be a teaching tool. Then there are those special times when you are minding your business, living your life, and things will happen around you or as a result of you that support others to learn, heal, and grow. The key to any of these experiences is to remain focused on your behavior, your responses and reactions, and your internal triggers, and to practice forgiveness.

Your connection to and remembrance of the presence of the Spirit of God in every experience relieves the need to figure out, Why did this happen to me? Look for your lesson, or be the willing object of the Creator's work. Spirit has no reason to ask what you did to contribute to the situation. It was a necessary detour on your journey. It is a function of your curriculum. Spirit will not "blame" someone for "doing something" to you. All parties in every experience are teaching and learning, whether or not they know it or accept it. Spirit is indifferent to good or bad. It knows that by universal law we are all held accountable. Spirit is doing its work. We must train our conscious mind to be in harmony with Spirit.

Forgiveness is a major step toward spiritual growth and development. It must come from the heart, not the head or the mouth. Forgiveness is the foundation of being in alignment with universal law because it requires a conscious effort toward understanding who you are and what your mission is in this life experience. Forgiveness is a major step toward maintaining harmony in the universe, because it creates peace—inward and outward. Forgiveness allows us to be free of the negative experiences of anger, pain, disappointment, guilt, and shame. When we are free, we are open to experience love, joy, gratitude, success, and peace. When we forgive, we learn. When we learn, we grow—mentally, physically, and spiritually.

If you are not receiving good things in your life, you need to forgive. If you are not giving freely and feeling good about it, you need to forgive. If there is anyone about whom you have painful or negative memories, you need to forgive. If you are feeling lonely, desperate, and confused, you need to forgive. Forgiveness is the spiritual laxative that purges the mind, the heart, and the spirit. The Holy Bible instructs us to forgive "Seventy times seven." The process for this depth of forgiveness is offered in *A Course in Miracles*, as the Forgiveness Diet. The Forgiveness Diet is a powerful and effective tool for releasing past hurts—those you remember and those you do not. It requires a commitment of 20 minutes in the morning and 20 minutes at night, and a brand-new notebook.

Giving Up for a Change

Select a time in the morning when you will not be disturbed. On a clean page in your notebook, number 1 through 35, skipping every other line. Write the following sentence 35 times:

"I [your name] forgive [a person you blame] totally and unconditionally."

Do not pick and choose who you will or will not forgive. Do not think before you write. Write whatever names come to mind. Try to write 35 different experiences. However, if one name or experience continues to come forward in your mind, it is fine to write it as many times as you think about it. When you have completed the exercise, take five to seven long, deep breaths, and close the book.

Repeat the exercise just before you go to bed. This time, write the following sentence:

"I [your name] forgive myself totally and unconditionally. I am free to move on to wholeness and completeness."

You may not know why you need forgiveness. It does not matter. Your spirit will know the reason.

You must repeat this exercise, every morning and every evening, for seven days, forgiving others in the A.M. before noon, yourself in the P.M. before midnight. If you miss a day, you must begin again. True forgiveness requires work. Missing a day reflects the resistance of your unconscious mind to releasing the pain. Be gentle with yourself and keep trying. Spirit will show you whether you have truly completed your task, so don't be alarmed if you see or hear from the very person you are forgiving. Pay attention to how you respond to the situation. When you have totally forgiven others and yourself, you will experience a new sense of freedom!

What I thought love was, I discovered it was not. Who I thought God was, I now know God is not. To recognize this was difficult. To understand it was almost impossible. To acknowledge it was heartbreaking. Learning you have been mistaken and maintaining your dignity is one of the most awesome and humbling experiences life offers.

— Iyanla Vanzant

What I Know Now

Forgiveness is a powerful act of self-love and self-discovery.
Forgiveness does not erase the memory
of an experience, it neutralizes its impact.
The deepest healing occurs when you can forgive
what you have told yourself about someone else.
Forgiveness is a state of being that
supports the unfolding of your authentic self.

Forgive everything! There are simply no words that adequately describe the power and efficacy of forgiveness. I will, however, offer you two words of advice: *Do it!* Until you are willing to forgive everyone for everything, every dastardly thing you believe they have done to you, you will be stuck in the muck and mire of recycling your past. You will have enough room in your heart and life for only temporary and fleeting moments of pleasure. You will live on the edge of waiting for someone else or something else to knock you down and run over your face. You will be unable to express true and authentic gratitude for the grace and blessings of your life. You will spend most of your time looking over your shoulder, comparing yourself to others, wondering why you can't have what they have. In essence, there will be a seed of misery in your mind, heart, and soul that will gnaw away at you, making even the brief moments of joy you experience difficult to hold on to. In the short run, you can become suspicious, anxious, sarcastic, and mean. In the long run, you will be bitter and wrinkled!

You can forgive, no matter what the person has done to you. As long as you do not forgive, you are locked into the memory of the event. One way to begin is to forgive yourself for anything negative you have ever thought, said, or done against anyone. When you begin the forgiveness process, you probably will not believe or feel what you are saying. Do it anyway! And, yes, you can forgive people after they die.

Make no mistake about it, to forgive someone you believe has hurt, harmed, or violated you is, in some way, no easy feat. However, doing so is a spiritual mandate for your healing, learning, and growth. To forgive the parent who abused, neglected, or abandoned you; to forgive the person who molested, raped, or violated you; to forgive the friend who betrayed or stole from you; to forgive yourself for the myriad of mistakes you have made has nothing—absolutely nothing—to do with *forgetting* what happened. What I know now is that forgiving any or all of these experiences is about practicing *good spiritual hygiene*. It is the only way to cleanse your heart and mind of your interpretations and judgments of the people and events designed by God to advance and support your spiritual evolution. Forgiveness leads to a shift in perception. It takes your attention from *why* something happened to the grace that supports and allows you to move through the experience. It transforms the blame into a blessing, the hurt into healing.

There is a deeper aspect of forgiveness that few of us recognize, and others refuse to accept. I admit that it is a difficult concept to grasp and heart-wrenching to practice. What I know now is that true forgiveness has nothing to do with anyone else. True and radical forgiveness is about *forgiving yourself.* Take a breath! Take a long, deep Cleansing Breath before you consider closing this book or throwing it across the room. The premise at the foundation of this concept is this: At all times, in all situations, under all circumstances, there is no one in the room but you and God. How you view, react to, and handle the experiences and circumstances with which you are confronted is a function of how you view and treat yourself and how you view and treat God. Everyone you encounter is an aspect of you and an aspect of God. How they behave is an aspect of your own consciousness calling forth an aspect of the consciousness of God within you. How you respond to their behavior points to the aspects of your consciousness that are either healed or require healing. The deeper your connection to the essence of God within, the more likely your response will be God-like—forgiving, merciful, compassionate, loving. The greater the level of disconnect or unconsciousness to the presence of God within you, the more human, helpless, and internally violent your response is likely to be. You will conjure up more anger, shame, guilt, and fear internally as a reaction to *what you have been through.* Forgiveness levels the playing field, allowing the human in you to surrender itself to the God in you.

Forgiveness, when you truly forgive yourself and others, will take you headfirst into a miracle: the miracle of release. Release is an experience of inner freedom, peace of mind, and clarity. Forgiveness releases your heart and mind from the stranglehold of anger, hurt, woundedness, and the other toxic emotions associated with what *they did* or *didn't do.* When the release happens—and it will happen—you have more energy to experience life and express love. Forgiveness, unconditional forgiveness, also releases you from the need and desire to watch for other people to get their just rewards—*the big payback.* Even when you are not aware you are watching for it, you are watching and waiting, mentally and emotionally. Once the release occurs, your mind is free to explore new horizons because you are no longer looking over your shoulder. The most important release occurs when you get the message, the lesson, the clarity that, as a result of whatever happened, you are stronger and wiser. Release therefore is experienced as a benefit, a bonus of forgiveness. There is nothing else you need to do to make it happen.

God's Ways Are Not Your Ways!

What I know now is that there is a temptation to apply human logic to things of a spiritual nature. We attempt to use language, logic, and the reasoning of our finite and tangible world in an attempt to understand and resolve experiences designed by the infinite, intangible mind of God. The result is confusion. The finite can never rationalize the infinite. The tangible cannot evaluate the intangible. Things of the Spirit can be discerned, understood, only by the Spirit. If it is of God and from God, it is only through a connection to God that you will be led to embrace, understand, and neutralize the impact on your tangible physical mind. This is where faith and trust inevitably kick in. When you know God and the spiritual nature of God in an intimate way—the kind of intimacy that grows from a consistent spiritual practice—you develop faith in your connection to the essence of God. You learn to trust that that connection—rather than what you know, what you can do, or what you wish to happen—will bring you through the experience. There is no logic, no reasoning, no rationale that can explain the connection. Either you have faith or you do not. Either you trust or you do not. What I know now is that through the experiences of life, even the ones I thought I would not, could not live through, my faith in my connection taught me to trust that, no matter what, I would be okay.

Here is another juicy tidbit that I have discovered about forgiveness. Most of the time when I thought I was angry, upset, or hurt about another person, including myself, I was really in a state of high pissosity with God. I believed that God had made a mistake, or that God was treating me unfairly, or that God was allowing someone to get away with something I determined was unfair or unjustified. I was superimposing my human logic onto the order of God's universe. I was trying to *out-God* God. I was attempting to reconcile the depth of the pain I was experiencing with the loving mercy I attributed to God. If God loves me, why would He let Boo-Boo or Fifi hurt me like this? If there is a God, why is this happening to me—again? Why aren't some of the people who hurt me or betrayed me repeatedly suffering the way I am suffering? That, I discovered, was the crux of my problem. I was mislabeling the experiences. I was judging my experiences and the people in those experiences as right/wrong, good/bad, fair/unfair without realizing that I was either teaching, learning, or functioning as the object of some higher plan and purpose.

What, you might ask, is the purpose of a child being raped, abused, abandoned, or neglected? Children are innocent! How do you rationalize a working mom on her way to the supermarket being killed on the freeway? Or a loving and devoted father being gunned down in the street and robbed of the $40 in his wallet? The short answer is that you cannot rationalize these events, and you may not understand that. You must remember that all people are here in life to work out their own personal and unique spiritual curriculum. How you respond to the events of your life and the lives of those you love is also a function of your curriculum. Forgiveness will help you to graduate from "special education"—the need to repeat a lesson over and over until you get the point.

When I was nine years old, I experienced a sexual violation by my uncle. Notice how I have labeled the experience. In common vernacular, I would have said: "He raped me." What I know now, after many years and layers of healing, is that to "language" it as a common human experience ("I was raped") makes me a victim rather than a teacher, student, or object of a lesson. It puts the emphasis on what happened to me and what he did, rather than on my response to the experience. For many years, I felt dirty, damaged, bad, and wrong. The sad part is that I didn't even realize the connection. Well into my adult life, the shame, hurt, and anger that I had not given my nine-year-old self permission to feel or express at the time seeped into my adult relationships, my finances, and every aspect of my consciousness. I would over-commit and underdeliver in an attempt to prove my worthiness. I would lie about who I was and what I could do in order to gain acceptance. I had a keen eye for the shortcomings of others, always trying to convince myself that I was better than they were because, deep inside, I did not believe I was. I could go on and on about the depths of my pain and dysfunction. Suffice it to say, I was a hot mess—internally and externally.

When the God-ordained time comes for you to heal, you will heal. Despite your greatest efforts to stay mad, be broken, or absolve yourself of taking full responsibility for the condition of your internal landscape—your mind, heart, and spirit—when the universe of God and life determines that enough is enough, you better buckle up! Healing will come to you in a seemingly incon-venient way. The first level of healing for me came as a result of a conversation with my stepmother. Although we had our ups and down, I knew in the core of my being that this woman loved, hon-ored, and respected me. On this particular day, she was my Bible. She spoke into my soul, into my very DNA, words that were so filled with the essence of God that my brain went into suspended animation and the Holy Spirit entered to realign my mind with the mind of God.

We were drinking coffee and talking about nothing in particu-lar when all of a sudden she looked me squarely in the eye and said to me: "What do you think he took from you? Did he take a cup of you? A pound of you? Did he take anything that really matters? Did he take anything that you cannot give back to your-self? As long as you stay mad at him, you are giving him way more than you think he took. You may never be able to forgive him for what he did, nor do you need to, but what you must do is forgive yourself for giving him your soul."

I was rendered speechless, not so much by what she said, but because of what I thought was her betrayal. She *knew* what had happened. She knew how my aunt had not responded to it, how my aunt tried to ignore what had occurred, and, in doing so, how she silently communicated to my nine-year-old self that I was not important. In fact, it was my stepmother, my best friend in the world, who had rescued me from my darkest memories of that God-awful experience. Now, she was, in essence, telling me it was *my* fault. I thought she was implying that it was up to me to clean up the mess *he* had contributed to in my life. This was unfathomable! I thought she had lost her mind. The good news is that I was so mad at *her* that I stopped being mad at *him*. The bad news is that it took me two years to realize that what she said was the God-ordained truth.

What I ultimately discovered is that I had, in fact, given that experience a front-row seat in my life. Everything I did not like about me became a function of having been raped. Everything I declared I could not do or had not done was an outgrowth of the trauma of that one experience. Every man who left me left because I was unworthy of love, because I had been violated. I was dirty and unworthy. Every experience of betrayal or disappointment opened the wound of that violation and poured a handful of salt onto it. What I know now is that I was using that one experience as an excuse to be irresponsible in my life, unaccountable for the condition of my heart, and derelict in my spiritual duty to lean on God rather than on my own understanding. I did not understand why it had happened to me. I know now that I chose not to understand. Instead, I had chosen to stay angry.

If I'm Okay, Then It's Okay, So Let's Get to Work!

The introduction of *A Course in Miracles* states the following:

> *This is a course in miracles. It is a required course. Only the time you take it is voluntary. Free will does not mean that you can establish the curriculum. It means that you can elect what you want to take at a given time. The course does not aim at*

teaching you the meaning of love, for that is beyond what can be taught. It does aim, however, at removing the blocks to the awareness of love's presence, which is your natural inheritance.

I was first introduced to the *Course* in 1978. At that time I understood it to be a book that would change the way you think. When I tried to read it, I did not understand a single word. Thirty years later, after much study, I understand that the *Course* is a way of life that supports you in experiencing and expressing more of God's presence in your life. God is love. The *Course* teaches you how to find the love, see the love, and be the love in every experience, because it shifts your perception from the past to the present moment. The *Course* taught me that my uncle was a teacher who came into my life because he loved me enough to teach me how to love myself. The *Course* taught me that I am never angry for the reasons I think I'm angry, and that if I seek the peace of God, I will find it. The *Course* taught me that my holiness in God can never be disturbed or diminished by a physical experience, and that forgiveness offers me everything I want. The *Course* taught me that my life has a function that God would have me serve, and that all things are lessons that God would have me learn. It was not an easy path or process but I learned that the only reason I had experienced everything I had experienced was to learn to love myself and others more. The only way I learned that lesson was to forgive myself for believing that I knew what anything meant in my life. That, too, was a lesson from *A Course in Miracles*.

I remember the day vividly. It was a warm Sunday afternoon in August. I was exhausted, sitting on the deck outside of my bedroom. My husband, the love of my life, sat down in the chair across from me and announced that he had decided to go forward with the divorce. Although we had been separated a little over a year, I was under the impression that we were endeavoring to work things out so that we could resume our lives and the vision for our lives as loving partners. It is probably good that I was in such a weakened state or I would have said or done something I would long regret. His words hit my heart like a plate filled with spaghetti in a greasy sauce. His words stuck to the fibers of my soul, then slid down the walls of my being slowly, very slowly, burning my insides with an indescribable heat. The response I recall giving was, "If that's what you think you need to do, I will support you." *Liar! Liar! Pants on fire!* He left, and I fell into a heap on the floor.

For the next year, when we did talk, it was not pleasant. He experienced me as trying to convince him to change his mind. I experienced him as giving up on us. When we did not speak, I cried, and prayed. I freaked and panicked. I blamed and projected. There was really little else I could do because at the time my eldest daughter was extremely ill. I felt as if I was being asked to choose between what I could do, needed to do, as a wife to save my marriage and my responsibilities to my child. There was no question that my daughter and my participation in her healing was my first priority. Rather than lean on my own will and understanding, I did what I knew I needed to do: I asked God to help me and show me what to do. From the depths of my soul came the words, *Be still and let him take the lead.* I knew enough to be obedient.

On what would have been our fifth wedding anniversary, I received a certified letter that contained the notice indicating that he had filed for divorce. I lost it! I literally lost every ounce of my good sense and all of my loving nature. I drove to the courthouse and filed a counterclaim, alleging all manner of misbehavior. I was not going to allow him to get away with suing me for divorce! He left! He broke his commitment to me! He violated our marriage! I was going to countersue so the world, or at least that one judge in that one court, would know what a lowlife he had really been. Then I heard it again: *Be still and let him take the lead.* Two days later I went back to the court and withdrew my petition. My daughter was ill, my husband was leaving me, and I was insane. Insane people must not be left alone with a pen! I did my best to stay away from him, and he returned the favor. Although we exchanged a few heated e-mails, what I know now is that it was all a part of my learning, growing, and healing. He was simply my teacher.

A little over a year later, I received an e-mail from him. At the end of the e-mail he wrote: "Oh, by the way, the divorce is final." I must have read that line 100 times, and each time my heart and mind sank deeper into despair. Surely he had lost his mind. He must be smoking or drinking some mood-altering substance, because I know *this man*, the man I have loved all of my adult life, did not just write me an e-mail about some insignificant thing, and then casually mention that we were now divorced. It is a really good thing that I had been deeply engaged in daily spiritual practice. It is even better that God knew I was in trouble, because in that moment I heard it again: *Be still and let him take the lead.* The "lead" had led us straight to the divorce court. The "lead" had led him right out of my life.

Surely, I thought, this is not the voice of God speaking! This is a mistake! This is wrong! Then I heard the voice once more: *What is the most loving thing you can do right now?* Kill him? I thought. No! No, no, that would not be a loving thing for me to do. What I can do is tell him how I feel. So, breathing and praying, I wrote to him and shared how I did not deserve to be notified in that way, that I felt it was both dishonorable and disrespectful. He wrote me back. He agreed and he apologized. I spent the next two years forgiving myself for believing that he was wrong for marrying me, that he was wrong for divorcing me, and, in my opinion, he was just *wrong* for being alive! It took me most of that two-year period to realize that *I* was wrong about believing he was wrong. What can I say except that I had to learn that it is okay to be wrong?

When it comes to forgiveness, the spotlight is always on *you*. As the *Course* teaches, you are never upset for the reasons you think you're upset. There is always something coming forward from your internal landscape that causes you to read more into an experience than is necessary, required, or productive. What I know now is that what we impose onto our current experiences are the shadows of past similar experiences. My husband divorcing me was a reminder of my daddy driving by with his other women in his car and acting as if he did not see me. It stirred up the feelings I could not express when I was pregnant at 16 and my son's father made it known to me and the rest of our high school that he had another girlfriend. It led me right back to the place in my heart where I had given my all to what I knew was a dysfunctional relationship, only to get beaten and left for another woman.

The experience of having my fairy-tale marriage end brought forward in my consciousness every ounce of unworthiness and self-loathing that I had hidden, buried, denied, and failed to acknowledge. I was angry with myself for all the times and all the ways I had ignored the urgings of my own soul, chasing what I thought would make me feel better; when it failed to do so, I would blame the other person. The simple truth is that he had changed his mind. He had decided that he did not want to be in a relationship with me any longer. His manner for coming to that decision was not pretty for either of us, but it was just that simple. Anything I imposed on it was my lesson, not his.

In the book *Radical Forgiveness,* author Colin Tipping offers four steps for us to consider when we find ourselves judging others, feeling self-righteous, or wanting to change the outcome of a particular experience. The steps include recognizing whether (1) you agree, (2) are willing to agree (even if you cannot do it right now), (3) are open to agreeing, (4) are skeptical about agreeing, or are unwilling to agree, that somehow you have created the situation in which you find yourself. The premise is that every experience is a creation of your own mind to support you in recognizing a core belief or wound that needs to be healed. The level of your willingness to accept your responsibility in the creation of the experience will move you toward or away from peace.

The second step Tipping offers is to recognize how you are judging yourself and others as right or wrong, good or bad. At this level, you must acknowledge and own your true feelings and love yourself anyway. Denying that you feel what you feel sets you up to be *un*forgiving. Instead, radical forgiveness requires that you feel it, acknowledge it, and forgive it. The third step asks you to be willing to see the hand of God in the experience, even when you do not understand why it is there. The fourth and final step is to choose peace over the toxic or disturbing emotion attached to the experience.

What I know now is that, had I not put my faith in the power of forgiveness, I would be babbling and drooling on some park bench, feeding the pigeons scraps of dry bread. Or I would be writhing in the pain of the foolish, self-debasing, ego-driven choices and bad decisions I have made. Without forgiveness, I would be saddled with so much guilt and shame about who I have been, where I came from, and the many, many missteps I have made along the way that you would not be holding this book. I am humbled and motivated to forgive when I think about all the times that *I* have been forgiven—by those to whom I have caused harm and by God. When I think about the awesome wisdom of God to provide us with a foolproof way to erase our minds, cleanse our hearts, and step into the healing grace of His love, my heart weeps with sorrow for all the time I wasted. Simultaneously, it weeps with joy and understands that *any moment can be the moment* when we can surrender, forgive, and experience God's love.

Got pain? Try forgiveness.

Chapter 10

RITUAL

Every morning, my grandmother would get up, wash, make a pot of coffee, place a chair in front of the kitchen window, and stare at a small, frayed black book. By 7 A.M., she was fully dressed, breakfast was ready, and the clothes my brother and I were to wear that day were laid out. I was expected to get up, make my bed and be washed by 7:15 A.M. We were blessing our breakfast by 7:30 A.M.

Every Monday, we washed the crystal and polished the silver. On Tuesday and Thursday, we took Father John's Fortifying Emulsion. The taste was beyond horrific, but not quite as bad as the castor oil we had to take every Saturday morning to keep our bowels moving. Every Thursday evening, we washed our clothes by hand on a scrub board. Every Saturday morning, we sprinkled the dry, starched clothes, rolled them, and placed them in the refrigerator to be ironed Saturday evening. We went to Sunday school and church every Sunday. We ate dinner every weeknight at 5:30 P.M. On Sunday, we ate at 3:30 P.M. I lived by Granny's strict schedule for the first 16 years of my life. At 16, I decided to do it differently.

My grandmother paid her bills on time from the money she kept in a hankie stored in her bosom. She never had a toothache. I don't remember that she ever had a cold. There was no dust in Granny's house. Her plants never died. She never went to school. Widowed at age 15, she never remarried. She had only one child, my father, and she never grew hair on her chin. My grandmother didn't know the exact date or year of her birth. In 1990, we guessed that she was 92 years old. She lived alone in Virginia and had full control of her faculties and bodily functions! She had never read a full-length book but could quote the Bible and the almanac! Granny couldn't spell *meditation,* yet she did it every day! She had never been to a workshop or a retreat, but she had a direct line to God; or at least that is what she told me, and I believed her!

At age 14, I discovered boys and fun. I rebelled against my granny's ritualistic schedule. At age 16, I had my first child! At age 19, I entered an abusive marriage! At 22, I had my first nervous breakdown! My grandmother did not visit me in the hospital. I never called her when I was released. At age 23, I began receiving public assistance. At age 25, I was virtually homeless! At age 29, I was in therapy! When I was 30, my husband broke my jaw, I had my second breakdown, my first breakthrough, and a long talk with Granny!

Grandma told me the importance of doing things on time. She called it "following God's clock!" Granny explained how the clock worked. The sunlight of the day is the best time to do the things that support life. The darkness is the time to restore and make medicine. Spring is the time of new growth and fresh starts. Summer is the time that will bring the benefits of what was done in the spring. Fall is the time of death—a time to eliminate the old, the worn out, the useless. Always, she advised, leave your bad relationships in the fall. Winter is the time to rest, plan, and rejuvenate. Grandma said that the sun is man's energy, the energy that supports life. The moon is woman's energy, the energy by which life is created.

On that day, my grandmother talked to me about what she called "women's business." My grandmother talked about the phases of the moon and the energies of the months. She said, "God has given us a clock. The same thing happens at the same time, year in and year out. If you follow God's clock, you will always be on time and you will get better at what you do. You never have to wonder about what's going to happen when you follow the natural clock; you already know! You can have a schedule if you like, but remember who owns the clock." What Grandma called "the clock" is what African people call "ritual!"

A ritual is a prescribed way of performing an act or certain acts. A ritual is the traditional or ceremonial approach to an event or series of events. African people are a ritualistic people. Tradition mandates that African people approach life events and actions ritually. Our ancestral cultures prescribe secret rituals, religious rituals, social rituals, family rituals, and personal rituals. These rituals create, utilize, and release energy. They demand and create sacredness.

In your journey toward spiritual evolution, it is self-supportive to develop a ritualistic approach to your spiritual practices. This means you should approach your prayer and meditation practices in the same way, at the same time, in the same place, as often as you can. Set realistic goals based on your circumstances and schedule. Begin by setting a time limit. About 10 or 20 minutes may be a good place to start. Make a commitment to continue the practice for a specific number of days, and honor that commitment. Select a location for your practice where you feel comfortable and where you will not be disturbed for the allotted time. Inform your family and loved ones not to disturb you during this time. This will elicit their support and respect of your time, as well as destroy your excuses not to continue, which are bound to arise as you attempt to discipline your mind.

If you have a special chair, garment, or other instruments you will use for your ritual, try not to use them at any other time. This will determine and preserve their sacredness. If you miss a committed time, do not be angry or distressed. Continue your activity at the next scheduled time. Feel free to perform your ritual at any additional time as you feel necessary. In any case, you should make every attempt to continue your ritual consistently for three months before you amend it, unless Spirit directs you to do so. Consistent practice helps you to develop discipline, which is a key element of spirituality. The following beginner's ritual may prove helpful for actual practice or as a guide for developing your own spiritual ritual.

Beginner's Ritual

It is recommended that you engage in this ritual every Sunday, Tuesday, and Thursday over a 90-day period. Do it before any other daily, morning activity, and repeat it after your evening bath.

- Arise 30 minutes earlier than usual.

- Do eight repetitions of Deep Breath.

- Draw water and perform the Head Blessing Ritual.

- Offer prayers for yourself, family, community. If you feel uncomfortable or unfamiliar with praying, you can read a psalm from the Holy Bible.

- Write down three questions about challenges or situations present in your life to which you are seeking an answer. (You can ask the same question on a maximum of seven different occasions, if the answer is not immediately apparent.)

- Next, do four repetitions of meditative breathing.

- Spend five to ten minutes in silence, focusing on the rhythm of your breathing. Use a journal to write down any thoughts or ideas that come to you while you are in silence. You can use an egg timer or alarm, or you can ask your spirit to make you aware when the allotted time has passed, in which case you will be alerted by a sound or feeling.

- Do four repetitions of Cleansing Breath before leaving your ritual area.

- Repeat the entire exercise again before retiring in the evening.

Ritual

Any moment could be the moment that
you have a breakthrough in Spirit.

— Rev. Lydia Ruiz

What I Know Now

Rituals are spiritual support systems that deepen
and enhance your spiritual energy and practices.
Rituals align your internal and external being with a specific intention.
The more you practice the more meaningful the practice will be.
Rituals engage the fives physical senses in a way that
provides a full-body experience of a specific practice.

Over and Over and Over Again

On the third Monday of every April and October, I am joined by seven other women at my dining room table. We practice deep, meditative breathing; we hold hands, and we pray. We call the names of 30, 40, or 50 women, blessing each one of them, and we pray again. We read certain scriptures from the Bible; we choose certain passages from *A Course in Miracles,* and again we pray. Then, we listen deeply and intently for guidance from the Holy Spirit. One by one, we share our insights, and after each one shares, we pray. It is a ritual that we have done the same way, at the same time, for 12 years in order to prepare for our semi-annual workshop that takes place the third Friday of every April and October. Our prayer and blessing ritual prepares us to support the women who come from all over the world for a weekend of sharing, learning, and healing. It also creates an atmosphere, an energy that supports our intention to be fully present and available in service for our sisters, the women who will participate in the Wonder Woman Weekend.

A ritual provides you with a spiritual support system because it taps into the intangible energy of the universe, creating an atmosphere that is conducive to, and in alignment with, your desires. Energy follows thought. Sending forth thoughts and words with a specific intention creates an energetic vibration that calls forth from the invisible, intangible realms that you have named. An intention is the act of mentally and emotionally determining and stating what your actions will be and what results you desire. Your intentions focus your mind, your will, and your spirit in a manner that provides you with a point of reference and a focus that become the guidelines you can use to create, re-create, and govern your choices and behaviors. What I know now is: *A ritual is the repeated practice of a specific behavior with a clear intention and desire that creates the atmosphere for the realization of a specific experience.* In many cases, a ritual has a religious or spiritual purpose. In other cases, it does not.

Every Christmas Eve for the past 20 years, my children and I pile into the car and go out in search of just the right Christmas tree. On Christmas Eve night, while I am seasoning the turkey and boiling potatoes for potato salad, my children decorate the tree. Now that I have grandchildren, they have joined in on the event. I heat apple cider, or whip up some other nonalcoholic concoction in the blender. We hoot and holler, turning my usually well-ordered home into an unsightly mess of paper, ornaments, and loose pine needles that trail from the door to almost every corner of every room. Once the children are asleep, I put the turkey in the oven and wrap presents. I usually finish at 6 A.M., 30 minutes before the children wake up to tear into the brightly wrapped packages. I love Christmas! Not just because of the religious and spiritual connotations, but because it is a ritual I can depend on to bring my entire family into one place with a common purpose.

On most mornings I wake up at 4:45 A.M. I have done it for so long that my body is now conditioned to do it without the help of an alarm clock. As soon as my eyes open, I slowly recite the Lord's Prayer and Psalm 27 at least three times. I then reach over to my nightstand, turn on the light, and grab my prayer journal. I write one page of prayer, acknowledging God for the blessings in my life. I confess my shortcomings, fears, and any concerns I may have. I thank God for my health, my children, my grandchildren, and whatever else may come to my mind. I close by making specific requests for myself and others. On certain days I will then get up and begin my day. On others, I turn off the light, roll over, and go back to sleep. This is my morning ritual, a practice that sustains me.

A Foot in Two Worlds

Alignment begins in the heart. It is through your heart that God speaks, guides, and directs your mind and your actions. Rituals are a way to bring your being and your life into alignment with the presence of good and God. What I know now is that many people are afraid of the word *ritual*. For many, it conjures up images of things that are considered to be spooky, dark, or ungodly. As a Yoruba priestess, a cultural custodian, I have learned the meaning and power of ritual, whether or not the practice is for a spiritual or nonspiritual purpose. All rituals are tied to a specific belief system. As a recovering Pentecostal, and New Thought Christian, I have seen and practiced many rituals that were called by other names, and thereby were deemed acceptable to the collective consciousness of the general population. While all people may not do the same thing in the same way, if it is a repeated practice that brings meaning to the participants, it can be and should be considered a ritual.

While we may not know it or call it such, we do rituals to create order, safety, and familiarity. Order is the first law of the universe. The universe of nature and life generates the reoccurrence of certain events without fail, at the same time, in the same way. Nature is orderly, and if we desire to be in alignment with nature, we must know and create order. We all strive to create and enjoy a well-ordered mind, life, and environment, whether in our homes, families, work environment, or communities. We engage in certain practices so that we will know what to expect, and so that we can experience the order of the familiar. A ritualistic practice or lifestyle need not be cause for alarm or speculation. In fact, it can

193

be a way to create a seamless connection between the spiritual and the mundane, the internal and external experience of life, the old and new worlds, and the private and public expressions of who we are and what we hold to be meaningful.

Women need rituals. It is a way to gather, purify, enhance, and direct our energy. Rituals support us in meeting the many demands on our lives. In the old-world ways of most indigenous cultures, women gathered to support and encourage one another. Whether they were washing clothes in a kettle, skinning and curing meat, or quilting and sewing for the needs of their families, women have always engaged in ritualistic practices. What transforms a mundane practice into a sacred ritual is intention and repetition. In the movie *Beloved,* when one woman was in trouble, a group of women stood in the front yard and prayed and sang. I could be wrong, but I don't believe they were responding to a call-to-arms e-mail that was sent out that morning. I saw and sensed that the group had long been engaged in the ritual of group prayer. This was not the first time they had come together to address a specific need. They were all wearing hats. They were all carrying Bibles. They all knew exactly what to do, because, I believe, they had done it many times before. There is nothing more powerful than a group of women gathered and moving toward a common purpose. It is a function of order and an outgrowth of their ritual. In today's fast-paced world, I continue to encourage women of all ages to gather and create rituals that support the individual and the collective consciousness of the group.

Rituals need not be collective or public endeavors. Private, solitary rituals and practices are equally powerful and important. My grandmother stared out of the window every day. My daughter baked cakes and cookies with her daughter every Tuesday. I use Monday, every week, as the day dedicated to my scrapbooking. What I know now is that every woman needs and can do rituals to feed, comfort, and develop her spirit. A nightly bath can be a ritual. A morning or evening prayer practice can be a ritual. Taking a day for yourself, withdrawing from the world, or doing something that calms and feeds your soul on a regular basis can be a ritual.

My best friend takes naps. Resting is her ritual. As a minister, she gives out a great deal of energy, and her naps help her to recharge her mind and body.

Whether for spiritual, physical, or emotional reasons, every woman can benefit from the practice of certain rituals in her life. Rituals create an ordered and sacred atmosphere. Whether for bathing, cleaning, or lovemaking, a ritualistic approach to certain activities can have a beneficial impact. The following is a Room-Clearing Ritual that I have shared with many women and practiced in my own home. I offer it to you as a place to begin if you are not accustomed to creating your own ritual practices. Before you conduct the clearing ritual, be sure that the space has been physically cleaned and ordered. This may mean you will need to dust, sweep, empty the trash, and put in order any papers and books.

Room-Clearing Ritual

For this ritual you will need the following:

- A pre-selected prayer, scripture, or affirmation.

- A spray bottle with eight ounces of water, ten drops of lavender oil, five drops of geranium oil, five drops of peppermint oil.

- Four small white candles. Tea lights that are self-contained work extremely well for this purpose. You may place one candle in each of the four corners before you begin your ritual. You will light them as a part of your clearing ritual.

- Choose a room in your home (this can also be done in your office) in which you desire to create a sacred energy.

- On the day before you perform the clearing, set your intention. State exactly what it is that you desire to create or experience in the space you will be clearing.

- On the morning of the clearing, restate your intention and ask your Higher Self for guidance.

- Approach the room or space with your intention in mind.

- Standing in the doorway of the space you intend to clear, speak aloud the selected prayer, scripture, or affirmation, and the purpose of what you are about to do. (At this point, you may enter the room to preset your candles. When they are in place, walk back to the doorway to begin the ritual.)

- From the doorway of the room, walk to the far right-hand corner. While facing the corner wall, spray your solution on the wall from the ceiling to the floor.

- Recite your selected reading aloud again. Speak your intention and desire for the space once more.

- Spray the wall again.

- Light the candle you have preset in this corner.

- Turning slowly and moving to the right, walk to the next corner and repeat the process until you have covered the four corners of the room.

- When you have completed the fourth corner of the room, without turning your back, walk out of the room. If there is a door, close it. If at all possible, do not return to the room until all of the candles are extinguished. If you use tea lights, this should take about two hours.

- If you are using a larger glass encased candle, allow it to burn for at least 60 minutes before you enter the room to extinguish it.

- Repeat this practice on the same day of the week, at the same time, every 30, 60, or 90 days. You can determine how often you will repeat the practice in response to your experiences.

Be mindful and take notice of how you feel in the space and what happens in the space once you have completed the clearing. You should immediately notice a difference. Also, remember that every ritual, whether for yourself, someone else, or a specific space has only the meaning you intend for it.

Chapter 11

ALTARS

A shrine or altar is an area of consecrated energy and a place for sacred rituals. Shrines are a principal element of African culture. The pyramids are ancient African shrines. Totems are shrines among the Native Americans. The Washington Monument is a shrine among Anglo Americans. Unfortunately, African descendants have been limited and imprisoned by the English language. Consequently, we are uncomfortable with and turned off by certain words.

In our individualized, computerized society, we are uncomfortable with the term *shrines,* so we have *altars.* As you will! An altar is used as the place of offering respect, honor, and celebration of spiritual energy. It is also considered an area of consecrated energy for sacred rituals such as prayer. An altar is a primary element of spiritual development, because it provides a visual and physical focus for your spiritual intentions, energy, and activity. An altar is necessary only to the degree that it enables you to focus your mind, house your sacred implements, and provide a consecrated location for your spiritual practice. Once you have erected your altar, it becomes the place to which you can come, daily or weekly, to pray and meditate. It is also a place to which you can come to just sit and focus or ground your energy.

An altar may be as simple or as elaborate as meets your needs and tastes. There are, however, certain protocols or formalities you are encouraged to follow if you are going to set up an altar.

- Place your altar in a place that is not heavily trafficked by daily family activities. An empty closet serves adequately for apartment dwellers. If you own or live in a home, try a secluded area of the attic or basement.

- Cleanse and consecrate the area in which your altar will be. Cleanse first by sweeping and mopping the area. This can be done with detergent, followed by an herbal washing. Sage, rosemary, or hyssop, boiled and strained, makes an excellent herbal cleanser. You may also add essential rose, myrrh, or frankincense oil to the water while boiling. After washing, you can smudge the area with incense. To smudge, place the burning incense in the selected area and allow the smoke to fill the space. Once you have consecrated the area, do not use it for any activity other than your spiritual practice (e.g., meditation, prayer).

- Cover your foundation (e.g., table, bookcase, etc.) with a white cloth. The color white indicates your desire to invoke and experience light and clarity.

- If you have any sacred items that you would like to place on your altar, be sure to cleanse and smudge them first. You can do this by passing them through the smoke of the incense several times.

Remember, you are a divine expression of the Creator. You have the ability and the right to consecrate implements for your sacred use. You may do this by cleansing the item and praying over it, recognizing its sacred energy and decreeing or affirming it suitable for your sacred use. The following items may prove to be beneficial for use on a personal Guardian Spirit/Angel Altar or Meditation Altar.

- A large glass or vessel of water.
- A candle or other form of light.
- Symbol of divinity, e.g., a bible, cross or ankh.

This simple meditation altar is established with water, flowers, candles, a statue of the Buddha and burning sage.

Ancestral Altars

There are many different kinds of ancestral altars, each one has a specific purpose and design. For example, an ancestral altar can honor historical or cultural ancestors, the ancestors of your family bloodline, or the elders of your community.

This ancestral altar was erected for a specific ancestor celebration. The fruit and food are a part of the ceremonial observance.

This "off of the ground" altar was created for a special ancestral celebration.

One common traditional altar (described below) should be set up on the floor because ancestral spirits help ground us and protect us in our earthly endeavors. The altar area should be encircled with white chalk, with nine lines drawn across the circle like the spokes on a bicycle wheel. Within the circle, the following items should be placed:

- Pictures of deceased family members or loved ones.

- Hats, pipes, canes, or other memorabilia of the deceased family members.

- Vessel of water (for purification).

- Cup of coffee (represents a product that has fallen from a tree).

- Small glass of honey (represents collective work).

- Small glass of molasses (represents the process of transformation).

- Small glass of milk (represents the nurturing essence of the mother).

- Two glass-enclosed white candles, to be placed on opposite sides of circle.

- Small bottles of clear liquor such as white rum, gin, or vodka (liquor represents an element that has gone through several processes to reach completion).

- Cigar, to be lit and placed over coffee cup (tobacco is a sacred herb of the earth).

Each of the liquid items will need to be replaced weekly. You may also put cloth dolls or masks in the circle to represent ancestral forces.

When burning incense at an ancestral altar, the following blends are particularly pleasing:

- Frankincense and myrrh—strength, purification, power

- Rosemary and lavender—purification, love

- Anise seeds and rosemary—spiritual clarity, purification

- Lavender and cinnamon sticks—love

- Sage, rosemary, and lavender buds—purification, wisdom, love

- Rose or sandalwood cones—love, prosperity

It is best to use fresh herbs on a charcoal block or *pure* incense sticks. Pure incense appears darker in color than those that contain sawdust.

Personal Development Altar

Water is the medium of spiritual purification. It is the element through which spiritual energy passes clearly and effectively. Water on the spiritual altar fosters clear, effective, and pure spiritual communication. Seven glasses of water are to be used on this altar. Each of the glasses is dedicated to one of the spiritual forces that inhabit every individual.

Personal development altars are established with seven water-filled glasses representing the spiritual forces that surround every individual and the seven levels of consciousness.

These spiritual forces include:

Glass 1: Ori, the spirit of your head

Glass 2: The spirit of your bloodline—parents (whether living or deceased) and ancestors (known and unknown)

Glass 3: The spirit/essence of masculine energy

Glass 4: The spirit/essence of feminine energy

Glass 5: The spirit/essence of the inner child

Glass 6: Karmic Spirits (any spiritual energy from past existences)

Glass 7: Spirit of the Creator, the Godhead that established the divinity of your life and all life.

The Personal Development Altar is to be set up on a table covered with a white cloth. The center, or Godhead, glass needs to be larger than the other six glasses. The glasses identified should be placed on the table in the order listed above. Before it is placed on the table, each vessel of water should be consecrated in the following manner:

Holding one glass at a time, at the center of your forehead, recite the following prayer:

I dedicate this water to the spirit of _____
[Fill in one of the spiritual energies listed, i.e. my head;
my bloodline—parents and ancestors; the masculine essence
of my being; the feminine essence of my being; etc. Feel free
to add or use the words that make you comfortable.]

*I dedicate this water for my spiritual purification, elevation,
and evolution. I dedicate this water so that the spirit of [fill in the
spiritual energy being used] will provide me spiritual assistance,
spiritual strength, spiritual clarity, and spiritual understanding.
I dedicate this water for my spiritual growth.*

The final vessel of water to be consecrated is the Godhead,
which will seal the table in light and divinity. The above prayer, as
well as your personal favorite, may be recited. You can also dedicate this glass with a special prayer for yourself. Once this glass is
placed on the table, you can light a candle and begin your spiritual
practice.

The water in each glass will need to be changed at least once
a week. Each time you change the water, you must rededicate the
glasses to the spiritual forces they represent. In the beginning,
you may notice tiny bubbles filling the surface of the glass. This
indicates that the spiritual forces are drawing and cleaning energy
from you and your environment. It is fine. The clearer the water
becomes, the clearer you will be. You can add a pinch of alum to
the six primary glasses to intensity the vibrations. A few drops of
mercury in the center glass will do the same.

Finally, please note that the above description relates to an
individual altar for spiritual development. It is not an ancestral
altar. An ancestral altar should be set up on the floor or on the
earth. An altar for spiritual development should be set up on a
table. I've reviewed here only the minimum requirements for
altars. If you feel the need or desire to consecrate a more modest
or a more elaborate altar for any purpose, I encourage you to con-
sult your spirit in prayer and meditation for guidance and instruction, then follow those instructions implicitly.

What I Know Now

*Altars are ways to nurture a relationship with the Divine.
An altar provides us with a place to cast
our problems into the arms of God.
Altars support us in developing a disciplined
practice and a devotional mind set.*

A Place to Be

My kitchen is the place everyone converges when I am the hostess of a family or social event. People seem content to squeeze themselves into little corners, to share the two stools that surround my very small, glass-top table, and to linger in the two doorways that lead to either the family room or the dining room. No matter how many times I suggest that they sit somewhere, they are unable or unwilling to tear themselves away from the happenings of the kitchen. In every home, there is a special gathering place. There is also a place to sleep, a place to cleanse the body, and a place for storage. Why, then, do we forget that we also need a place to rest, to think, to worship? An altar provides a home with just such a place.

An altar is a private and sacred space that provides the spirit a place for rest and focus. The owner's intention when constructing the altar, and choosing the objects to be placed on the altar, conveys the sacred stories and desires of the owner's heart. In this special place, one is connected to one's past, one's future dreams, and one's present experiences as revealed through prayers, songs, and even tears. For women, an altar can be a place of uncensored devotion and worship. It is an opportunity to say, feel, and do what her soul demands when, or if, it is not welcomed or accepted by the larger, male-dominated religious or spiritual community. In both African and Native American cultures, women have sacred altars and ceremonies where men's presence is forbidden. The women's prayers, dancing, and singing are centered on their concerns for themselves, their children, their families, and their clans. They give humble offerings of food, drink, and coins to establish a connection between the energy of the altar and the energy of their hearts, and between the energy of their intentions and the essence of their reality.

The practice of erecting altars predates most organized religions. In many early communities, shrines and altars were erected in the center of the village for the purpose of public communion and connection with the spirit world. In the absence of traditional communal or public altars, a personal altar can be a spiritual aid. In her book, *Beautiful Necessity*, Kay Turner states: "The intimacy of this very personal form of devotion is characteristically and profoundly female. Today many women are building altars for prayer, meditation and personal rituals." Altars give us a place to be, to focus, and to tap into the happenings of our minds and hearts.

I am fortunate enough to have an entire room that I have dedicated as my sacred space. In this room I have several altars, including a crystal altar, a meditation altar, and a prayer bowl altar, where I keep several crystal bowls into which I deposit my written prayer requests. I have also erected altars for special needs and occasions. After losing my brother, I created an altar in his honor. I kept pictures of him and us as children, the program from his funeral service, and two gifts he had given me over the years. Whenever I felt myself grieving for him, I would sit in front of his altar. In this space it was safe for me to cry, to remember, to pray, and to write in my journal the many things I never said to him. My brother's altar became my safe place to grieve. This is where I deposited the energy of my sadness. As time passed and I came to a place of peace about his transition, I dismantled the altar. Whether you are like me with an entire room, or you have only a small table in a corner, it is important to realize that energies converge at the site of your altar. It is not a passive or mundane space. As a result of your intention and interaction, the energy from your psyche and soul, an altar becomes the meeting point of your spiritual and mundane essence. This energy can anchor you, give you strength, and provide you with permission to explore the realms of your inner landscape.

Feel free to bring special objects and items into the sacred space of your altar, should you choose to erect one. My first eagle feather has a special place on my meditation altar. It was gifted to me by my sister-friend Waunetta Lone Wolf. Although Waunetta surrendered her life to lung cancer, through her feather and *cha-nupa* (sacred pipe), she and I are still connected as sisters. When I hold the feather or her pipe, it helps me to remember her and all of the wonderful things she taught me. You may have seashells, pictures of special occasions and people, or sacred objects like crystals, stones, or prayer books, all of which could have a safe place to be on your personal altar.

In the original text of this work, I shared with you the process for erecting and maintaining several types of altars. You may choose to create one or all of them. Whatever you choose, I encourage you to be mindful that you deserve and have the perfect right to establish an altar that honors your connection and devotion to your spiritual essence. Take a day to gather your supplies.

Take the time to clear and cleanse the space you choose. Put your heart and your prayers into the clearing and organizing of the objects that will live on your altar. Light a candle. Burn some incense. When everything feels just right, sit and pray. Then, sit in silence and connect with your breath. Listen for the beating of your heart. Feel the beauty and power of life as it moves through your being. If you are so inclined, before you rise and leave your sacred place, I welcome you to read, aloud or silently, the following translation of Psalm 76 as written by Sister Nan C. Merrill in her book *Psalms for Praying: An Invitation to Wholeness;* personalize it by changing "our" to "my" and "us" to "me."

Psalm 76 from *Psalms for Praying*

In loving places, O Beloved, are You known,
Your mercy extends to all on earth.
Your abode has been established in our soul,
Your dwelling place in our heart.
You break down our walls, our anger, fear and doubt.
Glorious are You, more majestic than the everlasting mountains.
That which is haughty within us is brought low,
Our greed brings us to ruin.
The violence that we harbor turns in upon ourselves.
In your loving mercy, O Beloved,
You raise us up with Love.
For You fill us with wonder.
You who know our innermost being,
You forgive us and raise us up.
From the depths of our soul You call us to love,
to grow toward harmony and wholeness.
You well up in our hearts with injunction
to liberate all the oppressed of the earth.
Surely our fear-filled hearts will one day praise You.
Abandon yourself to the Beloved with confidence;
And receive the blessings of Love from the Heart of your heart,
From the One who forgives your transgressions,
Who welcomes you home with joy!

— Sister Nan C. Merrill

Chapter 12

SPIRITUAL BATHING AND PURIFICATION

When she opened the front door, I fought to stifle a scream. Her skin was as black as coal! Her eyes were piercingly white. So white that I could see them through the dark lenses of her sunglasses! Her head was wrapped in what appeared to be a red bed sheet. The piles of cloth on her head matched her long red dress. The ruffled dress resembled the style worn by mammies on old TV shows, complete with a red-and-white-checkered apron. The 12-inch cross around her neck hung from a thin piece of clothesline.

"Mother Mary?" I asked.

She didn't answer. She told me to step back from the front door, walk back down the stairs, and wait at the door she indicated. She slammed the door in my face before I could even move! Obediently, I walked down the steps to the basement door. A small voice in my brain was laughing hysterically when suddenly the door flew open! Before I could say a word, Mother Mary threw a bucket of ice-cold water in my face! I stood there dripping wet, trying to catch my breath!

"Come on in, sweetheart!"

I stepped through the doorway saying a silent prayer: *Dear God, when am I going to learn?*

As I sat shivering, Mother listened intently to my story. No money. Trying to finish school. Bad relationship ended badly.

Can't eat. Can't sleep. Mother sick. Father couldn't care less. Losing my mind! Mother's eyes seemed to be piercing my skin as she stared at me. She was fondling the huge cross around her neck when she finally said, "The devil hates the cold, you know!" She stood up and walked away, leaving me in the dimly lit basement room that resembled a church. There was an ancient piano, chairs set up auditorium style, a cross on every wall, and a stack of hymnals on the floor.

"The devil likes black people!" She was yelling out from another other room. "He is particularly fond of black women. You know why?"

"No, why?"

"Because they're weak!"

My political intelligence was immediately offended!

"They've been weak every since the old African mothers stopped teaching about God and His medicine. They been weak since they straightened their hair and put on panty girdles. They weak 'cause they sleep in them big, fat, pink hair rollers! You can't hear God talk through hair rollers, you know!"

I thought to myself, *Oh God, what am I doing in this basement with this crazy woman?*

Mother Mary called out, "Come to me, sweetheart." I laid my wet coat on a chair and walked into the next room. Mother was standing beside a shower stall. She had a white plate in her hands. Quickly, I scanned the bathroom. There was a glass-encased candle on a shelf in every corner. To my left, there was a shelf with six or seven candles of different colors, with a picture of a saint next to each one. There was a sweet-smelling smoke swirling around Mother, which made her seem like an apparition. On the wall directly in front of me, above Mother's head, was a huge poster of the Virgin Mary, and, just like the vision I had had so many years before, the Virgin was a beautiful black woman!

Mother told me to kneel down. She placed the plate on top of my head and started singing. She was singing so loud and off key, I was embarrassed for her. She started praying. She was calling the names of people I didn't know. In the process, she called my father, Horace, and my mother, Sarah, whose names I had not mentioned. Her words wiped the embarrassed smirk right off my face! Now she was speaking in a language I couldn't understand. Somebody understood her, because I heard the answers. There were two distinct voices. One male. One female. Both loud. I didn't dare open my eyes.

"Get in the tub!" *Who was she talking to?* Then she screamed. "Get up! Get in the tub!" Scrambling to my feet, I half stepped, half fell into the shower stall.

"Put your hands on the wall! Spread your legs apart!"

Obediently, I followed orders as I thought to myself, *Please don't let her kill me!* I felt her hands ripping at my clothes. One yank and my $30 sweater was gone! Ripping. Tearing. The skirt fell off! Now the scissors! Bra first, panties next! The yanking at the panty hose almost spun me around!

"Face the wall! Don't look back! Don't ever look back!"

My toes were curled as if gripping at the tile, and my fingers lay plastered against the walls of the shower stall. The first blow came to the top of my head.

She was singing some crazy-sounding song as she washed my body with eggs! From the top of my head, across my face, down my back, and on to my legs! I could feel the egg shells cutting my skin. I couldn't open my eyes. I tucked in my lips to avoid the taste of the raw eggs. Abruptly, she stopped. I could hear her step away. She was praying again.

Without warning, Mother doused me with another bucket of water. She started scrubbing me down, then she handed me her tools. Lemons!

"Wash your face and your privates!"

As I washed, she poured. Ice-cold water!

"Stomp on those clothes!"

I was shivering, stomping, scrubbing myself with the lemon rinds.

"Jump on those clothes! Stomp it out!"

I jumped, shivering and scrubbing! It was a frenzied experience.

"Tell him to get back!" Mother gave me a whack on the bottom! "Tell him to leave you alone!" I don't know who "he" was, but I was screaming at him, "Leave me alone!" I was stomping and screaming. Shivering and screaming! Scrubbing and screaming! Mother gave me more lemons. I was frantic! I scrubbed my arms, legs, face! Under my breast and my privates! I was screaming at the top of my lungs when I heard Mother's calm, melodic voice. "Now, don't hurt yourself, baby. It's gone!" I think she meant "he's gone," but I thought it better not to ask her for a minor grammatical correction.

When I fell to my knees in the stall, Mother was ready with another bucket of water! This time, the water was warm and sweet-smelling. Gently, she stroked my body to remove the egg shells and lemon rinds. She was humming now. "You got a change of clothes?" I shook my head to indicate no. Mother walked away, leaving me exhausted on the shower-stall floor. I heard her go up and come back down the stairs. "Put this on, but don't dry your body." I got dressed.

When I came out of the bathroom, Mother just stared at me.

"Now, don't go feelin' ashamed because your breasts hang! Any breast that nursed babies is supposed to hang!"

I was wearing a parrot-green crocheted sweater and a red skirt that was four inches over my knees. My brown ankle boots were soaking wet from the first dousing. "You look much better! You are such a beautiful woman. I don't know why you let people make you feel ugly!" I didn't even care how she knew. I felt 100 percent better. Light-headed, but better!

Mother took my hands and prayed with me. She told me to go home and be good to myself, as if I knew what she meant. At the time, I had no idea. Mother told me that God had given me special blessings. My problem was, I didn't realize how specially blessed I was! Mother kissed my forehead. She told me that her work was free, but when I could, send $250 to a post office box. The church, she said, needed my support. I picked up my dripping wet, wrinkled coat, threw it over my arm, and headed for the door. Mother called out to me, "Eggs are sacred forces of life. Lemons cut bitterness! When in doubt, just get in the water." I told her thank you and left. More than three months later, when my life had leveled out nicely, I sent her a money order as she had requested.

As a nurturing source for life, water is the most powerful healing natural element ever known to man. All natural sources of water carry the "mother force" of the universe. Water soothes, heals, nurtures, and cleanses. Water—the warrior, the protector— is always available. If you cannot get to a river, a lake, or the ocean, you can always immerse yourself in the bathtub! The essence of water impacts and transforms your consciousness because its presence brings forth new life. Water nurtures your being because it symbolizes the protection of the womb.

Talking, praying, affirming your desires in or over water is a powerful way to put the universe on notice that you are in need. Sprinkle perfumed water around the house to create a clearing and refreshing energy. Place a clear glass of water under the head of your bed to remove cloudy energy that may be blocking your memory of dreams. Keep large vessels of water around the house to draw and clear negative energy. Drink plenty of water daily, to keep your system flushed. Water is the mother of life! Keep that energy alive!

To give your bathwater an extra healing effect, you can add a few drops of an essential oil or a handful of herbs. Oils provide stimulation to the central nervous system and the spiritual centers (A'se). Herbs create a vibratory energy force around the physical body, and attract similar energy from the universe. Both herbs and oils have a healing affect on the mind and body and should be used in hot water.

Wade in the water.
Wade in the water, children.
Wade in the water.
God's gonna trouble the water.

— Negro spiritual

What I Know Now

Water is the most powerful element in the universe.
Spiritual bathing and cleansing neutralizes
the energy we attract in our daily interactions.
Bathing can be used to cleanse the
body or infuse it with a desired energy.
Bathing is considered a personal, cultural, and spiritual practice.

Rub-a-Dub, You Don't Need a Tub

I have a confession. I am and have been for quite some time a "soap whore." I have an incredible stash of roughly 300 bars of soap that I have collected from South Africa, western Africa, Europe, and various shops throughout the United States. When I see or take in the fragrance of a certain soap, I am immediately transported to my bathtub. I imagine myself reclining in warm scented water, slowly and methodically massaging my body with the bar or ball of fragranced delight that the world calls "soap." I have and will spend any amount required to get some new kind, new fragrance, or new shape of soap that promises to do things that may or may not be possible. My most expensive soap acquisition is a 3.5-ounce block scented with mimosa and lily of the valley. It cost me £32, which at the time calculated to $59.60. I have an awesome and constantly growing collection of soap that I store in various baskets and on various shelves, from the linen closet to every one of the three bathrooms in my house. I must also admit that the collection has now invaded my lingerie drawer.

Making soap is a vehicle of self-loving, self-supportive indulgence. A few years ago, I took a soap-making class, intent upon using my knowledge of herbs and essential oils to create a line of products that would bear my name and support women in their quest to elevate their energy and/or their spiritual vibration. My first batch of homemade soap produced a batch of green gook that refused to produce lather during the 15 minutes it took me to scrape it from under my fingernails. *I'm better now!*

Sometime ago, I had to admit that I had run out of space. I asked my friends and loved ones who have supported me in my socially acceptable addiction not to gift me with any more soap, recognizing that it had become essential for me to work through my vast supply. I have been in recovery for about two years now. I am not allowed to buy anything that bubbles unless it is specifically manufactured for the washing of dishes or clothes. It is incredibly hard to watch the contents of my baskets and shelves, once filled to capacity, slowly dwindle away before my eyes. But I know it is for my own good. I cannot just buy the soap; I also have to use it. Okay! I admit it! Soap is not an essential element of spiritual bathing or cleansing. I just told myself that it was so that I would have a legitimate reason to buy something I really love.

Spiritual bathing and ritual cleansing of the body is an ancient tradition that has been practiced in most cultures around the world and is recommended in the Bible. One of the most well-known bath formulas is mentioned in Psalm 51, in which the herb hyssop is used for purification from sin. Whether for hygienic, recreational, or religious purposes, the practice of bathing can be found in the most ancient cultures and has a very specific meaning for the people of that culture. In many cultures that predate the Bible, the bath maker would add scents, minerals, herbs, roots, and tree bark to the water, depending on the condition and purpose of the bather. The oldest ritual baths involve the use of pure water from a running stream or river or water from the sea. This recommendation can be traced back to the Jewish-Kabbalist tradition. In Judaism the *mikvah,* or ritual bath, must be made with free running water.

What I know now is that our skin is our largest organ of elimination. In the same way sweating eliminates toxins from our body, what we put *on* our skin infuses the body. Bathing, while often thought of as a private experience, has in many cultures been considered a sacred, leisurely, and ritualistic public practice. In Rome, for example, bathing was considered a communal activity, and as such it was conducted in public facilities that resemble the spas and health clubs of our modern society. Among Roman royalty, it was not uncommon to find a series of rooms or even a separate structure dedicated to the purpose of bathing. In public Roman bath houses, men and women gathered to submerge themselves in expensive and vibrantly scented waters at certain times of the day before they went to work or worship.

In Japan, wooden bathing structures called *ofuro* or *furo* boxes have been an integral part of the culture for many centuries. A traditional *ofuro* is made from hinoki wood that is virtually unique to Japan. Although it is now very rare, this wood is golden in color and has a heavy lemon scent that tends to diminish about a year after the wood is cut. The first rule of bathing in Japan is that the bath is not the place to clean your body. Baths are designed for the purpose of purification and relaxation. Historically, the proper way to bathe in Japan was first to rinse yourself before entering the bathtub, or *ofuro*, using a bucket of cold water that you poured from head to toe. Today a cold shower is an acceptable alternative.

The Japanese believe that bathwater should not contain any soaps or bubbles. Instead, they use a collection of bath salts prepared for the specific effect you desire. The water of a Japanese-style bath is as hot as you can take it. You must immerse yourself up to the neck for a minimum of 15 minutes, allowing the energy and scent of the bath salts to support you in relaxing and drifting away. Once you have soaked, you leave the bath and go to the shower to clean yourself. When you have completely scrubbed and rinsed your body, you reenter the bath for another 15 minutes. A traditional Japanese bath is completed with yet another cold shower. After the combination of hot immersion and cold shower, you will have released toxins and relaxed the mind, and you will emerge feeling like a new person. The aspect the Western world would probably have difficulty accepting is the sharing of bathwater; if someone else is bathing after you, it is expected that you will not let the water out of the *ofuro*. Since the water is only for soaking, it can be used by multiple people.

Wading in the Pool of Possibilities

One of my favorite spirituals is "Wade in the Water." I am not sure why this song holds such a deep meaning for me, but there are times when I hear it and weep from the core of my being. When I researched the song many years ago, I discovered that no one actually knows its author. Like so much of the music handed down through the generations of Africans who became slaves, there are no records of how certain songs came into being. I did discover that the song is believed to have been originally sung to warn and encourage runaway slaves to walk in the water instead of on the land on their journeys north, in order to avoid dogs and trackers. Some sources believe that the song was a sort of calling card for Harriet Tubman as she led the Underground Railroad, ushering slaves to freedom. Still others believe that the original meaning of the song comes from John 5:4, which reads: "For an angel went down at a certain season into the pool and troubled the water; whosoever then first after the troubling of the water stepped in was made whole of whatever disease he had" (King James Version).

"Trouble," as used in the lyrics of the song, refers to stirring up or infusing with presence. For the slaves, the water was a place where they could find and be covered by God's presence. For the sick, the water was considered a place of healing. What I know now is that whether you are afflicted by some sort of enslavement or a physical, mental, or emotional disorder, water is a safe and healing haven.

In Yoruba culture, Yemoja is the name for the essence of God that is found in the salty waters of the ocean, which cover 96 percent of the earth's surface. Yemoja is considered to be the mother of the universe. In some cultures she is considered the Black Madonna and is depicted holding a baby, which represents her connection to human life. In other cultures, she is recognized as the Earth Mother, or Divine Mother, who covers the earth. From the core of Yemoja's being, all life is formed and nurtured. Her body is the ground from which we receive food, her heart is the moon that determines the tides of the oceans. Osun (pronounced *o-shun*), on the other hand, is the essence of the Creator found in the "sweet waters"—the rivers. The Yoruba believe that Osun's heart is the needle that God used to weave together the fibers of the world, making it a cohesive place for the promulgation of life in all of its forms. Osun symbolizes family and love, the two things every living being must have in order to evolve in consciousness and life. Whether or not you embrace the philosophy or culture of the Yoruba, it is easy to see that water, whether for bathing or recreation, holds a sacred meaning among indigenous people.

In 1999, Dr. Masaru Emoto stunned the scientific and the layperson's worlds with his controversial claims that human thoughts, when directed toward unfrozen water, will create water crystals that are either beautiful, ugly, empowering, or harmful, depending upon whether the thoughts are positive or negative. His book *Messages from Water* indicates that we can alter the character and energy of water with prayer, music, spoken words—even by attaching written words to a container of water. The controversy of his work has little to do with whether or not his results are accurate. The scientific world takes issue with his methodology, ignoring the fact that water is a living element that can and will respond to the energy it receives. In my home, I use water that is stored in five-gallon glass bottles. I use the word stickers offered on Dr. Emoto's Web site to charge my water. The stickers are plastered all over the bottle. Every time I look at the water bottle, I am sending the mental energy of the words into the water. When I go to the beach, my first order of business when I step into the water is to pray. I ask the essence and energy of the water to cleanse and restore me in any way it sees fit to make me a better person and servant to humanity. When I cross or pass a river, I touch the center of my chest, over my heart, and say thank you.

My point in providing you with all of this delicious information is to say that bathing, particularly with a spiritually grounded intent or purpose, is a good thing. Water is a living element. As such, whether it flows from the pipes in the projects or a ramshackle cabin in the deep woods, you can infuse its essence with a conscious and beneficial intent. I encourage you always to draw your bathwater consciously, to prepare the environment of the room in which you bathe sacredly. It is also a good idea to use your time in the bath to release or infuse your being and essence with whatever it is you desire or require at the time. If you are bathing to release, I do recommend a shower immediately following the bath. If you are bathing to infuse yourself, I encourage you not to dry off, but rather allow your body to air dry. As with any sacred or spiritual practice, do not be afraid to experiment and try new things. As long as you have a clear intention, it is a safe bet that you will not cause harm to yourself or anyone else in the process. Above all, enjoy yourself!

Chapter 13

HELP FROM PLANET EARTH

The Convent for the Order of the Holy Mother is located in a small, suburban town 60 miles outside of Detroit. Over 250 acres of land, including a small lake, a corn field, and every type of tree imaginable, it's not what I thought a convent would look like! It was beautiful! It was serene. It was an ideal location for self-searching black women on spiritual retreat! At first, I felt a little uncomfortable going to a convent. I wasn't a Christian. Most nuns are white. I still had a tendency to use four-letter words. And where was I going to smoke? However, once I set foot on the property, I knew that something miraculous was about to take place.

It was early Saturday morning when my spiritual Sister and I began the workshops. "Creating a New Reality"—that was our goal. For six hours, Shaheerah and I taught about the power of the mind, the value of the spirit, and the wisdom of God. We conducted meditations, visualizations, and soul-freeing exercises. A mother who had not spoken to her son for six years came to realize that she would see him again. A woman who had never spoken in public stood up and gave a ten-minute speech about the pain in her life! A woman who had come to the retreat by mistake and knew no one in the group decided to stay! One by one, people began to realize their beauty, their power, their connection with the Creator! We cried about it! We sang about it! We made a miracle scorecard! At the end of the first session, we had chalked up 15 miracles! It was time for dinner.

I decided to take a walk. It was a beautiful day. The grass was freshly cut; the pine, oak, and elm trees offered shade from the sun. The energy was flowing through my body at 75 miles an hour! I needed to be grounded, to get centered. I walked to a large, open field where the earth seemed to meet the sky. I lay on the ground in spread-eagle fashion and began to pray. I had been lying there for about ten minutes when I realized I wasn't alone! There seemed to be a misty fog hovering over me! There was a sweet smell in the air and a cool breeze. I wanted to open my eyes, but I couldn't. Suddenly, my stomach did a somersault as if I had just plunged down the first hill of a roller coaster! The fog became denser, and I could feel it on my skin. Now, I was scared!

As I began to breathe deeper, I heard the voice: *What do you want?* It was a heavy, deeply male voice. It was gentle but stern. My mind was fuzzy. I couldn't figure out if I was asleep or awake. I could feel the sun shining on my skin, and, although my eyes were closed, I could see the fog. I heard it again: *What do you want?*

"Oh s--t, God is talking to me!"

I knew I had gone over the deep end! Then I felt bad for cursing. Suppose it really is God? Now I've cursed at Him! But why would God be talking to me? I don't believe this s--t! God is talking to me! The sweet smell was lingering under my nose! I could hear my heart pounding in my ears! My eyes were closed, but I could see everything! I wanted to turn my head to actually see, but I couldn't move! "You're crazy!" I told myself. Then I heard myself saying, "God *is* talking to you." Then the voice came again. This time, it was louder, firmer, and right in my ear! *What is it that you want?*

My mind was both blank and flooded with thoughts at the same time. What are you supposed to say when God asks you what you want? All of the spiritual theory I knew went right out the window! I was struggling to figure out what was happening. All of my self-value and worth issues were staring me in the face! Why would God take the time to talk to *me?* Here I was, a lowly human, trying to do my spiritual work, struggling with my own issues, and God, Himself, was talking to me! How did I know this was real? Somehow, I just knew it, and it scared me half to death!

Did I ask God for a cure for AIDS? No! Did I ask God for the secret to a wholesome, prosperous life? No! Did I ask Him to eradicate poverty? Racism? Did I speak to God about my feelings regarding the abuse of women and children? No! I had been praying for more than 30 years for all the things I thought were politically and spiritually correct. I had prayed for clarity, guidance, and understanding. I had children who needed protection, friends who needed help, and clients who needed salvation.

And then the voice came for the fourth time: *What do you want?*

I responded, "A car!"

I was embarrassed for myself. How could I waste this glorious opportunity? As soon as the words were out of my mouth, everything became frightening still. I thought I was dead, but the voice came back.

What do you believe about a car?

Oh, God, now what do I say? The words rolled off my tongue. "I believe you need money to get a car."

You don't need money to get a car. All you need is an idea. A car is simply an idea in your mind. Your mind is in My mind. All I do is create ideas. You bring my ideas into the world.

I couldn't speak!

The voice came back: *If you keep your mind stayed on My mind, you can have anything, because all things are My ideas. You are an idea in My mind! You belong to me!*

On a very, deep level of my being, it all made sense. If God is the source of all life, then everyone and everything belongs to God. The thought crossed my mind: "Well, how come we can't get things together?" The answer came quickly.

Your ego is in the way and sends you on a search for things you already have! Still your ego, and keep your mind on Me.

The fog lifted. My eyes opened. I knew it had been real!

I sat up slowly, trying to make sense of it. The earth beneath me felt alive. I could feel it pulsing. The trees seemed to be watching me. There were several birds walking within 12 inches of me. I could hear the sound of a waterfall that I could not see. I tried to stand up. I was floating! I could smell the flowers. It seemed as though I could see for miles. I felt a peace and stillness within myself that I could not explain! When I finally stood up and turned around, I noticed a 20-foot marble statue of the Virgin Mary! She was looking directly at me! My heart jumped. I shut my eyes. When I opened them, the statue was gone. Six months later, with a $37,000 student loan in default, an overdrawn bank account, and $15 in a savings account, I was *given* the title and keys to a new car! When I changed my mind, my ideas, my beliefs, and the circumstances of my life changed.

The Creator has placed at our disposal a wealth of natural energies that are willing and useful healing tools. We need only ask, and the help is there for us.

Trees

These mighty friends are elemental symbols of wisdom. They are tangible signs of transformation and growth. Trees are receptive and energizing. They stand as symbols, representing and demonstrating our endless source of supply. Imagine that every leaf on every tree represents an idea, a possibility. Imagine that every tree you pass on the streets or roads is a demonstration of the things you can be or have in your life. There is no shortage of possibilities in life, and every possibility is within your reach. We can also talk to trees, particularly elms and oaks. Weeping willows are eager receptacles for our sorrows—they take our tears and transform them into beauty! Trees are a solid support system.

An excellent clearing ritual can be performed at the foot of a tree. Dig a small hole in front of the tree or near the roots. Lie flat on the earth and talk directly into the hole. Talk as though you were speaking to a person. If you are expressing pain, sorrow, fear, and so on, tell the tree exactly what the cause is and how you feel about it. If you are making a request, be specific. Talk about the situation, what you are feeling, and propose an outcome. When you have fully expressed yourself, re-cover the hole. Ask the tree to take your concerns and turn them into something beautiful! Another simple clearing process is simply to sit on the earth with your back against the tree and talk out your concerns. Whenever you download your difficulties into the earth or at the foot of a tree, always thank the tree and leave an offering—pennies, a flower, fruit, or a prayer. In essence, you are paying for the work the tree will do.

Rivers

Rivers are the sweet waters of the universe. They represent the energy of Venus, the planet that rules the energy and flow of love and money. The river is always flowing as a representation of the movement of love, wealth, community consciousness, and emotional well-being. Rivers attend to the day-to-day flow of life: how we respond to it and how we overcome the challenges we encounter. Rivers encourage us to learn how to flow with the tides of life.

Sitting on a riverbank, talking aloud about your emotions, is an excellent cleansing ritual. Releasing and clearing emotions about relationships should be done at the river. Praying for specific information, direction, and guidance can also be done at the river. When praying or meditating at the river, it is helpful to ring a small, brass bell while you are praying to clear and uplift the energy. When you are done, leave an offering of honey or yellow flowers. The offering of honey can be poured into the river while you are ringing the bell and praying. I would encourage you to taste the honey before pouring it so that the words you speak will be sweet. You can also leave an offering of five pennies, five nickels, or five dimes. The number 5 represents the energy of the river. It is the number of family, flowing energy, and fulfillment. It is important that you never throw garbage into the river, nor should you leave any discarded items at the riverbank.

Oceans

The ocean is the ultimate "Mother Force" of the universe. Like the amniotic fluid that nurtures life, the ocean is a supportive, protective, nurturing, and healing energy. You can take all of your troubles to this Mother. She is an enduring source of strength!

Like all mothers, the ocean energy is primarily concerned with health. For us, that translates to mental, physical, and spiritual health. Meditation and prayer at the ocean is one of the most powerful and effective healing tools at our disposal. The ocean is littered with the bodies and spiritual energy of African ancestors! They live because the ocean supports life in many forms. When you go to the ocean, be humble and respectful. Do not wear shoes, fancy clothing, or makeup. Make your prayer with outstretched arms. Always take an offering of fruit, molasses, blue cloth, or silver coins. Leave your offering at the water's edge.

The ocean is the best place to cry. (The river can also take your bitter tears and sweeten them.) When you cry at the ocean, Mother will wash away the source of your tears. Be very mindful of what you ask for at the ocean's shores because these things will ultimately shift or change. Once you have shared your concerns with the Mother, you may recognize people, conditions, and situations leaving your life. It is important that you resist the temptation to fix, change, or hold on to them. The Mother cannot heal or transform your concerns if you get in her way. Because the Mother energy of the ocean represents intuition, once you ask her for assistance, you will intuitively know what to do and how to do it.

Mountains

If you want peace, mental clarity, tranquility, and understanding, go alone to a mountaintop. When you want to forgive or be forgiven, dress in white and go to a mountaintop. For evolution, quick resolutions, and instant mental illumination go to a mountaintop. It is there, in the heights of the mountains, that the Father resides! For these purposes, it is not necessary to scale Mount Kilimanjaro. A simple road trip through the mountains or a weekend of solitude in a cabin in the mountains will suffice.

Taking a ride through the mountains is a powerful mental-clearing ritual. Find a quiet place where on the side of the road where you can look down and see a countryside. Take a single coconut, hold it in the center of your forehead, and speak your prayer or concerns aloud. When you have finished, place the coconut in a well-nestled place and leave it. (The coconut would not be considered an unwanted item because it is a natural element.) Once you have spoken aloud, spend 20 to 30 minutes in silence, eyes closed, with the palms of the hands turned upward. End your prayer/meditation with joyous thanksgiving. Never tell anyone what you've asked for and never ask for it again! Mountain energy is a slow energy. However, it is the most precise and concrete energy available to us on the planet.

Fire

Fire creates the direct link for communication between man and the Creator. It is a powerful cleansing way to release energy into the universe. Fire carries a vibratory presence that permeates the tangible and intangible energies of the universe of life. It represents illumination at the spiritual level and transformation on the physical level. With candles we can use fire for illumination and transformation in our everyday lives.

Candles add vibration to the prayers we offer and the requests we make. The body of the candle holds the thoughts; the flame sends the thoughts into the universe. The color of the candle represents the energy we desire to create. The flame of a candle carries that energy upward and outward. Candles are strongly recommended for those of us who lack the discipline to repeat the same prayers/affirmations daily, as well as those of us whose faith is strong enough to ask for it once and then surrender our attachment to the outcome.

I have discovered that my greatest outcome has unfolded when I charge a seven-day pull-out candle. These are the large candles that come in a glass jar. When you have a specific request or situation that requires healing or transformation, hold the wax candle in your hands while you pray or speak about it, and then place the body of the candle back in the jar. In this way, your thoughts and your energy are captured and held by the candle wax then released into the universe as the candle burns down. As with anything spiritual, you get out of it what you put into it! When "charging" your candle, be relaxed, be clear about what you are asking for, and be positive. (Note: Always keep a lit candle in an open, stable location. The higher, the better. Place your burning candles on a saucer or in a shallow bowl filled with water.) Select the color of candle that vibrates the level of energy you wish to attract (see below).

Color

Color represents the wavelengths of light that emanate from or reflect an object. The vibratory effects of color emit energy, and influence the mind, emotions, and energy in the atmosphere. Color sends a message and draws upon the energies of the universe. The decor of our homes, the clothes we wear, and even the food we eat carry the vibratory effects of color. We can create and dispel energy by the clothes we wear, because they radiate the energy of our being. Choose your colors carefully so they are attuned to what you feel or what you desire to draw to you.

Color: Vibratory Principle

The richer and deeper the tone, the stronger the vibration of the color.

- Red—passion, courage, connection, survival

- Orange—energy, dynamic force, fertility, motivation

- Yellow—mind, intellect, optimism, personal will

- Green—love, prosperity, success, versatility, supply, forgiveness

- Blue—inspiration, religion, devotion, healing, artistic ability, vision

- Purple—high spirit, holy, divine radiance

- Brown—stability, sustenance, practicality

- Pink—universal love, tenderness, innocence

- White—clarity, innocence, wisdom, strength

- Black—absorption and destruction of negative energy

Returning, Returning, Returning to the Mother of us all.

— from "Returning" by Jennifer Berezan

What I Know Now

The physical earth represents the physical body.
It is our responsibility to walk harmlessly on the earth.
Every element and aspect of the earth offers and
provides support for healing and evolution.

Wallowing in the Mud

One of my favorite places to visit is Sedona, Arizona. The sight of those huge, red clay mountains transports my mind to total peace and my spirit to heights difficult for me to establish in any other environment. In Sedona, the air seems cleaner than any other place I have been. I love to walk along the flowing rivers and sit in the quiet of the valleys between the mountains. Whenever I visit Sedona, I collect rocks—huge, beautiful rocks. On my last trip, I collected so many rocks I had to ship them home, which cost over $200. I am not ashamed of spending that much money for a box of rocks; they allow me to keep a piece of Sedona with me forever. The rocks live in my garden and remind me of the beauty and power of this God-created space.

I love dirt. I love the way it smells and the way it feels in my hands. I frequently lie on the earth, digging my fingers down beneath the surface, resting my face against the coolness, a practice I associate with lying against the Mother's breast and listening to her heartbeat. In Native American culture, the earth represents the Mother. It is characteristic of the warmth, comfort, and security we all need and seek in life. The earth has a hard exterior and soft interior. It holds what Native cultures call Turtle Medicine. Like the turtle, the earth's movement is slow, persistent, and determined. Its progress is measured by slow, methodical steps that always yield powerful, positive results like the seasons that govern the planting and harvesting of crops. It would do us well to honor and follow the earth's lead, planning our lives in alignment with the seasons.

As the earth moves, it gives rise to cleansing time, growing time, flowering time, harvesting time, and renewal time. We call these times summer, winter, spring, and fall, without a true understanding of how the earth's movement and energy influence the ebb and flow of our experiences. What I know now is that winter is the time for us to rest and renew. The cold, frost, and snow encourage us to slow down, go within (physically and spiritually), and rest. Spring is the time for us to awaken and plant. With a

234

rested body and soul, we can plant the seeds of our vision with new actions and behaviors. Between spring and summer we have the flowering and growing time, the natural unfolding of all we have planted. Summer is when we ripen and reap the rewards of what we have planted—mentally, emotionally, and physically. Fall is the most appropriate time for us to evaluate and cleanse. This is the time to reflect and release those things and those people who do not support our growth and healing. Although we have a close affinity to the earth, few of us have an understanding of how our lives and personalities are influenced by the seasonal characteristics of the earth's movement and nature. As a result, in today's world, many of us live chaotic and imbalanced lives. In essence, we are *out of order.*

In the Bible, the book of Genesis is the story of creation. It reveals the step-by-step process employed by God for the creation of the fullness of the earth or life as we know it today. From nothing, God called everything into being, including light and dark, water, plants, birds, animals, and the human being. Beyond the religious interpretation, there is important symbolism behind the creation process. Genesis is a directive for how we are to live on the earth. God spoke and things came into being: This reminds us of the power of our words. Everything God spoke into being had a purpose: This is a reminder that we must use our words and resources to create purposefully. Creation is a function of vision and intention. I particularly love the part that reads: "He rested." This first book is a reminder that speaking positively, creating intentionally, and resting periodically is a powerful way of living on the earth.

Coping with Critters

Over the years, I have frequently ignored the power of the God-given creation process. I have been overcommitted, overworked, and totally disrespectful of the signs and wonders the earth provides to keep my mind, body, and soul balanced. The good news is, I now know enough to recognize when my life is out of balance. The bad news is that I have frequently ignored that information. One year, however, I made a faithful attempt to help myself find clarity and balance. I was physically exhausted, mentally bewildered, emotionally drained, and teetering on the brink of financial ruin. Drawing on my Native American ancestry, I knew it was time for a Hanblecheyapi, a vision quest—a ceremonial retreat of fasting, prayer, and meditation—where I would examine my soul, seeking guidance and direction in life. A vision quest is one of the seven main rites of many Native Nations. A traditional quest is usually undertaken during teenage years; however, it can be taken at any time with the guidance of a teacher or Medicine Man to restore balance in your life. As a solitary journey into the wilderness to commune with the earth and nature for the purposes of personal growth, a vision quest will bring you face-to-face with your inner self, the good and the not so good.

It was the dead of winter when I called my teacher requesting his support for my quest. I arrived on the reservation in South Dakota to discover that winter in the plains has a completely different meaning than winter in the city. It was –15 degrees during the daylight hours. No one dared to guess what it would be at night. Warfield, my teacher, decided that I would do the entire quest in the *Inipi*, the sweat lodge. He gathered six men from the community who had volunteered to gather the rocks and build and keep the fire burning for my quest. I was humbled to tears to know that these men, who did not know me, would endure such inclement weather to support me in my time of need. It was a reminder that the earth and those connected to it will never fail us.

I entered the lodge with nine elders who came to pray for me. When the first seven stones were placed in the pit of the lodge, the heat forced me to remove my sweatshirt and pants. One by one, the elders sang and prayed for me, my vision, and my future, as soft tears streamed down my face. By the time they were done, there were 21 stones in the pit that gave off a beautiful amber glow in the pitch-black darkness. The heat was intense. I would guess that by the time the initial two-hour ceremony was complete, the temperature in the lodge was at least 110 degrees. I also knew that it would not stay that way. Warfield gave me my final instructions, and he and the elders left me to pray and sweat alone.

The lodge was warm and toasty for a long while. Then, as the rocks in the pit cooled off, I could feel the bitter cold seeping from the earth. During the ceremony I had taken off all of my cold-weather clothing, which I now could not find in the pitch-black darkness. Wrapping myself in the available towels and blankets, I spent so much time bracing myself for the anticipated onslaught of cold that I could not pray. Once the cold set in, I was no longer seeking a vision; I was protecting my physical body from the frigid temperatures. I could hear the fire crackling outside the lodge. I knew there were rocks on the fire, and that at some point, one of the brothers would come to place those hot rocks in the pit in the center of the lodge. They did not come fast enough. Once I started shivering, my future was not the issue. Mentally, I began to prepare myself to freeze to death in the Black Hills of South Dakota.

As I sat in the lodge shivering, I tried to pray. I tried to meditate. I tried to ignore the fact that I really needed to pee. I failed miserably at all of the above. I laid down. I sat up. I rocked back and forth, side to side. The lodge was so dark, I really couldn't see anything, and every few moments, I blew out through pursed lips to see the frost of my breath. I kept remembering Warfield's last words to me: "Stay inside. Do not lay the pipe on the earth. Let the Mother nurse you back to peace." Was I supposed to pee in my clothes? In the lodge? Was I supposed to go outside near the fire and pee on the sacred grounds? My mind was spinning, my bladder was filled to capacity, and I didn't hear anyone approaching the lodge to help me or save me except the coyotes that were howling in unison right outside the door of the lodge.

Although I had been specifically instructed by Warfield not to drink anything for at least 24 hours before entering the lodge, I had been disobedient. I had been fasting from food for seven days when I took the flight from Maryland to South Dakota. The pressure of the flight made my mouth so dry it felt like my tongue was covered in fuzz. I knew it was wrong, but that physical experience

overwhelmed my mind and led to a conscious act of disobedience. I guzzled down a 16-ounce bottle of water on the plane and
another eight ounces walking through the airport. In fear and
shame, I didn't bother to mention this to Warfield. As a result, he
did not have the opportunity to give me proper instruction. I was
about to pay a huge price for my disobedience, and, in the process,
I would learn a powerful lesson.

I am not sure how long I had been in the lodge when I felt
forced into making a drastic decision. Either I would pee in the
sacred lodge, or brave the subzero temperatures and the coyotes
to pee near the fire. I decided the latter made more sense as long
as I did not put the sacred pipe down. It, I thought, would protect
me from being eaten alive by the wild beasts that had gathered
outside.

Realizing that there were rocks somewhere in the lodge that
I could not see, and that were possibly still hot, I felt around the
earth for the edge of the lodge. Pulling at the blankets and other
coverings that had been secured over the lodge to keep it airtight,
I also discovered that the ground was frozen. My bladder was
demanding that I find my way out quickly or run the risk of sitting in wet clothes that would surely freeze. Pulling and tugging, I
lifted the lodge covering high enough to look out. I could see the
glare of the fire blazing and two eyes staring back at me. Clutching
my pipe, I retreated into the lodge. Crawling along the edge of the
structure, I moved what I thought was a reasonable distance and
pulled up the coverings in this new location. Now, I was directly in
front of the fire; I figured that if I went out here, the coyotes would
probably not approach me. Still clutching the pipe, I lay on the
earth and slithered through the small opening. Dressed in a tank
top with the bottom half of my body wrapped only in two yards of
African print cotton, I made my way out of the lodge. Crouching
low to the ground, I surveyed the landscape for a suitable place to
relieve myself. What I saw were multiple sets of eyes to the right,
to the left, and directly in front of me. It scared me so bad, I peed
right in front of the lodge, staring into eyes that were close enough
for me to touch.

I knew enough not to make any quick movements, so I stilled my body and my breathing. Somewhere within me I realized that it was below zero and I had very few clothes on. Still, I dared not move. I closed my mind, clutched the pipe, and began to pray. When I did, I felt the warm tongue of a wild coyote lick my face. As the tongue moved across my cheek, I prayed and cried—for how long I do not know. Then, suddenly, I realized that I was not afraid, nor was I in danger. Every prayer I had ever prayed for guidance and protection flooded my mind. I opened my eyes, stared deeply into the fire, and continued to pray. I felt warm and clear and peaceful. Slowly, I lowered myself to the ground and slithered back into the lodge, where I covered myself with the blankets and went into a deep sleep. I was awakened by Warfield's voice. It was daylight and a day later.

What I know now is that we can become so attached and addicted to our physical senses and comfort that we dishonor, disrespect, and ignore the natural movement and symbols of the earth. The number one addiction of the human race is control. When we cannot control a thing, we fear it. We fear the unknown, we fear change, we fear risk, believing that if we cannot control an outcome, we may not be able to avoid some unknown harm or danger. Each of these things brings us face-to-face with our perceived weaknesses and limitations. In these moments we forget our connection to God and the earth. We discount or ignore our oneness with all things. We doubt ourselves and imagine the worst possible outcome rather than faithfully calling upon and relying on the guidance of our spirit, which is available at all times in all situations.

The demands of the physical body and senses can be overwhelming, creating a sense of urgency that no amount of prayer seems to quiet. Driven by our physical senses, we will say and do things that take us further away from the very thing our spirit yearns for: a closer connection to God, God's love, and God's protection.

Honoring Mother Earth

The physical earth as we know it is changing, and so are we as the earth's inhabitants. Along with the global warming of the planet, we as human beings are contributing to and experiencing the influence of the earth in ways that were once considered impossible and implausible. Many of us are recognizing our connection to our planet and promoting lifestyles that support or advance an ecofriendly co-existence between humans and the natural elements. What I know now is that, from a spiritual perspective, we are being forced to awaken and change.

Several years ago, I adopted a policy of harmlessness. This means I do not kill anything. I do not swat or stomp bugs; I do not litter; and I endeavor to remain mindful of the costs of advancing my physical comfort. For several years, I stopped eating meat. Unfortunately, my body rebelled, and I was advised to add organic poultry and fish back into my diet. Living a spiritually grounded and empowered life does not mean we must move to a mountaintop and exist on a diet of leaves and bugs. It does mean that we must be conscious of how our demands and behavior impact the environment. We must learn how to respect the ebb and flow of the earth. We must contribute to the proliferation of life. We must make peace and order priorities in our lives.

I live in a remote area of Maryland where farms still exist. I am often sad to see the number of townhouses and condos built on the land that was once inhabited by God's creatures. Road kill has increased while, at the same time, the massive homes that were built are being foreclosed on. Somehow, we must find and restore balance, realizing and embracing behaviors that honor the purpose and intelligence of nature. Strengthening our inner connection to God strengthens our inner connection to all things. Nothing is separate from anything else; the connective consciousness of life is everywhere. What we see and experience around us is the manifestation of an invisible creative process that occurs within physical bodies, senses, and personalities. With these things in mind, we must remember that the earth supports and assists us in the ever-evolving process of life. As such, we owe it to ourselves and to God to respect and honor the bounty of the earth.

While we all cannot live in a mountaintop villa, at the shores by the ocean, or on a farm, there are things that we can do that will support the reestablishment of peace and order on the earth. Our speaking, for example, can change from violent to peaceful. We can use the horns of our cars to warn other drivers rather than to bully them out of our way. We can use trash cans instead of sidewalks to dispose of our fast-food wrappings. We can request paper instead of plastic at the supermarket. What I know now is that every little bit counts, and while everyone cannot do everything, we can all make an effort to honor the Mother for all she gives to us.

Chapter 14

SPIRITUAL CODE
OF CONDUCT

When I first heard the phrase, *"Talk the talk and walk the walk,"* I really thought I knew what it meant. Of course, I didn't! I had built my spiritual foundation on self-deception. I was doing all the right things, praying the right prayers, putting forth the right image. However, inside, I was still avoiding myself, blaming others for my shortcomings, and using my spiritual knowledge as an escape. I still had fears. I still hated my father. I was not living up to my full potential, and I told lies. Everything was going great!

I really believed that I had sufficiently covered my weaknesses. I thought if I continued reading books, going to workshops, and saying the right things to the right people, everyone would know how wonderful I was. I made one deadly error. In an earnest prayer, I asked Spirit to put me on the right path to do my life's work. I really meant it, and, of course, Spirit answered my prayer!

I was well on my way to becoming a sought-after spiritual teacher. I could demonstrate my knowledge in writing and through speech. I had gained the confidence of many people, even though my life was a mess. I was involved in a triangular relationship with a married man. I was up to my neck in debt. My children were unhappy and acting out. I kept teaching and writing. I convinced myself that it was a test, that if I kept doing the spiritual work, everything would work itself out. It didn't matter that I was miserable, as long as I was able to keep up a good front. The facade continued for quite a while; then I prayed again and the walls came tumbling down!

One of my students became seriously ill. She was in the hospital. It was my duty as her spiritual teacher to go see her. When my student called, I promised to do something for her, but I was otherwise occupied. I hung the telephone up and forgot all about my promise. My male friend had told me that he was going back to his wife. I had never told anyone that he was still with her. I had led everyone to believe things were fine with us, so I had no one to talk to. I couldn't admit that I had been lying all along. I retreated to my bed to cry.

When my student was released from the hospital, she called me. Refusing to admit my own troubles, I told her I had done what I had promised to do. My promise had involved another person. In essence, I lied. When I tried to get in touch with that person, I couldn't. My intent, at that point, was to backtrack and do what I should have done in the first place. Better late than never. Months passed, and everything seemed to calm down. My student recovered. My boyfriend came back. Life was livable again. Every now and then, my student would raise the issue. I always brushed her off, saying that I was trying to locate the person. I tried for six months to get in touch with this person, to no avail. My student didn't question me, and I didn't bring it up.

One bright Saturday, the telephone rang. It was a friend of the person I had been trying to reach. He told me that he had spoken to my student and that she had expressed her concerns. He had contacted the person I had been trying to reach. He had no idea what my student was saying. Could I please clear this matter up? My ears got hot. My head was swimming. My lie was about to unravel. My student would know I had lied. My friend would know that I had not done what I was supposed to do, and his friend would know I had lied on him. *You get exactly what you pray for.* You may not like it, but you *will* get it!

I told my friend I would clear it up, but the truth was that I didn't know what to do. I needed to save face. No, what I *needed* to do was get on the path. But I didn't want anyone to know what I had done. I had told a big fat lie, and they already knew. But I could fix it. I couldn't think. I couldn't speak. I sat down on the bed and cried. Crying is so wonderful. It really purges the poison in our minds. The key is to cry with an agenda. As I cried, I got in touch with everything I felt. I was tired of trying to live up to the false image I had created. I was tired of pleasing people. I was tired of lying, making myself out to be something I was not. I was afraid of failing, and I was afraid of succeeding. I really felt alone in the world. I had been trying to make people like me. I was really confused, with no idea who I was or what I really wanted to do. I wished everybody would leave me alone so I could take time to get myself together. I was born on a Sunday, and every truly transforming experience I have had has occurred on a Saturday. I now realize that if I deal with pain on Saturday, then I will be *re*born on Sunday!

My first instinct was to lie. I couldn't face the fact that everyone would know what I had done. I had failed in my responsibilities as a spiritual teacher. I had lied. I had misappropriated someone's money. I had been involved in a relationship with a married man. What would people think about me? What would this mean to the following I had built up? How would I ever face these people again? My ego was frantic and kept showing me images of my destruction. I saw people laughing at me, ignoring me, and taunting me. I could hear the stories and see people's reactions. I thought about all the people who would find out and what they would say. I finally admitted that I didn't care; what I wanted was to get right within myself. It was then that I knew the strength of my spirit. I truly wanted to do the right thing, so I did.

I went to my desk and took out a pad. I wrote my student and my friend. I told them exactly what had happened. I admitted to the lie. I explained my motives without blaming anyone else, and I asked for forgiveness. By the time I had written the two letters, I wasn't crying anymore. I felt peaceful and strong. It wasn't as bad as I thought it would be. I felt free. I mailed the letters and locked myself in my bedroom for 16 days. I didn't answer the telephone.

I didn't talk to my children or anyone else. I knew a part of me was going to die in that room; but I also knew I was ready to let that fearful, angry, unworthy, people-pleasing aspect of myself go to its final resting place.

So many of us think that if we act like a thing doesn't exist, it will just go away. When you are on a spiritual path, you must come face-to-face with yourself and acknowledge all of who you are. Only through this process will you will grow and become the embodiment of a true spiritual consciousness. We cannot teach what we do not know. We cannot talk what we do not walk. If we resist this truth, we create pain for ourselves. Learning and growing spiritually does not have to be painful. We make it painful by resisting the unpleasant parts of ourselves. Acknowledging the dysfunctional and unpleasant aspects of who we are is an essential part of the spiritual purification process. We must clean ourselves out in order to be purified and prepared to serve God and others. We must face and release the thoughts, habits, and beliefs that limit us. The fears of the old self must die in order for the new spiritualized self to be born. In order to do this, we must embrace and live by a code of conduct that embraces spiritual law.

In the quest for spiritual purification, enlightenment, and evolution, there are specific principles and understandings one must accept and incorporate into a life philosophy. The Spiritual Code of Conduct provides a basic framework for the development of individual desire, thought, and action that embodies the true nature of Spirit. It is not enough to pray, meditate, and visualize. One must reprogram one's thinking and indoctrination in order to absorb and be aligned with the principles of universal law. Purification embodies more than the elimination of toxins and meat from the diet. True spirituality requires acceptance of self as an expression of the Creator, and recognition of that same quality in all others. Our actions must be guided by spirit. The Bahá'í faith teaches, "Nearness to God is likeness of God," which means God-like principles must govern our behavior at all times.

The Spiritual Code of Conduct requires accepting your "oneness" with the Creator as the source of power, knowingness, truth, and order in your life. The code is judgment-free. It is the "I Am" principle, which acknowledges every individual as a unique expression of the Creator on a mission to serve the whole. For women, the following principles compose a Code of Spiritual Conduct that will result in the purification of the individual for the evolution of the entire group.

Unconditional Love

- Eliminates fear.

- The nonjudgmental acceptance and practice of good-will for yourself and all others exactly as they appear to be (e.g., beyond their behavior) in the moment.

- Not to be confused with lust, or with love of another because he or she loves you.

Unconditional love means to see everyone and everything as an extension of yourself, and to act toward others as you would want them to act toward you. Surrender of judgment, criticism, and ego is imperative. Unconditional love is evaluated by your ability, in any given situation, to work toward the best possible outcome for everyone involved. It is evaluated by the question: Am I promoting and/or creating what I would want for myself?

Truth

- Eliminates the misperceptions of the ego.

- The immutable laws of the universe that are in alignment with the mind of God as they operate in the physical world reality.

- Not to be confused with what you know or believe based on your knowledge and experience.

A life of spiritual integrity and empowerment requires you to know truth, accept truth, speak truth, teach truth, and seek truth. Truth is not what you believe based on your individual belief system. Truth is consistent throughout the universe because it reflects the mind of God. It reveals and produces joy and peace for everyone. It is evaluated by the question: Is what I am thinking, saying, and/or doing a reflection of what I know about the nature of God?

Willingness

- Eliminates resistance.

- The ability to accept what happens in the moment as the divine order of what needs to happen.

- Not to be confused with willfulness or doing whatever you want.

Willingness is the surrender of self-centered desire. It eliminates limitation of thought and action in response to misperceptions of reality. Willingness means doing whatever is required and in alignment with spiritual law, whether you want to or not. It is an act of faith and is evaluated by the question: Is God's will greater than my will?

Righteousness

- Eliminates manipulation.

- The right use of your mind, speech, talents, and resources in service to the highest good for yourself and others.

- Not to be confused with "I want to be right!"

Righteousness requires the purification of thought and desire in service of the truth. You must do what is most appropriate and loving considering all involved. It is evaluated by the question: What is the best possible thing to do/say that will create harmony or balance for all?

Responsibility

- Eliminates blame and projection.

- The ability to respond with a conscious intent without doing harm.

- Not to be confused with self-sacrifice and self-denial, or actions that impress others.

Responsibility is the willingness to be held accountable for every thought, word, and desire that manifests and motivates your behavior. It is evaluated by the questions: How did I contribute to this situation, circumstance, in which I find myself? And, what have I learned as a result of what I am experiencing?

Discipline

- Eliminates procrastination.

- Repeated actions that demonstrate internal and external cooperation in alignment with a specific intention.

- Not to be confused with selfishness, or self-denial.

With discipline, thoughts and actions are manifested in an orderly and consistent relationship to goals and responsibilities. Discipline is evaluated by the question: Am I doing all I must do to realize my vision, without harming myself or others?

Humility

- Eliminates feeling used or manipulated.

- Living, giving, and sharing from a heart-centered, egoless manner in service to others, without regard for reward or recognition.

- Not to be confused with being a doormat or sacrificing the self to please someone else.

Your actions must be prompted from a posture of service to the Creator and not for the satisfaction of the ego. Humility is giving for the sake of it, and not to promote self. It is evaluated by the question: What do I hope to gain for myself?

Compassion

- Eliminates false responsibility.

- Empathetic presence that inspires, motivates, and encourages rather than overpowers.

- Not to be confused with sympathy.

Compassion is the ability to place yourself in the position of another, without judgment, criticism, or the need to control. It is the realization that everyone is fully capable of resolving their difficulties and challenges, then standing with them in that awareness.

It is evaluated by the question: Am I my brother's keeper? And the answer is: No. I am my brother.

Perseverance

- Eliminates mental and physical weariness.

- Consciously committed action toward a desired outcome.

- Not to be confused with stubbornness or reckless action.

Dedication and commitment to a stated goal, even in the face of adversity, equals perseverance. When moving in truth and righteousness, one must know that the best will manifest. It is evaluated by the question: Am I being true to my stated intention?

Patience

- Eliminates hasty or unconscious choices.

- Courageous inner strength born of trust and humility.

- Not to be confused with laziness or inactivity.

Patience is accepting the concept of divine order for the perfect outcome of all situations, in relation to the Creator's goals. Patience is evaluated by the question: Is this the best time for the manifestation of my desire?

Speaking with a Conscious Tongue

- Eliminates negative words and energy.

- Not to be confused with speaking your mind, or saying anything you feel.

We must be mindful of the energy that our words create. Because every word we utter is a prayer, we must always speak in a manner that promotes love and harmony. Speaking consciously is evaluated by the question: Are my words kind, necessary, and for the highest good of everyone involved?

Selflessness

- Eliminates quest for ruthless power.

- Inner security that serves the heart and overrides the demands of the ego to conquer.

- Not to be confused with doing something to get something, or acting to get approval or acceptance.

Selflessness is a state of being and behavior that nurtures and supports others and promotes universal truths. It is evaluated by the question: What can I do to serve and support others in this experience?

Tithing

- Eliminates supporting unworthy spiritual sources.

- Grateful giving and sharing of resources to a person or place that encourages or supports your spiritual growth.

- Not to be confused with the obligation to give or pay for spiritual guidance.

Tithing requires one to give freely to the source of one's spiritual education for the purpose of maintaining that source. The universal law of reciprocity states that what we give, we get back one hundredfold. Tithing enacts this law.

Adherence to the Spiritual Code for Conduct supports the establishment of boundaries for our daily interactions and interpersonal relationships. These boundaries, or any boundaries of behavior that are grounded in spiritual principles, support and create a shift of mental, emotional, and physical energy. The result will be a more balanced, harmonious, and orderly approach to activity. For women on this spiritual path, this specific Spiritual Code of Conduct is in keeping with the ancient Kemetic (African) principle of Ma'at, as symbolized by the feather.

The Code of Ma'at

Ma'at is the intuitive sense of law and order that is aligned to and in harmony with divine and universal law, not the law of man. It is learning from within, based on who you are and what you have come to this life to learn and do! It is the foundation of life, symbolizing truth, righteousness, and moral conduct (intent). Ma'at encourages love, the principle of giving and asking nothing in return. It judges the heart, not the deed or external appearances. It is the universal law that evaluates the intent of your criticism and the truth of your actions.

When we pass from the physical to the spiritual plane (transition from life to death), Ma'at is the principle by which our life will be measured. If your heart was placed on a balancing scale with the feather of Ma'at, would the scale balance out? Using the Spiritual Code of Conduct as the tool by which we measure our lives will create peace within our heart toward others and within the world. It is this peace that will balance the scale of Ma'at.

On the path toward spiritual enlightenment, it is easy to mistake the lower nature of the ego as a newfound spiritual power. We can justify almost anything by saying, "Spirit told me..." or "My spirit says [thinks, feels]..." However, if we have not achieved a true spiritual consciousness, we are simply using spirit as a scapegoat for the ego. One must be cautious not to allow human emotions to color the principles of spirituality. Remember, spirit is energy! Consequently, there are spirits of light, as well as spirits of a lower, darker nature. Spirits of light follow universal law. Dark spirits satisfy human lusts and weaknesses. We create energy and attract spiritual energy that matches the level and state of our consciousness

As human beings, we are innately committed to the satisfaction of our physical senses. We are led by those things we can see, hear, touch, smell, and taste. We are socialized in a society that emphasizes tangible evidence as a source of security and control. We are trained and encouraged to accumulate tangible things to substantiate what we know and have. A brilliant, enlightened spiritual being becomes suspect without a degree; yet, a dark-hearted, egotistical individual with a degree is held up as a model being. As difficult as it may be, those on a spiritual path must seek to have a clear conscience and a personal sense of integrity, regardless of whether the outside world recognizes the light.

Unfortunately, satisfying the demands of our physical nature usually puts us in violation of universal law. Because our physical senses are enslaved by our will and ego, we are motivated to be in control of people and situations. Will and ego, ruled by emotions and perceptions, places the individual self first, whereas Spirit recognizes the Creator as the First Cause, the creative power in all things. The physical nature will use dark energy to achieve light, while Spirit moves in the light to achieve enlightenment. Unless we adhere to spiritual principles to govern our thoughts, conduct, and words, we will create harm and discord. And it is in this environment that dark spiritual energies are attracted to us for strength.

What we draw to us is what we are. Whatever the condition of our external life, it is a reflection of our internal state. For every physical sense, there is a spiritual equivalent. The physical eyes are related to the third or spiritual eye, located in the center of the forehead. The third eye sees truth from a universal perspective; physical eyes can relate only to what we know. The sense of hearing is related to the heart. The heart is centered in unconditional love, while our hearing is limited to emotions. The sense of touch is related to the life center, located in sexual organs. Touch is a function of desire, which must be purified by denial and sacrifice. The sex organs are the root of satisfaction of all lusts, not just the sexual. The sense of smell is related to the solar plexus, located in the center (stomach) region of the body. The solar plexus is the seat of our ability to make decisions, while the stomach is satisfied by the conscious will.

When we are motivated by satisfaction of the physical, without consideration for the spiritual, we fall into the trap of doing "what feels good." What feels good is not always best for us, in the final outcome. When we experience misfortune, delay, and disappointment in our physical life, it is a reflection of an imbalance in one of our spiritual centers.

As women, many of us are desperate to find a way out of our suffering, pain, and immobility. Most of us want peace and happiness. We are taught to look for happiness in things and people. We are indoctrinated to seek peace in what we are doing, rather than in who we are! Most of us are trained to be dependent and irresponsible, expecting others to create our happiness. We live according to roles, as opposed to purpose. These are the life issues that take us out of alignment with the laws of the universe. We will remain slaves to our weaknesses, our fears, and the lower nature of our human consciousness, until we surrender our will and ego to Spirit. As long as we continue to do what we *think* is right, without clear guidelines to know what is right, we will remain limited.

A spiritual brother of mine, who is of the Bahá'í faith, teaches that the only way to determine if you are in compliance with the Spiritual Code of Conduct is through a process of self-accounting. We must take ourselves into account each day to determine if we are moving in a spiritual light. This brother taught me that, before retiring each day, you must review your actions—from the last thing you did, to the first. After listing your activities, you should ask yourself the following questions:

- Who did I serve today?
- Who did I help today, without asking for payment?
- With whom did I share some knowledge today?
- Did I speak consciously today?
- Did I keep the agreements I made with myself today?
- Did I keep the agreements I made with others today?

As much as possible, your thoughts, behavior, and words should be in alignment with the code. When you miss the mark, don't beat yourself up. Forgive yourself by making a commitment to do better the next day. With patience, perseverance, and a conscious commitment, you will become more consciously enlightened.

Oh, my Glorious Lord, help me to
refrain from every irregular inclination;
To subdue every rebellious passion;
To purify the motives of my conduct;
To conform myself to that meekness
which no provocation can ruffle;
To that patience which no affliction can overwhelm;
To that integrity which no self interest
can shake, that I may be qualified
to serve Thee and teach Thy word.

—`Abdu'l-Bahá

What I Know Now

*Your life is a demonstration of your relationship
with God. Every behavior is a function of conscious
or unconscious choice. Knowing and embodying
spiritual principles transforms reactions into responses.*

A Prideful Encounter

I had already missed my submission deadline, so I was on a crash schedule to complete the book. I was working 14 to 15 hours a day, eating once, if I remembered, and sleeping in my clothes. Everyone I knew and loved did their best to leave me alone. They called only to make sure I was still breathing, knowing I would simply grunt my responses to their questions because all the words I knew were pouring out of me as my fingers tapped the computer keyboard. It was two o'clock in the afternoon when my significant other called. I was still wearing my pajamas. I tried. I really tried to pay attention to what he was saying because I had summarily dismissed him for the past two days. Typing slowly, hoping he would not hear the sound in the background, I still found it necessary to ask him to repeat every other statement. He tried. He really tried to bring me up to date on the events of his life. Failing miserably, he finally conceded.

"Go back to work, baby. I'll talk to you later."

"No, no, sweetie," I insisted. "I'm sorry. Now what did you say?"

He knew better. "No, you go back to work. Call me later."

He hung up long before I did. In fact, I didn't take the telephone away from ear until the operator told me hang up the telephone if I wanted to make a call.

As soon as the telephone hit the cradle, I got the message. It was as if a very tall, very stern teacher was whispering in my ear. Although the tone was gentle, almost soothing, I knew I was in trouble.

Are you so busy that you don't have time to let him love you?

My heart sank and my mouth instantly became dry because I knew it was true. There was more.

The way you treat him is the same way you treat God—too busy to be loved.

I thought I was going to faint. Thank goodness I was sitting down. Instead, I dropped my head in shameful horror.

As my mind took me back over the past two weeks of my life, the best I could do was assume the position. I put my hands up over my head and spoke aloud, "I surrender." I knew I was caught and convicted of bad behavior. I had been driving myself to the point of exhaustion, dishonoring my body and my mind. I was not being kind or loving to myself, and I was extending the same disservice to those who loved and cared about me. My son had arranged for me to have six hours of treatment at a day spa. I had canceled twice because I had to finish the book. My sweetie checked in every day, sometimes twice a day, and I hadn't taken the time to be present and speak to him. Friends wanted to cook for me. I told them no, thank you. Hour after hour I sat to meet the demands of a schedule that I had created, a schedule that I had convinced myself was necessary. I tried to tell myself, "You gotta do what you gotta do," but the Holy Spirit was not going to let me get away with it. *If God is love, and if He loves you, then you are too busy for God.* With that, I turned off the computer and got in the shower.

There was a time when I could convince myself that almost anything I did was okay as long as I did it for the right reason. *I'm better now!* What I know now is that you cannot violate spiritual law or a Spiritual Code of Conduct for any reason and get away with it. When you are out of order, you are out of order. Period! That 24-hour schedule our bodies are accustomed to must include time for eating, sleeping, and other life-giving and productive activities. When we push the body beyond its limits, we harm ourselves and others. We overload our circuits, place undue pressure on the bodily systems, and disrupt the orderly flow of life that is gifted to us. Because the body is the temple of the Spirit of God, it must be valued and honored. It must be nurtured and cared for. It must be fed and washed. I know these things, and, yes, even me, Lord! I forget. I push the limits. The good news is that I have a relationship with the spiritual realm that offers me loving and gentle correction when I push the envelope too far. This day was a day when I was totally on the brink of violating everything I knew, because for just one second, I tried to ignore the voice of Spirit.

Self-Correction Is Essential
to the Spiritual Code of Conduct

The moment I stepped out of the shower I called him back and apologized. Because he loves and supports me, he offered me an escape route.

"It's really not a problem. I know you're busy."

I was tempted, but I also knew better.

"Thank you, my love." I wanted him to really hear me because I knew it was a lesson for both of us. "But it is unacceptable to me and to God that when you show up in my life to love me, I am too busy to be present. If God is love, then you are a manifestation of God's love in my life. I create my own schedule. I make time for what I think is important, and anytime I don't have time to receive love, yours or God's, I need to reevaluate my schedule."

The telephone line was silent. I was just about to say hello when he responded, "I am overwhelmed because I know I do the same thing."

I asked his forgiveness several times before he could respond. When he did and we hung up, I ran a bath, broiled myself a nice piece of salmon, made a salad, ate, bathed, and I took a nap. When I awakened three hours later, the book was still there, my mind was clear, and I was in alignment with what I know to be true; God works through a rested mind and opened heart.

Governing your life by a Spiritual Code of Conduct means having a set of guidelines, standards, and/or boundaries for self-correction. You don't have to wait for some disaster to befall your life or body before taking course-corrective action. It is your spiritual responsibility to honor yourself and your life in the process of serving God. We can make an excuse for almost anything. We can always find a good reason to be self-abusive, self-righteous, and, often, self-destructive. As my coach Steve Hardison once told me, "Your life will only work to the degree that you refuse to accept or offer excuses for bad behavior." It is not personally productive or spiritually conducive to engage in bad behavior, even when you have perfectly legitimate reasons to do so. Bad behavior is not only what you do or say to others, it is also what you think about, do to, and speak to yourself. In many instances, we take on more than is required in service to an unconscious need or an unhealed wound. We deny our own needs and desires, believing that's what is required to provide adequate service to something or someone external to ourselves. This is not to say that there won't be occasions when we are required to go the extra mile to complete a task or honor a commitment. We must be mindful not to make a steady diet out of late nights, missed meals, broken nails, tired feet, bird baths, and quick showers.

Over the years, the code for my spiritual conduct has evolved. I have become clearer about my weak spots, committed to eliminate my mischievous behavior, and conscious of the myriad of tricky methods I employ to escape my spiritual responsibilities to myself. My current spiritual code focuses on building spiritual character, spiritual integrity, and spiritual strength. It is my deepest desire to be the best me I can be in service to God, myself, and my purpose. I also want to be around for a long, long time, fully-able and productively contributing to the evolution of human consciousness. I know how slippery I can be, so I started with a clear intention. I share that with you now, as well as my new code, encouraging you to consider them for your own practice so that we may all evolve together.

Spiritual Code of Conduct Prayer

*It is my sincere, reverent, and humble intention
to open my heart and lay down all defenses.
I ask for and open myself to receive correction and direction from the
Holy Spirit as it relates to any limitations present in my consciousness
as a thought, feeling, belief, attitude, judgment, projection,
perception, learning, or pattern of behavior that in any way hinders,
blocks, delays, or obstructs my willingness, readiness, or ability
to make self-loving, self-honoring choices in every aspect of my life.*

*I ask that the parts of me that are ready to be healed and the parts
of me that resist healing be brought into submission and service of
God's will for the highest and greatest good of all involved.*
Let it be so!
And so it is!

Act as If You Know the Truth

- *Never Underestimate Your Own Need, Ability, or Power to
  Effect Change in Your Life*

When I was 20, I knew everything I needed to know. I checked
in with other people only to make sure I was right. When I was
30, I knew everything and felt it was my duty to let others know
what I knew. When I was 40, I realized that I didn't know much,
and half of what I did know had changed since I first knew it. At
50-something, I remember less than half of what I thought I knew.
My point is, we are changing, moment by moment. Internally and
externally, new information is always being presented to us. It is a
mistake to believe you know all there is to know about anything
or anyone, including yourself. Be willing to be a student of life
forever. Be willing to grow. Be willing to learn. Be willing to heal.
Make your internal landscape your homeroom class, and check
in frequently. Make your external world of experience your study
hall, where you observe, take notes, and sharpen your skills.

- *Mind Your Own Business First*

One of the most powerful lessons I garnered from my study of Byron
Katie's The Work is: Stay in your own car. I expanded that notion to:
Stay in your own car, in your own lane, on your own road, in your
own world. This is a spiritually advanced way of encouraging you to
mind your own business before you go out helping people or telling
them how to do what they do. As a recovering control freak and
the mother of adult children, I have found this concept particularly

helpful. After a consistent and conscious practice of self-reflection, I discovered that my drive to fix, change, or correct others was actually of function of the things *I* feared. And the things I wanted to correct in my children were the things *I* was ashamed of or guilty about in myself. I also noticed that each time I attempted to drive someone else's car—in other words, fix their life—something in my own world crashed. Well, of course! If no one is driving my car—meaning my life, my mind, my heart, and my affairs—it is headed for danger. I also realized there was a distinction between *helping* someone and *supporting* him. "Help" meant I was attached to the outcome. "Support" meant I waited to be invited in, and did only what enhanced harmony in my own life.

- *Seek Harmony*

What I know now is that harmony is a higher principle than balance. Very often, as we strive to achieve balance, we actually create an environment for the polarity, or opposite, which is *im*balance. Harmony means creating a life in which everything gives to and supports every other aspect of your life. Creating harmony encourages us to give time and share time with others doing those things that are life-affirming, life-supporting, and life-enhancing. It requires that your mind and heart, your work and play, your physical reality and spiritual reality enhance each other and add value to others.

- *Replace External Referencing with Inner Authority*

Hear Ye! Hear Ye! Calling all overcommitting people pleasers! You have the inherent right, ability, and power to determine what goes on in your own life. In fact, you are the only one who gets to say what goes on in your life. Your inner authority is the producer and director of your authentic identity; it is the aspect of your being that is a demonstration of God. One of your purposes in life is to awaken to this aspect of your being, and to celebrate it in all that you do. You cannot stand fully in the truth of your being if you make the needs, demands, acceptance, and approval of others more important than your own inner voice. Stop it! Putting the voice of others before your own voice is an example of poor spiritual hygiene.

- *Stop Being Bad and Wrong*

I have done many things in my life that I am not proud of, and God still loves me. I know this is true because it was the grace of God's love that has taught me to distinguish between the belief that I am *bad to the bone* and the belief that I have a latent propensity for making unwise, uninformed, or downright stupid choices and decisions. Like everyone else, I am a creation of God. This means that our essence—our core—is pure and innocent. This is a truth that cannot be altered by any mode of dysfunctional behavior. Believe in your goodness! Affirm your divinity!

- *Take Your Rightful Place*

For some reason (most probably because someone told us) we believe that it is pleasing to God and obedient to Spirit to deny our gifts and power. Some of us have difficulty accepting a compliment. We deny our beauty, question our innate talents, and undercharge for the expert services we offer to the world. We embrace a false sense of humility because we have been socialized to believe that it is bad or wrong to a have a sense of pride in who we are or what we do. I encourage you to be mindful that there is a distinction between self-aggrandizement and honorable self-affirmation. Your rightful place is in the latter.

- *Go for the Joy!*

What I know now is that happiness is a temporary condition that arises from external stimulation. Joy is a state of mind and being that feeds and nurtures the soul. Many things that make us happy satisfy the demands of the ego. Joy is a Spirit-driven, Spirit-

263

TAPPING THE POWER WITHIN

given experience. When we have joy, we are centered in the heart, grounded in calm, and unshaken by the world at large. Joy is a function of knowing the truth, trusting the truth, and living the truth of your being. When you have joy, you don't worry about losing it. Quite often when we have an experience of happiness, we are watching and waiting for the next shoe to fall.

Now That You've Got It, Use It at Your Discretion

My heart weeps with joy when I realize all that I have experienced, learned, and been able to share with you. Yet I also understand that your expectations and commitment to practice will determine the outcome and what you receive. As with anything of a spiritual nature, there is no way I can tell you what to expect. Spiritual healing, growth, and evolution is a process, much like the turning of leaves, the growth of body parts, and the graying of hair: it just happens! Neither you nor I can pinpoint the exact moment you will have a full-body experience of your spiritual connection to the Creator of your life and all of His creations. However, when it does happen, you will know it.

Nothing can help you unless you *believe* it can help you! If you have read this book believing it will provide you with information, then that is exactly what you have gotten. Nothing more, nothing less. And that may work for you. If you believe this information can help you achieve clarity, peace, strength, health, love, or good fortune, then that is what you will see manifest in your life. Where the mind goes, the life follows! If you believe you are too far gone, too messed up, too confused to make sense of the things I have shared in this book, then you will believe it has been a waste of your time. You and what you believe are the key factors in all of your experiences.

There will be people who are in total disagreement with as much as 75 percent of what I have shared. There will be others who will use some and discard the rest. To yet others, these pages will contain the revelation they have prayed to receive! No matter which category you fit into, this book will bring you exactly what you have been looking for. Actually, this book does not tell you anything you do not already know! The keys to your kingdom are within you! Having the keys, however, can be very frustrating if you do not know which doors they fit and if you don't have the faith to unlock them. What this book does is structure the mechanics. Spirit will give you exactly what you need, when you need it, if you are honestly searching. With that in mind, I leave you with the words of a song written by my spiritual sister and friend Rickie Byars Beckwith and her husband, my brother Rev. Dr. Michael Bernard Beckwith:

I release and I let go, I let the spirit run my life.
Now my heart is opened wide because I am only here for God.

Chapter 15

PRECAUTIONS
FOR YOUR
JOURNEY

The level of crisis we create in our lives is amazing! Unnecessary—but amazing! For me it was a financial crisis. My life consisted
of people coming to cut something off, to repossess something, or
to put me out of somewhere. As a child, I was never taught how
to budget. Like my parents, I lived hand to mouth. I believed I did
not have enough money to save, so I never did! I wanted so much,
while believing I had too little. When I did have money, I bought
what I wanted in rebellion against my lack of things. When the
financial crisis hit me, I beat myself up for what I had done with
my money.

I had a million reasons for not paying my bills: My public
assistance budget wasn't adequate; the children needed shoes; I
deserved a new dress. Many of my friends who were also on public
assistance would sympathize with my plight. We would borrow
and lend money among ourselves, as we bemoaned our fate. It
never once dawned on us that *we* were responsible for creating the
life we desired and for better budgeting. Instead, we would gather
and share war stories. One day, at a round-table discussion of our
poverty, one of my friends suggested that "someone must have
done something to me!" That was the only explanation she could
come up with for her continued bad luck. She told us that, where
she came from, people would burn candles, make a special powder,

and drop it at your door, and do things with your picture. If they wanted your man, they would go to all lengths to make your life miserable. Some of the women laughed. Some asked probing questions. I kept my mouth shut and made a mental note!

Without a clear understanding of what to look for, I set out to find a spiritualist who could tell me if something had been done to me, too! The newspaper was full of advertisements. I was drawn to an ad that read: "It takes a special power to clear financial blocks— I've got it!" I called immediately to make an appointment.

As soon as I walked in the door, I knew it was a mistake, but, believing I was desperate and helpless, I decided to keep my appointment. The waiting room was cluttered with people, furniture, knickknacks, newspapers, and dust! None of that bothered me, but the darkness did. The room *felt* dark. When "Dr. Bones" called my name, I jumped to my feet. He led me into the kitchen, where he had a candle, several glasses of water, an opened Bible, and hundreds of jars of "stuff." He turned the pages of the Bible and, without asking my name, began to tell me about my life. My mother's death. My neglected childhood. How many children I had and the order of their birth. My faltering relationship and my financial devastation. I was shocked!

He made up a little jar of something. I was to wash my hands three times a day for ten days. I gave him $50. If things did not improve, I was to come back on the tenth day. After I left his office, I was sticking the key in my apartment door before I fully realized where I was or how I had gotten there. Ten days later, the telephone was disconnected, I owed two months' rent, and the refrigerator was bare! I called, and Dr. Bones instructed me to come right over.

This time, Dr. Bones let me in on the seriousness of my problem. Somebody had "fixed" my boyfriend so that he would leave me. He had brought an evil spirit into my house, and that was why our relationship was going sour! The spirit, Dr. Bones said, was in my stomach. What I needed to do, he said, was take my panties off and let him place some Run, Devil, Run! oil in my vagina. It would cost another $75, with guaranteed results. Reality hit me with a blast!

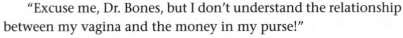

"Excuse me, Dr. Bones, but I don't understand the relationship between my vagina and the money in my purse!"

He became very stern.

"If you want to get your life together, stop acting foolish. I see hundreds of people a week. What makes you think I want you?"

My memory scanned the waiting room. I was the only person younger than 50!

"I'll tell you what. Give me the oil and I'll put it where it should be!"

Reluctantly, he handed me the bottle of Run, Devil, Run! oil, and pointed me toward the bathroom. My pants were around my ankles, and I was sniffing the bottle of oil when the doctor crept into the bathroom. When our eyes met, I knew instantly that my telephone bill would not be paid and that I would probably get evicted! "Please don't" were the only words I could speak. I am not sure whether or not there was smirk or a sneer on his face, but I do know that something dark and evil passed between us. When it did, I made the first move. Scrambling into the corner, trying to pull my pants up, I dropped the bottle of oil!

"Oh s--t!" He screamed at me. "Look what you're doing!"

Dr. Bones was on his knees trying to save the oil. I stepped over him, grabbed my things, and left! Three blocks away, I started crying. I cried all the way home!

Why is it that we must be in a state of desperation before we look for God? Marianne Williamson, author of *A Return to Love*, says, "A nervous breakdown is an opportunity for a spiritual breakthrough—the chance for God to clean up your spirit and life! A nervous condition means you are not getting the point!" I was definitely on the verge of a nervous breakdown!

I spent the afternoon moping around the house. Each time I thought about the "doctor," I would cry harder and louder. How was I supposed to know he was a rip-off? He was using a Bible for God's sake! The $125 I gave him would have paid some part of the telephone bill! I sat on the edge of the bed for hours, letting the thoughts flood my mind. I was SOS—stuck on stupid—and it was embarrassing. Working very hard not to be disgusted with myself, I noticed a newspaper on the floor. Without thinking, I picked it up and started thumbing through. Just below the advertisement for Dr. Bones, I saw an ad that read: "Free consultation by telephone!" Now, just how dumb can I be? Dumb enough to call! I went to the corner telephone booth. The line was busy for 15 minutes. Then, on my very next call, a woman answered on the first ring, saying, "Let us pray."

For the next several minutes, a soft melodic voice filled my mind! I was told how beautiful I was, and how much God loved me! I heard a plea go up for my clarity, safety, and peace! I was reminded that anything I needed to know, I already knew! I was told that anything I wanted or needed, I already had! I was instructed to confess my heart and ask for forgiveness and guidance. I was told to get "still" and let the love of the Almighty fill my mind! I was further instructed not to eat or speak for the next six hours, and that the answer would come, no matter what the question was. In 14 days, I was to put $25 in an envelope and send it to PO Box GOD, the code for Box 764, in Brooklyn, New York! I went home and followed all of her instructions. Seven days later, the telephone was back on, the refrigerator was full, and the rent was paid up to date! I put $100 in an envelope and mailed it to Mother Mary!

This is not an easy task you are about to undertake, yet it is a necessary one! You are about to alter your conscious and unconscious state! You are attempting to shift and manipulate energy! You are moving to touch the foundation of your being! You are going to meet challenges and obstacles. *You, yourself, are going to be the greatest obstacle you will encounter!*

Change is difficult. Change is frightening. Change is constant. Change is inevitable. Change is an "inside job"! As you begin to change, something deep inside of you is going to resist your efforts. You will gravitate to what is known, what is familiar—even those thoughts, habits, and people who have not been positive in your life. Remember, once you commit yourself to a path of spiritual growth, spirit will give you what you need, when you need it! Do not be surprised by anything you see, hear, or experience that shakes some belief you have held! Simply affirm for truth to be revealed, and for strength and understanding to be provided.

You may begin to notice that your thoughts and feelings about certain things and people will change. Trust your head! Understand that feelings are "e-motions"—the energy that moves us from one place to another. You are moving from one level of spiritual consciousness to another. Your emotions will move you from thinking and behaving in a nonproductive manner to a more productive manner, by revealing to you all nonproductive forces. Remember, however, that the choice to move remains yours! Spirit will not move you for you! Affirm for clarity and direction to act and move in the best way for the benefit of all concerned.

You should not discuss the intimate details of your ritual, experiences, and revelations with too many people. If you are not clear or sure of anything you experience, pray and meditate for guidance. Know that "when the student is ready, the teacher will appear!" Do not look for someone to do it for you! What you want is for someone or something to provide you with guidance and assistance. This may come in the form of a book, a lecture, a dream, or even a television commercial! Be on the lookout for your answer and, above all, *trust your head.* It will tell you what is right for you!

Another helpful hint is to keep a journal of your thoughts and experiences. This is a way to keep your mind clear while you are evolving, and a method to solidify your thoughts. You can capture in your journal writing what is hard to capture in thought. When you can read your thoughts, you find the realities as well as the inconsistencies. Above all, writing is a release! You can release and clear your mind to receive new and improved information, which will aid in your growth.

Finally, be very careful of what you say during your development process. Never say "never!" Avoid "I can't," "I don't know," and "I am confused." Keep your thoughts and words to, and about, yourself positive and encouraging! Do not talk about what you do not want—"I don't want to stop," "go," "fail." Speak about yourself and what you desire in positive terms. Avoid the temptation to condemn, judge, or speak negatively about anyone or anything during this time. As your spiritual vision and your understanding sharpen, you will recognize that things are not always as they seem! You want to avoid negative pronouncements that you may later be forced to retract. Above all, stay up, stay open, and stay in tune. Spirit will pave the way. Walk in balance, with faith in your divinity!

So do not throw away this confident trust in the Lord.
Remember the great reward it brings you! Patient endurance
is what you need now, so that you will continue to do God's will.
Then you will receive all that he has promised.

— Hebrews 12:35-36

What I Know Now

You can delay, avoid, and resist spiritual growth, but
you cannot fail. Everything you experience is a lesson you
must learn. Do not discount your lessons. Healing and
growth are natural processes, so keep it simple.

Let Eyes That Can See!

In my mind, I was simply being a good Yeye. That's what my grandchildren call me; it is the Yoruba word for "grandmother." I took my youngest grandson, Ade, to get his eyeglasses repaired. He was born with an underdeveloped muscle in one eye. We recently discovered that the eye has no sight, which makes it necessary for Ade to wear glasses to protect and strengthen the eye that does have vision. When we arrived at LensCrafters, I discovered that they were having a sale. An extensive eye examination was only $39.99. Being the highly skilled shopper that I am, I could not pass up a sale, so I signed up for an eye exam. It was a truly enlightening, high-tech experience. I was particularly fond of the part where, without notice, a machine squirts air into your eyes to test you for glaucoma. It was shocking! It was surprising! The results of my eye examination were equally shocking and surprising!

I had no idea that I could not see! According to the examination results, I needed not one, but three pairs of eyeglasses. I needed a pair for reading, a pair for driving, and a pair for working on the computer. I vehemently refused to purchase three pairs of glasses. I bought two because they had nice frames. If I have to wear glasses, they must be fly. No horn-rims. No rhinestones. I'm talking diva-fly eyewear! But I digress.

The optometrist explained to me that vision normally wanes with age. I supported her in establishing a new belief: *Your vision changes with usage.* Fortunately, as the doctor explained, your eyes will adjust to the degree of strain you place on them, or the degree of defect that is present. Eventually, you become unaware that letters are not as big as they once were. You adjust the distance at which you hold a document in order for you to be able to read the fine print. When you can't read it, you try to remember what it says from a time when you could read it. Or, if you're like me, you go to the discount drugstore and find a snazzy pair of magnifying eyeglasses. My point is: How many of us walk around without the slightest clue that *we really cannot see what we are looking at? Or the things we are looking for?*

Reluctantly, I put the driving glasses on to see if they made any difference. Cars suddenly became closer, license plates got bigger, and street signs were readable. At first, I was horrified. No wonder I kept getting lost, missing streets, turning the wrong way. I thought of all the accidents I could have had. Then I realized that I had no way of knowing that my vision was diminishing, because my eyes had adjusted themselves to accommodate the deficiency. Such is life, and such as it is *in* life. We cannot change a thing, alter a condition, or improve ourselves until we become aware that there is a problem, limitation, or deficiency. Until we gain awareness, we have a tendency to accommodate conditions, to tolerate a limited perspective, and to allow ourselves to believe that some things have gone awry (which, by the way, has nothing to do with us). Yes, awareness is a very important principle. Without it, you can crash and burn in your own ignorance and resistance. With it, things become clearer, easier to see, and so much easier to change.

Awareness is the cornerstone of self-discovery, self-realization, and spiritual empowerment. Awareness of self, needs, values, talents, latent gifts, abilities, and of desires to serve, give, receive, grow, shine, and be authentically present in every aspect of your life puts you in the driver's seat. Awareness of beliefs, distorted perceptions, inappropriate and unproductive behaviors, and of secret, silent, unconscious addictions and attachments gives you power— the power to make the choice to change. Without awareness, you are merely the passenger in a car with worn tire treads, on a long and spiraling road. Traveling in the dark of night, you just don't know if you're going to make it to your destination, or what shape you will be in when you get there, because you can't drive and the driver's been drinking. Until we are aware, we are powerless to make conscious choices. Once we become aware, choice becomes a responsibility we willingly embrace rather than a task we avoid. *Awareness is a key element of spiritual growth, healing, and evolution.* Like me, once you become aware of what is possible for you, no matter how far-fetched it may seem to you and everyone else, you cannot resist every opportunity to make your vision of yourself and your vision for your life a reality.

You know better than anyone else what you need to do and what no longer serves you. Looking outside of yourself for your answers will inevitably prove dangerous and disappointing. Believing that someone else knows more, or is more spiritually gifted than you are, can result in your being deceived or disappointed. The only thing others have that makes them more grounded, focused, or evolved is awareness. They are aware of God's presence within; they are aware of the process for tapping into that presence; they are aware of the moments when they receive inner guidance, and they are aware of the benefits of following the inner guidance they receive. The only thing any of us needs to experience and express the authentic identity of our God-like Self is the awareness that it actually exists and the acknowledgment of our desire to be a demonstration of all that it is. We must desire a spiritual expression because that is the truth of our being. Walking a spiritual path in an attempt to escape or avoid the trials of being human simply will not work. God loves a joyful giver. When you give yourself and your life over to the Spirit of God for healing and evolution, you must do so with no strings attached.

On a Clear Day

When this book was published 20 years ago, the commercial literature available that addressed the process of spiritual growth and healing was limited. There were classic books written by authors that many in the new world of self-help still may not know. The point is that today the market is flooded with an abundance of theories and practices designed to support the average person with the information and tools necessary to tap into her spiritual power, whether or not she has a religious or spiritual foundation. Why, one might wonder, if this is the case, are there still so many people faltering, suffering, and experiencing discontent? What I know now is that many of us still do not know what we are seeking. We embark upon a spiritual search with a preconceived idea of what we should experience and what we can expect as a result. Few of us understand our need for mental or emotional healing. Others dismiss the connection between our physical-world experiences and our spiritual curriculum. In large order we know the words and mouth them with great skill and enthusiasm, but when it comes down to it, we simply do not want to do the work. It is time-consuming, frightening, and sometimes looks as if we are getting nowhere fast!

Healing, the restoration of wholeness, the evolution of consciousness, the expression of unconditional love that flows from a forgiving heart, and the development of spiritual discipline all require work—deep, inner work that will, more often than not, show us things about ourselves that we would rather not see. In lieu of doing the work, we become seat warmers at spiritual workshops. Rather than taking that long hard look in the Mirror of Self, we read the books and quote the authors. We have become so accustomed to living in a society of microwave meals that we tend to seek shortcuts to feeling better and acquiring more knowledge about things of a spiritual nature.

True spiritual inner power can result only from an almost ruthless commitment to do the consistent, sometimes arduous work required to free your mind from every false thought; to heal your heart of every toxic emotion; to cleanse your life of every dysfunctional behavior; and to be, do, and have only that which is in alignment with the divine mind of God. And the work required is an ongoing process that presents both overt and sometimes hidden rewards. What I know now is that anyone on the path of spiritual evolution must realize that she will not get full-time rewards for part-time practice. When it is your desire to make God, your spirit, and a life of spiritual integrity a priority, the blessings you will receive are not for you alone. They are to serve as a demonstration of what is possible to others.

The following is offered as an updated version of precautions for your spiritual journey:

- Begin an active and continuous process of self-care and self-nurturing. It is essential that you learn how to love yourself as you move through the process of mental and emotional healing that leads to spiritual transformation.

- Do not ignore or dismiss your right and ability to make conscious choices of what is right for you regardless of the circumstances that confront you in any given moment.

- Practice forgiveness at every opportunity. Once you have forgiven, forgive again.

- Focus your time and energy on a deeper realization,

experience, and expression of love rather than an elimination or a change of external influences and experiences.

- Do your own independent investigation of what is true, loving, and nurturing for your soul as it relates to God and things of a spiritual nature. Once you do, seek and find the sacred text that validates and elevates your experience. Live the wisdom of that text.

- Be mindful not to dismiss or ignore the active presence and value of your ancestral culture in your spiritual development.

- Be aware that all spiritual work is a divine opportunity to re-create your internal landscape. It is a journey toward wholeness, meaning a state of conscious holiness, which is the truth of your being.

- Know that your spiritual evolution is a lifelong process. There are levels of self-betrayal, self-abandonment, and self-hatred that will continue to come to the surface. This does not mean that you did anything wrong, or that you are not doing something right. Keep working with yourself and within yourself.

Ask! Knock! Receive!

As you begin or continue on your path of spiritual evolution, enlightenment, and empowerment, I suggest that you pray for a deeper awareness of your divinity, your nobility, and your ability to discern between the truth and that which is not. I insist that you pray that those aspects of yourself that are ready to heal and grow be stronger than those aspects that are afraid to heal, grow, or change. Set a clear intention to remain open to the most appropriate steps for your spiritual evolution, and surrender all expectations of what can or may happen. Above all else, pray earnestly that your journey to wholeness, healing, and transformation of your mind and heart be easy, gentle, and divinely directed. Spiritual work is not a job. It is a privilege. Just as it is a privilege to be alive at this time in the history of the world, it is a privilege to endeavor to live the best life possible.

Suggested Reading

Beckwith, Michael Bernard, Rev.: *Forty Day Mind Fast Soul Feast*
An internationally recognized minister, teacher, and metaphysician, Rev. Beckwith teaches us how to tune out the *chirping* noises of the world and focus the mind on the inner presence of God. Through this process, the mind becomes a compass that will continually turn and tune you into the presence of Spirit.

Clark, Glenn: *I Will Lift Up Mine Eyes*
An amazing story and process offered by the author that details how to become totally dependent on God.

Ferrini, Paul: *Silence of the Heart: Reflections of the Christ Mind*
Spirituality is not just an ascent into the light—it is also a descent into the shadowy world. Without the descent, we would not develop the strength and wisdom we need to be keepers of the flame. In this work the author brings us *Reflections of the Christ Mind* that facilitate a deeper understanding of the requirements for living and loving fully.

Foundation for Inner Peace: *A Course in Miracles*
The *Course* is arranged throughout as a teaching device. It consists of three books: the 622-page text, a 478-page Workbook for Students, and an 88-page Manual for Teachers. The order in which students choose to use the books, and the ways in which they

study them, depend on their particular needs and preferences. The *Course* teaches that there are only two emotions—love and fear—and offers an understanding of why forgiveness is the road to inner peace.

Hurnard, Hannah: *Hinds' Feet on High Places*

This is the story of a young woman named Much-Afraid, and her journey away from her Fearing family and into the High Places of the Shepherd, guided by her two companions, Sorrow and Suffering. An allegory of a devotional life, the book takes its title from Habakkuk 3:19, "The Lord God is my strength, and he will make my feet like hinds' feet, and he will make me to walk upon mine high places."

Johnson, Deborah L. Rev.: *Letters from the Infinite: The Sacred Yes*

Each letter is a conversation, discrete in its own message. The lessons are universal, addressing the human condition common to us all. They provide solace, insight, and inspiration for our hurts, fears, hopes, hesitations, and aspirations.

Johnson, Jesse and Melva: *Mining for Gold in Your Relationships*

The stories of 14 real-life people who have used the author's MFG process to transform their relationships. The steps are simple, easy to understand, and extremely effective.

Jones, Laurie Beth: *Jesus, Life Coach: Learn From the Best*

Jesus had three years to train the 12 disciples, yet in that time he managed to turn a group of ragamuffins into "lean, clean faith machines." The book—divided into four critical sections: Focus, Balance, Productivity, and Fulfillment—presents a faith-based coaching program with Jesus as the model and delving into the principles Jesus used to transform those around him.

Kinnear, Willis Hayes: *The 30 Day Mental Diet: The Way to a Better Life*

Like every other diet, this one requires that you follow it through to the end. While on this diet, you'll encounter numerous ideas that may be somewhat new. But they are ideas whose nutritious value and productivity can result in a greater degree of health, happiness, or success.

Katie, Byron and Stephen Mitchell: *Loving What Is: Four Questions That Can Change Your Life*

The Work consists of four questions that, when applied to a specific problem, enable you to see what is troubling you in an entirely different light. As Katie says, "It's not the problem that causes our suffering; it's our thinking about the problem." Contrary to popular belief, trying to let go of a painful thought never works; instead, once we have done The Work, the thought lets go of us. At that point, we can truly love what is, just as it is.

Katie, Byron and Stephen Mitchell: *A Thousand Names for Joy: Living in Harmony with the Way Things Are*

This is a sweet, gentle book that supports the reader in understanding and seeing beyond the emotional impact of an experience to the lesson and the joy. Simply magnificent!

Miller, Patrick D.: *The Book of Practical Faith*

Faith can be sensible and savvy, and practicing it daily increases its reliability. Yet faith is also tinged with mystery, for it is the connection to our unknown potential and the power of creation. Faith is the way out of misery, the way into self-knowledge, and the way toward a more effective and fulfilling life.

Morrisey Manin, Mary: *No Less Than Greatness: Seven Miracle Principles That Make Real Love Possible*

The author affirms that love is our birthright—and learning to love well is life's greatest lesson. She shows that we are not alone in our search. When we learn to ask for and listen to divine guidance, we access a different kind of wisdom, a new kind of hope.

Muller, Wayne: *Legacy of the Heart: The Spiritual Advantages of a Painful Childhood*

The author does a masterful job of translating the most common and most painful experiences of childhood and how to heal the heart of the effects in order to live productively as an adult.

Tipping, Colin C.: *Radical Forgiveness: Making Room for the Miracle*

The concept of *Radical Forgiveness* enables us to see the spiritual meaning in any situation, the big picture. When we can see it, we are able to recognize that life is divinely guided and unfolding for each of us exactly how it needs to unfold for our highest good. We are able to surrender to the flow of life and to learn that ultimately, there is nothing to forgive.

Watson, Alan and Robert Perry: *A Course in Miracles Workbook Companion*

This book takes the 365 lessons from *A Course in Miracles* and breaks them down into daily lessons and practices.

Werber, Eva Bell: *Quiet Talks with the Master*

This is one volume in a four book series that offers insightful, channeled meditations by the author. Each meditation, offered in the first person, is like a direct conversation between the reader and the Creator.

About the Author

Iyanla Vanzant is the founder and executive director of Inner Visions International and the Inner Visions Institute for Spiritual Development. She is a Yoruba priestess and an ordained minister in Christian New Thought. The author of 13 titles—including five *New York Times* bestsellers, and the Inner Visions Series of Meditation CDs—she is the former host of the television series *Iyanla* and co-host on the NBC daytime reality show *Starting Over* as well. The proud grandmother of five, and avid scrapbook enthusiast, resides in Maryland.

Inner Visions Institute for Spiritual Development

Personal Development
Spiritual Life Coaching Certification
Ministerial Orientation

The curriculum of the Inner Visions Institute for Spiritual Development has its foundation in the exploration of universal spiritual laws and principles. The principles are the basis for:

- Identifying and clearing unconscious or non-productive thought and behavior patterns.

- Developing a spiritual consciousness and embracing a spiritual identity.

- Developing an understanding of how your unique identity has been impacted and enhanced by life experiences.

- Balancing the demands of external or physical life with the desires of the internal or spiritual life.

It is our intention to guide and support our students through the experiential process of remembering and embracing their Divine nature.

We believe that the Divine nature of every individual is supported and enhanced through knowledge and integration of universal laws and spiritual principles. What we teach is not new. However, we share with our students a new process and format for incorporating these ancient principles into daily living.

Our curriculum provides the student with a first-hand knowledge of how to utilize the power of their Divine and spiritual nature as a basis for all of life's experiences. With this understanding, students are empowered and prepared to make better choices resulting in a more fulfilling life. For more information, or to be placed on our mail list to be informed about upcoming events, we invite you to visit our Website: **www.Innervisionsworldwide.com**

Titles of Related Interest

DVDs

YOU CAN HEAL YOUR LIFE, the movie, starring Louise L. Hay & Friends
(available as a 1-DVD program and an expanded 2-DVD set)
Watch the trailer at: **www.LouiseHayMovie.com**

BOOKS

NEVER MIND SUCCESS...GO FOR GREATNESS!
The Best Advice I've Ever Received, by Tavis Smiley

YOU CAN HEAL YOUR LIFE, by Louise L. Hay

CARD DECKS

EMPOWERMENT CARDS: A-50 CARD DECK, by Tavis Smiley

EMPOWERMENT CARDS for Inspired Living, by Tavis Smiley

TIPS FOR DAILY LIVING CARDS: A 50-Card Deck, by Iyanla Vanzant

UNTIL TODAY CARDS: A 50-CARD DECK, by Iyanla Vanzant

All of the above are available at your
local bookstore, or may be ordered by visiting:

Hay House USA: **www.hayhouse.com**®
Hay House Australia: **www.hayhouse.com.au**
Hay House UK: **www.hayhouse.co.uk**
Hay House South Africa: **www.hayhouse.co.za**
Hay House India: **www.hayhouse.co.in**

We hope you enjoyed this SmileyBooks publication.
If you would like to receive additional information, please contact:

SMILEYBOOKS

an imprint of:

Hay House, Inc.
P.O. Box 5100
Carlsbad, CA 92018-5100

(760) 431-7695 or (800) 654-5126
(760) 431-6948 (fax) or (800) 650-5115 (fax)
www.hayhouse.com® • www.hayfoundation.org

Published and distributed in Australia by: Hay House Australia Pty. Ltd.
18/36 Ralph St. • Alexandria NSW 2015 • *Phone:* 612-9669-4299
Fax: 612-9669-4144 • www.hayhouse.com.au

Published and distributed in the United Kingdom by: Hay House UK, Ltd.
292B Kensal Rd., London W10 5BE • *Phone:* 44-20-8962-1230
Fax: 44-20-8962-1239 • www.hayhouse.co.uk

Published and distributed in the Republic of South Africa by:
Hay House SA (Pty), Ltd., P.O. Box 990, Witkoppen 2068 • *Phone/Fax:*
27-11-467-8904 • orders@psdprom.co.za • www.hayhouse.co.za

Published and Distributed in India by: Hay House Publishers India,
Muskaan Complex, Plot No. 3, B-2, Vasant Kunj, New Delhi 110 070
Phone: 91-11-4176-1620 • *Fax:* 91-11-4176-1630 • www.hayhouse.co.in

Distributed in Canada by: Raincoast • 9050 Shaughnessy St.,
Vancouver, B.C. V6P 6E5 • *Phone:* (604) 323-7100 • *Fax:* (604) 323-2600

Tune in to **HayHouseRadio.com®** for the best in inspirational
talk radio featuring top Hay House authors! And, sign up via the
Hay House USA Website to receive the Hay House online newsletter
and stay informed about what's going on with your favorite authors.
You'll receive bimonthly announcements about: Discounts and Offers,
Special Events, Product Highlights, Free Excerpts, Giveaways, and more!
www.hayhouse.com®